THE Jazz Guitar HANDBOOK

Rod Fogg

The Jazz Guitar Handbook

Rod Fogg

A BACKBEAT BOOK
First edition 2013
Published by Backbeat Books
An Imprint of Globe Pequot
4501 Forbes Blvd, #200,
Lanham, MD 20706
www.rowman.com

Devised and produced for Backbeat Books by
Outline Press Ltd
2A Union Court, 20-22 Union Road,
London SW4 6JP, England
www.jawbonepress.com

ISBN: 978-1-4803-4104-3

A catalogue record for this book is available from the British Library.

DESIGN: Paul Cooper Design
EDITOR: John Morrish

Printed by 1010 Printing, China

Distributed by NATIONAL BOOK NETWORK

contents

contents

contents

contents

contents

Introduction

This book is a thorough guide to playing jazz on the guitar, starting at near-beginner level and progressing smoothly to an advanced standard. The musical exercises are demonstrated on the included CD and appear in both tablature and standard guitar notation. Backing tracks are also on the CD for your individual practice. Technical tips and notes on theory appear alongside the examples, highlighting important points as they come along. Many of the musical examples are written in the style of the great jazz guitar players, opening up possibilities for further study.

The roots of jazz are in the blues, but it became a distinct form after it emerged from ragtime music at the end of the 19th century. Ragtime was mostly composed and therefore lacks the improvisation that is one of the essential ingredients of jazz. But it swings, in a fairly stiff way, and when it was added to the mix of ingredients found in New Orleans at the turn of the 20th century – blues, folk songs, European art music, hymns and spirituals – it created a stew from which an exciting new music could emerge. To happen, this needed a cosmopolitan city with a wide range of different nationalities and cultures: French, Spanish, English, Irish, Scottish, Native American and, of course, African.

Since jazz began with the blues, we begin with the blues in this book; the simple harmonic basis of the blues encourages a relaxed and progressive approach to improvisation. Once blues harmony and soloing have been grasped we will be well placed to deal with the complex harmonic and soloing concepts found in modern jazz.

During the course of the 20th century, jazz developed and absorbed music from all around the world, a process that continues today. Jazz is a style, but it is also an approach or philosophy. You can play a song straight, or you can play it jazzy. You can play a part 'as written', or you can take the jazz approach and improvise or embellish. Jazz is not easy to define, yet most of us can recognize it when we hear it. A bass riff, a drumbeat or a saxophone lick can sound jazzy regardless of context. And many of today's music styles have absorbed elements of jazz: contemporary styles such as house, hip-hop, rap, and even metal owe something to jazz, because they are based on a beat that became commonplace in our music through jazz.

Over the course of its development, jazz has changed its nature about every ten years, taking on new influences and often making earlier definitions redundant. Many have tried to define jazz, and it is tempting to side with stride pianist Fats Waller, who is credited with saying, "If you don't know what it is, don't mess with it." So here's a catch-all which hopefully will not be out of date anytime soon; to be jazz the music must swing, or possess a rhythmic intensity or groove equivalent to swing; it must also have elements that are improvised, or, if fully composed, must be composed so as to suggest improvisation.

This is imprecise, but it has the benefit of fitting pretty much all the music that can be called jazz, right from the two-beat ragtime at the start of jazz to the big band arrangements of the 1950s and on to the dissonant free improvisations of the modern avant-garde. Since its inception, jazz has been music of rhythmic force, melodic invention, spontaneity, group interaction and an open-ended philosophy that views any harmonic progression as a potential basis for improvisation. It includes some of the most sublime music ever created and is an enduring joy and rewarding challenge for musicians of all standards and persuasions.

Now let's start learning how to do it.

Rod Fogg
London 2013

HISTORY
Jazz and jazz guitarists

■ Out of the blues

■ The guitars

■ The players

■ The electric guitar

■ Hot Club

Out of the blues

Jazz grew out of the blues, and the instrument of choice for most early blues singers was the guitar. We can safely assume, then, that the guitar and its ability to play chords rhythmically in all keys was influential on early jazz. Unfortunately the sound recording industry in those days was in its infancy so we have no idea what that music sounded like. The closest we can come is the blues recorded in the 1920s by artists such as Big Bill Broonzy, Blind Willie McTell, and Blind Lemon Jefferson.

Some blues songs were played fingerstyle, keeping a bassline going with the thumb while picking lead riffs and lines with the fingers. Others were played with the pick, mainly playing chords using downstrokes on downbeats but adding occasional basslines, solos, breaks and riffs. This was particularly useful when playing rhythm in small groups or duos, and as early jazz was a band activity it is fair to assume that this was the way the first jazz guitarists sounded.

The Buddy Bolden Jazz Band, one of the first bands playing the ragtime music that evolved into jazz in New Orleans around 1895, had a guitar player, Brock Mumford. But they left no recordings, so Mumford's contribution to their sound is again a matter of surmise. As cornets, clarinet, and trombone made up the bulk of the rest of the band it may not have been very audible.

In fact, you can search long and hard in the first recordings of jazz to find a guitar player. Back then, banjo was king; its fierce penetrating clang could match the frontline instruments in volume before the invention of amplification. Unlike the piano, which was the banjo's main rival as chording instrument, it was portable and you could carry it on a strap while you played. This made it handy for joining in the marching bands that were, and still are, a feature of life in New Orleans. Despite its volume, however, banjo has one important weakness; it does not sustain well. As the simple 'two-beat' ragtime forms of jazz that were popular in the first two decades of the 20th Century gave way to smoother 'four in a bar' swing flavours, the guitar, with its smoother, mellower, and more sustained sound, came to prominence.

This rise coincided with the adoption of the string or 'upright' bass and the gradual decline of the tuba as the bass instrument of choice in jazz bands. Jazz was moving from street and raucous barrelhouse to club and speakeasy, and growing in sophistication as a result. In those days the bass was often slapped (a technique in which the strings are made to hit the fingerboard and produce a percussive slap either with the bass note, or on the offbeats when in cut time). That meant another percussive instrument like the banjo was unnecessary. Add a set of drums and that really is too much slap, clunk, and thud and not enough actual harmony. The guitar has a smooth quality that blends well with the upright bass; with six strings it is also capable of a wider range of chord voicings than the banjo. Guitar manufacturers began to strive to produce larger, more powerful instruments that could be heard in the bars and clubs in which this more mature, urban form of jazz found a home.

The guitars
Gibson were at the forefront of this evolution, launching the jazz stalwart L-5 in 1923. Strangely enough, this revolutionary guitar design, which did so much to enable guitarists to compete in volume with the jazz bands of its day, was originally conceived as a member of the mandolin family. Mandolin orchestras had been popular for some time but by the time the L-5 came along the mandolin had declined in popularity in favour of the tenor banjo.

The L-5 was the world's first production 'f-hole' guitar (almost all earlier guitars had either round or oval sound holes), and featured the carved top and back that was developed by Orville Gibson in the 1890s for his mandolins and guitars. Carving a top is a laborious process, beginning with a solid piece of wood and then removing wood

1929 Gibson L–5. The world's first production f-hole guitar.

1937 Epiphone Emperor. A large arch-top with a carved top and back.

1933 Harmony Cremona. The first arch-top from the mass-market maker, which was owned by mail-order company Sears Roebuck.

1936 Stromberg Deluxe Arch-top. These guitars, produced by Elmer Stromberg in Chicago, are today highly collectable.

from top and bottom, firstly with a drill and subsequently with rasping tools, to create the arched top and back found on these 'arch-top' guitars. Orchestral cellos and violins are built in much the same way. The L-5 is still in the Gibson inventory today, testament to its efficiency at fulfilling its intended role.

The L-5 was not as loud as the 1920s banjo, which possessed a tone ring, flange, and resonator intended to add volume. It did, however, have a bright tone and penetration in its upper register, coupled with warmth and sustain low down. Designed by Lloyd Loar, a significant figure in the history of guitar development, it had several distinguishing features in addition to the f-holes, such as the fingerboard raised off the top, and two parallel braces or 'tone bars' under it.

The back and sides were birch at first, in common with all Gibson guitars of the

1935 Gibson Super 400.
Introduced in 1934, the Super 400 cost $400, almost twice as much as the L-5.

period, but in 1924 this was changed to maple. The neck was maple with an ebony centre laminate, in common with high-end Gibson mandolins from the time; most guitars in the Gibson line at this point had a mahogany neck. The neck joined the body at the 14th fret, which made access to the high notes slightly easier. Early L-5s were 16 inches wide and are today not as highly sought after by players as the 17-inch examples brought in around 1934. Lloyd Loar left the Gibson company in 1924, having overseen the production of fewer then 30 L-5 guitars.

Considering the suitability of the arch-top guitar for playing in the jazz bands of the day, it is strange that as late as 1930 the Gibson range still consisted of just one arch-top, the L-5. In 1931 Epiphone, a prominent banjo maker, introduced a line of nine 'Masterbilt' f-hole arch-top guitars. In response, over the next two years Gibson introduced three new 16-inch models, though none was higher in quality than the L-5. There were also two smaller 14¾ inch models. In 1933 another competitor entered the market, when Gretsch introduced a line of arch-tops. The budget market was catered for by guitars from Harmony and Kay. In the early 1930s even Martin, renowned for its roundhole flat-top guitars, introduced a line of f-hole arch-tops, though without much success.

In 1934 Gibson sought to steal a march on the competition by introducing its 'advanced' arch-tops, enlarging the body width of the four 16-inch models to 17 inches. In the following year the smaller models also advanced to 16 inches, and then two new 14¾-inch models joined the line. Finally, in late 1934, a new deluxe model was introduced. It was 18 inches wide and was as expensive as it was huge. It included a leather-covered case and was priced at $400 – an incredible sum for the time – and named the Super 400.

Size wars soon broke out in earnest. Epiphone and Gretsch came out with new models as large or larger than the Super 400. Similarly, the luthiers John D'Angelico and Elmer Stromberg began building 17- and 18-inch models to order. By 1940

Stromberg was building 17⅜ and 19-inch guitars. Other developments included the introduction of cutaways; at first, cutaway L-5 models were called 'Premier' and labelled L-5P. Later, a cutaway was designated by a C after the name. Until the invention of the electric guitar, the acoustic arch-top, usually strung with heavy flatwound strings, was to be the defining sound of jazz guitar.

Radio and recording

Developments in the recording industry played a key role in the growing appreciation of the guitar and its emergence as more than just a rhythm machine. Thomas Edison invented the first practical sound recording and reproduction system in 1877, recording onto waxed cylinders. Gramophone discs were invented in 1889 and represented a considerable step forward; they were louder, had two sides, and were easier to manufacture and transport. Until 1925, however, all sound recording was mechanical; that is to say that the sound waves would vibrate a diaphragm attached to a needle which would physically cut a groove in a disc. On playback a needle and diaphragm would reverse the process by vibrating in the groove; the resulting sound wave would be amplified by an acoustic horn.

By 1925 developments in the world of microphones and amplification led to the first electric recordings, in which recorded sound was captured by a microphone and amplified before being etched onto a disc. On playback, the vibrations picked up by the needle were also amplified to be reproduced through loudspeakers. In the studio the guitarist could be seated nearer the recording equipment than the louder instruments, and a balance achieved within the band that would have been impossible in a live situation. Once microphones were in common use it became possible to capture the delicate nuances of acoustic guitar far more accurately than by the earlier mechanical methods.

Radio also played a part in the emergence of the guitar from the rhythm section. The earliest experiments in public broadcasting date from around 1910, and by the 1920s regular radio programmes were being broadcast, with tube-powered receivers available to receive them. For a typical music broadcast, performers and presenters would gather together in the studio and everything would be broadcast live; the guitar's melodious sound came across well when broadcast over this basic equipment, and its small voice could again be dealt with by varying its distance from the microphone.

The players

Eddie Lang and Lonnie Johnson share the honours as the first guitar virtuosos of jazz. Eddie Lang was associated with the Gibson L-5 for most of his career. Johnson's choice of guitar is less clear; in early pictures he is shown playing a 12-string flat-top guitar with a round hole. It seems he often removed one of each of the top two paired strings, thus creating a 10-string guitar. This gave him four pairs of strings in octaves, with the top two single strings useful for single-note runs and bends. Born in New Orleans to a musical family, Johnson travelled to Europe in 1917 as part of a musical revue. On his return to New Orleans he found that his whole family, except for one brother, had died in the influenza epidemic that swept the world in 1918. He settled in St Louis and began playing locally.

Lonnie Johnson's first record contract (with the 'race' label Okeh) was a prize in a blues talent competition, and with his fine blues voice he subsequently found it hard not to be pigeonholed as a blues artist. In 1925 he made his first recording under his own name, 'Mr Johnson's Blues', on which he sings and plays guitar with piano accompaniment. It was recorded using the old mechanical process, and the guitar is thin and not particularly audible except in the breaks in the vocal. It is still worth checking out; you'll hear fluent single-note soloing and arguably the first recorded guitar parts to use string bending – impressive by any standards.

One year later, with 'To Do This You Gotta Know How', we can hear Johnson's first record using the electrical process. It's a solo and the guitar is more distinct and three-dimensional. It is also an even more impressive example of his playing. He tunes his lowest two strings down a whole step for this track, giving the tuning D G D G B E. The recording is in E, so we could guess he's capoed at the second fret, although there is much debate about how reliable the

Eddie Lang

mastering process was in those days. It also seems to have been common practice for record producers or record company owners to deliberately speed up recordings to make them more impressive; for this reason it can be hard to judge whether the guitar was capoed, tuned sharp, or tuned normally but speeded up in mastering.

By 1927 Johnson was recording in Chicago as a guest artist with Louis Armstrong & his Hot Five, playing on four classic tracks, of which 'Hotter Than That' is the stand-out masterpiece. It features Johnson riffing under Armstrong's scat singing. In 1928 he recorded with Duke Ellington, and can be heard effortlessly coping with the fast tempo of 'Hot And Bothered' and riffing freely in the background on the strange minor-key tune 'The Mooche'. Later he recorded with The Chocolate Dandies; 'Paducah', a slowish blues in E-flat, is well worth a listen for his two fluent solos, and he is equally unperturbed by the complex harmonies of the Hoagy Carmichael standard 'Stardust'.

Eddie Lang could not have had a more different background to that of Lonnie Johnson. Of Italian-American origin, he was born Salvatore Massaro and chose the name of a local basketball hero for his professional career. His father was an instrument-maker who saw to it that his son learned to play guitar, banjo, and violin. During his school days he became friends with the jazz violinist Joe Venuti and chose to concentrate on guitar. Some of his earliest recordings are with the Mound City Blue

Blowers, a novelty band that featured kazoo and comb-and-paper among the lead instruments.

Lang and Venuti recorded many duos together, which demonstrate Lang's robust rhythm style of strummed chords mixed with bass runs, lead lines, chord breaks, and intros. 'Wild Cat' is a good example, along with 'Stringing The Blues', their first ever recording together. Their output was consistently high in quality and represents some of the finest hot guitar and fiddle ever recorded.

In 1928 Lang recorded with Johnson under an assumed name (Blind Willie Dunn) because the racial restrictions of the day prevented black and white musicians appearing on records together. It seems that few people were fooled into thinking it was anyone other than Eddie Lang. That two such gifted guitarist should be alive at the same time, right at the beginning of the instrument's emergence, is remarkable in itself; that someone at the Okeh company had the foresight to get them to record together is something for which all jazz enthusiast should be grateful.

Freddie Green

During the course of the next year Lang and Johnson recorded ten remarkable

duets; highlights include 'A Handful Of Riffs' and 'Blue Guitars'. Lang mostly takes the rhythm part while Johnson mostly plays lead; however, they are evenly balanced in the recordings and their respective parts fit together seamlessly. These recordings are not merely historical pieces; they set the style for hot jazz guitar for the coming years and have a charm and vivacity time has not dimmed.

After their sessions, Eddie Lang returned to working with Joe Venuti and also recorded some fine duets with the young guitarist (and former banjoist) Carl Kress. 'Pickin' My Way' is a good example of their excellent work together. Lang played with many other leading jazz artists, including Bing Crosby, but sadly he was to die unexpectedly in 1933 as a result of complications after a tonsillectomy operation. Lonnie Johnson continued his career as a blues singer, gradually fading from public attention until the blues boom of the 1960s resurrected his career.

Many more swing-era guitarists deserve a mention. Al Casey played for many years with Fats Waller, where he mostly played rhythm. He can be heard out front however, on 'Buck Jumpin'', which demonstrates his relaxed, blues-flavoured single-note style. Freddie Green was the most successful rhythm player of them all, spending almost 50 years as the heartbeat of the Count Basie band. He rarely soloed, but was indispensable in the big band's rhythm section.

The electric guitar

Even though the L-5 was loud for a guitar it was still not really loud enough to compete in a live situation with the brass instruments that made up a typical jazz band. As the music had progressed from Dixieland to swing, bands had also grown in size, with whole sections of saxophones, trumpets, and trombones now appearing. In the studio, the guitarist could be positioned in such a way as to still be heard, and as a result several guitarists of the next generation began to emerge. These include the aforementioned Carl Kress, who also worked extensively as a studio musician backing the popular jazz singers of the day. Teddy Bunn recorded with Duke Ellington's band in 1929 and with the The Spirits Of Rhythm, a very popular vocal group in their day. George Van Eps was the son of Fred Van Eps, a famous banjo player from the ragtime era, and split his time between bands and studio work. He subsequently developed a seven-string guitar (with an extra bass string tuned to A) which he used for most of his long career.

Microphone technology was improving, and Eddie Durham, guitarist with the Jimmy Lunsford band, spent much of the 1930s experimenting with microphones inserted into guitars and with amplifiers that he built himself. When playing live, Sy Oliver, the band's vocalist, would bring his microphone over to the guitar on the bandstand for Durham's solos. Using a microphone to amplify a guitar in those days could cause all kinds of

George Van Eps

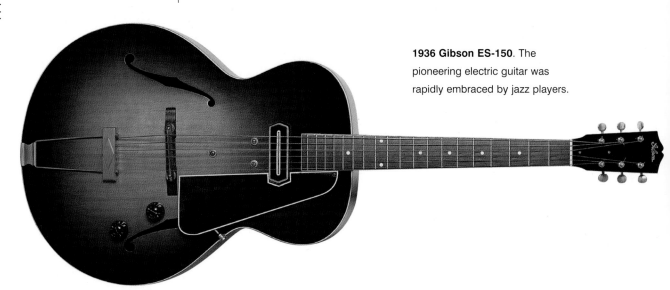

1936 Gibson ES-150. The pioneering electric guitar was rapidly embraced by jazz players.

problems, including boxiness of sound, picking up unwanted noises, and howling feedback. On 'Hittin' The Bottle' he can be heard recording with one of the first 'resophonic' instruments (which produced sound using a built-in mechanical resonator).

In 1931 the manufacturing company that subsequently became Rickenbacker invented the 'frying pan' electric guitar, a Hawaiian-style instrument designed to be played flat in the lap with a steel bar. (Hawaiian music had been a fad since around 1915.) It was an immense success, and sold well, together with its matching amplifier. Next, Rickenbacker launched the electro-Spanish, the world's first production electric guitar. At that time 'Spanish' guitar meant an instrument intended to be held vertically rather than flat in the lap. It was not successful – its tiny body and large pickup were too strange for most players.

The pickups on electric guitars are fundamentally different to microphones. They work on a principle known as 'magnetic induction' and as a result are often today called 'magnetic pickups'. If you place a magnet in a coil and vary the magnetic field, for instance by rotating the magnet, a current is generated in the coil; electrical generators work on the same principle. In the case of an electric guitar pickup, the vibration of the string affects the magnetic field and generates an alternating current of matching frequency in the coil. This extremely small current is then sent to the amplifier, where the circuitry makes it powerful enough to drive a loudspeaker.

The feasibility of an electromagnetic pickup had been demonstrated by Rickenbacker, and in 1936 Gibson introduced the pickup-equipped ES-150 and its companion EH 150 amplifier. Eddie Durham adopted one straight away and used it on tour with the Count Basie band in 1937. When the tour arrived in Kansas City, Durham was heard by Charlie Christian, a young, up-and-coming guitar player who had himself been trying to solve the problem of amplifying the guitar. He soon acquired an ES-150 of his own and proved to be a fast learner; after a few years' hard work he found himself at the top of his profession, playing with the Benny Goodman band.

The technology had arrived, and the guitar world needed another innovator to take the instrument in a new direction. Christian himself wrote an article in *Downbeat* magazine, extolling the virtues of his amplified guitar, and just as rapidly as the 1920s banjoists had abandoned their instrument in favour of the guitar, acoustic guitarists began to take up the electric instrument in the 1940s, hampered only by the manufacturing problems that were caused by the Second World War.

Sadly Charlie Christian was to die young, of tuberculosis, and as a result his entire recorded output spans just two years, beginning in 1939 and ending in 1941. Its influence, however, is colossal; there seems to be something of his style in virtually every jazz guitar player who has followed him.

Charlie left us around 25 recordings with the Goodman sextet and septet, a distinctive small band that left plenty of room for his inventive improvisation. There are also two takes of 'Solo Flight' with the Benny Goodman Orchestra in 1941 (the out-take is sometimes called 'Homeward Bound'), a feature number which is all single-note guitar. Some of his lines suggest the emerging bebop, while in other places he quotes some classic blues licks reminiscent of Lonnie Johnson; it's all held together by a powerful sense of swing and a big, bright, fat jazz sound, solidly recorded and powering along at the front of the big band.

Brochure for Gibson's ES-150 Electro Spanish Guitar.

'Seven Come Eleven' stands out among the sextet and septet recordings, its quick, string-skipping riff demonstrating Christian's powerful right-hand technique. 'Airmail Special' and its out-take 'Good Enough To Keep' are also good examples of the inventive riffing style that he brought to jazz. 'Waiting For Benny', a jam session recorded while the musicians awaited their band leader's arrival, is also revealing of his ability to spontaneously invent and develop a riff. Although not really a bebopper himself, Christian was a regular at the nightclub Minton's Playhouse, the home of jam sessions involving Thelonious Monk, Dizzy Gillespie, and Charlie Parker, the leading lights of the emerging bebop movement. Luckily, a jazz enthusiast named Jerry Newman recorded a jam session at Minton's in May 1941, and this can be heard as the track 'Swing To Bop' (based on the chords of 'Topsy'). Freed from the tight arrangements that were characteristic of the Benny Goodman band, Charlie Christian takes chorus after chorus of open-ended inventive soloing.

Hot Club

Meanwhile in Europe, a virtuoso guitarist of Gypsy origin had been listening to Eddie Lang and Lonnie Johnson. Born in 1910 in Belgium, Jean 'Django' Reinhardt was already a noted musician, mainly on banjo, when at the age of 19 he was severely burned in a caravan fire. His left hand was so badly injured that it seemed unlikely he would ever play again. However, such was his determination and innate musical ability that he completely reworked his technique to use primarily his first and second fingers, retaining the limited movement in his injured third and fourth fingers for chords when necessary. He played a distinctive acoustic guitar, the design of which was a collaboration between the French Selmer musical instrument company and the Italian guitarist and instrument designer Mario Maccaferri.

Superficially, the recordings of the Quintet of the Hot Club of France, a band featuring Reinhardt on acoustic guitar and Stéphane Grappelli on violin, are not so very different from the violin and guitar recordings of Eddie Lang and Joe Venuti. However, both Reinhardt and Grappelli were schooled in the European tradition of popular songs, waltzes, French musette, and Gypsy songs that made up the vernacular for the street musicians of Paris in the 1920s. Couple this with Grappelli's melodic sense of swing and Django's seemingly endless box of tricks – intense vibrato, tremolando chords and single notes, string bends, glissandos and almost unbelievably fast one-finger chromatic runs – and you have a recipe for music of incredible longevity. All around the world today there are 'Hot Club' bands paying tribute to Django's 'jazz band without drums'.

Django Reinhardt with Stéphane Grappelli (left) and Louis Vola in the Quintet of the Hot Club of France.

1932 Selmer Maccaferri Orchestra. Selmer was a saxophone company that joined forces with guitarist Mario Maccaferri to produce this innovative instrument.

Unlike Charlie Christian, Django Reinhardt produced a truly prodigious output. From his first guitar sessions with The Quintet of the Hot Club of France in 1934 until his death in 1953 he produced a great many recordings that are today available on multiple boxed sets of CDs. Such is his stature in the guitar world that he is a serious candidate for "the greatest guitarist who ever lived", a remarkable achievement when you consider that he never learned to read or write music. Highlights from the early years include 'Dinah', with Django's chord intro and humorous solo, the rapid 'Tiger Rag', and 'Oh Lady Be Good'. In the latter tune there is a unison guitar and violin introduction, and Django barely refers to the tune in his opening solo, choosing instead to take two wonderful choruses of improvisation. Notice also the change of key after the violin solo and the reappearance of the introduction in mid-song before the return to the original key. These three tracks alone demonstrate a remarkable maturity in the Quintet's music, and all were from the their first recording session, in December 1934.

At a later recording session, in January 1938, the quintet recorded 'My Sweet', 'Souvenirs', 'Daphne', 'Black And White', and 'Stompin' At Decca', notable because, of the eight tunes recorded that day, these five were original Reinhardt/Grappelli compositions. 'Daphne' and 'Stompin' At Decca' are particularly popular with Hot Club fans around the world. The other three tunes recorded that day were 'Honeysuckle Rose', with its distinctive Reinhardt/Grappelli-composed intro and outro, and classic versions of 'Sweet Georgia Brown' and Cole Porter's 'Night And Day'.

In 1939, at the outbreak of the Second World War, the Quintet was on tour in London. Grappelli decided to stay put, but the rest of the band hurried back to France. Django reformed the quintet, with Hubert Rostaing's clarinet replacing Grappelli's violin. He also added drums, thus moving a little closer to the Benny Goodman sound. American jazz records were banned by the Nazis, giving an unexpected boost to the jazz musicians of France, whose music was seen by the French as being subversive of the Nazi order. Django soon became famous and popular across society, and his

Stochelo Rosenberg

second recording of his own composition, 'Nuages', in 1940, became a huge hit.

After the war Reinhardt and Grappelli recorded again, but by 1949 the relationship had petered out; there was no big bust up, but it seems that by mutual agreement they both wished to move on to new territory. By this time, Django was playing an electric guitar and showing the influence of bebop. A simple man, with no great need for luxury, he seems to have been happy to live in a kind of retirement, close to his family and playing music only when it suited him. Some electric guitar recordings from this period show a man who had somehow lost his voice – the acoustic guitar seems to have been a more perfect fit for Django's whimsical genius. There are still some great tracks, however – 'Porto Cabello', a Reinhardt composition from 1947, demonstrates that although the sound was different the musical delicacy and technical wizardry were still present. Sadly Django was to die in 1953 at the comparatively young age of 43 years.

There are more than 850 recordings of Django's virtuoso playing, and he is responsible for an entire genre of jazz, with many fine guitarists following in his footsteps. Among these are the Ferret (later Ferré) brothers Boulou and Elios, sons of Matelo Ferret and nephews of Baro Ferret, both former Django accompanists. In the 1980s Biréli Lagrène emerged as a virtuoso at the age of 12. Although many of his later recordings steered towards the mainstream, he has recently returned to his Gypsy jazz roots. Modern successors to Django include Stochelo Rosenberg, Angelo Debarre, and Fapy Lafertin, all of whom demonstrate an astonishing level of virtuosity.

Bepop and beyond

In America, bebop, or 'bop' as it is also known, never fully caught on with the general public, even though it could be viewed as a natural development of the harmony, chord voicings, and improvisations of the swing era. From the viewpoint of the second decade of the 21st century the furore that bop caused among critics – it was described variously as "the end of jazz" or "chaos in music" – seems bizarre; modern ears hear it as one more stepping stone in the evolution of jazz. The distinguishing features of bebop are worth pointing out, however, because they became standard practice in the jazz to come.

Tempos, for example, became faster – leading to the complaint that the music was too fast for dancers. This was music for a sophisticated, intellectual type of jazz fan – one who was expected to sit and listen. It is no coincidence that this was the era when jazz began to move out of nightclubs and restaurants and into the concert hall.

Generally speaking, swing improvisers had followed the cadential structure of the music and mostly phrased in two- and four-bar patterns. Beboppers tended to phrase across barlines and cadential structures; often resolution of a dissonance would be delayed, or sometimes anticipated, so that the soloist was 'ahead' of the music, creating an urgent, edgy quality. This edginess is also found in the unadorned unison playing of the 'head' or tune of the piece by the trumpet and sax. Unison playing is stark and focused – it says: "this is our statement; we do not compromise".

The biggest change was to the rhythm section. No longer did drummers play "four on the floor", hitting the kick drum on every beat. The beat was now played on the ride cymbal and hi-hat, leaving the toms and kick drum for accents – "dropping bombs", as it became known. This left the bass with a more prominent role, not just outlining the harmony but also providing the essential pulse of the music. In turn, this also freed guitarists from the need to lock with the bass and drums and lay down a solid four-beat rhythm as heard in Dixieland, swing, and big band jazz. Bebop guitarists, like all modern jazz players, 'comp' their chords; in other words, they freely place simple chords or extended harmonies where they most ensure the rhythmic drive of the music and punctuate or comment on the soloists' efforts. All these changes are now standard practice in today's jazz, and earlier methods are mostly reserved for deliberate recreations of older styles of jazz.

With the death of Charlie Christian, the early days of bebop had no real champion on guitar, but Christian-inspired guitarists soon began to appear. The Nat King Cole Trio was responsible for the emergence of two guitarists who followed in Charlie's footsteps. Oscar Moore spent more than ten years with the pianist/vocalist, contributing fluent single-string solos and delicate rhythmic chord work. The subtlety of the Nat Cole Trio marks the emergence of jazz as chamber music (there was no drummer), and Moore's vital contribution can be heard on tracks like 'Body And Soul' or his own composition 'Lament In Chords'. Oscar Moore was followed in the Nat Cole Trio by Irving Ashby, making his auspicious debut with the band at Carnegie Hall. Tracks like 'Top Hat Bop' are good examples of his cool, swinging blues licks and long, well-shaped phrases.

Les Paul, another guitarist from that era, is a difficult character for jazz enthusiasts. He spent most of his life as a pop artist and is mainly remembered for his development of multitrack recording and the solid-body Gibson guitar that bears his name. Nevertheless, he was an adaptable musician and took part in the first Jazz at the Philharmonic concert in 1944 in Hollywood, along with Nat King Cole. One of the first Americans to recognise the genius of Django Reinhardt, Paul had prodigious technique and often tinged his solos with wit and humour. 'Bugle Call Rag', from the above Jazz at the Philharmonic session shows him in fine form, as do his recordings with Willie Smith and his Orchestra, such as the blues 'Willie Weep For Me'.

Guitar developments

The ES-150 was always a basic guitar, and it was only a matter of time before Gibson began to develop more upmarket models. These included the ES-250, an electrified version of the 17-inch L-7 acoustic, and subsequently the ES-300, which was the first electric guitar to have the jack socket mounted in the side of the lower bout rather than as part of the tailpiece. The ES-350, released in 1947, was essentially a cutaway ES-300.

The warm sound of an electric arch-top guitar is due in part to the air in the hollow body; these guitars sound fundamentally different to the solidbody guitars invented by Fender in the 1950s. However, electric arch-tops do not need the expensive carved tops and solid timbers required on acoustic guitars like the L-5. Pressed, laminated arch-tops are cheaper to make and their stiffness makes them more resistant to feedback. In 1946 Gibson introduced the budget ES-125, with a laminated top and back that was pressed rather than carved.

1949 Gibson ES-175N. The first version of this guitar, with a single P90 pickup.

This in turn led directly to the development of one of the most successful jazz guitars of all time, the ES-175, with its sharp Florentine cutaway, laminated/pressed construction, and single P90 pickup. A twin-pickup version followed in 1953 (the ES-

1953 Gibson ES-175D. The first twin-pickup version of the celebrated jazz guitar, which is still in production today.

1948 Gibson ES-350. This was a single-cutaway version of the earlier ES-300.

175D), with separate volume and tone controls for each pickup and a selector switch. In 1958 the pickups became humbuckers and the guitar has changed little since then. Herb Ellis (who later played the similar single-pickup ES-165), Jim Hall, Pat Martino, Joe Pass, and Pat Metheny are just some of the jazz players who have at one time or another been closely linked to this one guitar.

Another innovation in 1958 was the development of the Gibson ES335, a thin-body arch-top that had a solid piece of wood down the centre of the body with hollow wings with f-holes on either side. Part of a range of semi-solid guitars that included the ES-345 and ES-355, this guitar was in time to become popular with blues artists and with those seeking to fuse jazz and rock in the 1960s, not least because it was more resistant to feedback at loud volumes than the standard arch-top guitar.

1958 Gibson ES-335TD. The 335 series was the first of the thinline semi-acoustics. It had humbucking pickups as standard.

Guitar pickups

Prior to the development of humbucking pickups, all guitar pickups consisted of a single coil surrounding a magnet; most Gibsons in the 1950s were fitted with a bright but fat-sounding single-coil pickup known as a P90. Humbuckers (or double-coil or twin-coil pickups) use a phenomenon known as common mode rejection to reduce hum in the guitar output. They consist of two single coil pickups side by side, wired in series, wound in opposite directions, and with opposing magnetic poles directed towards the strings. This arrangement cancels out any electrical hum induced in the pickups, while reinforcing the desirable signal created by the vibration of the strings.

Gibson employee Seth Lover was responsible for the development of Gibson's humbucker design, and these pickups have been seen on most of Gibson's guitars since being introduced in 1958. Humbuckers also have the benefit of a more powerful output than a single coil, and because they slightly cancel some higher frequencies they can tend towards a fat middly tone, particularly from the neck pickup. It is certainly true that as the 1950s progressed into the 1960s jazz guitar tones became less bright. However, it is a cliche that jazz players all play on the neck pickup with the tone rolled back; listening to Joe Pass or Wes Montgomery reveals a sound that, although fat, still has plenty of power to cut through.

Joe Pass

The 1950s

The 1950s brought the 'cool' era, and saxophone, in the hands of musicians like John Coltrane, was king, along with the trumpet explorations of Miles Davis. The decade also saw the arrival of the long-playing 33rpm record; jazz gradually became an art form devoted to albums of music rather than single tracks as it had been in the era of the 78rpm disc. Jazz was becoming more mature, to be listened to in the home, with a risk that it might veer too much towards 'easy listening'. There were yet more great guitar players in this era, however, many of whom steered a successful course between commercial studio music on the one hand and successful jazz outings on the other. Top of the list of high achievers, and both with long careers, were Barney Kessel and Herb Ellis.

Kessel played in many West Coast bands and recording sessions before his breakthrough in 1952 with the Oscar Peterson Trio as part of a 14-country tour with Jazz at the Philharmonic. Among his early work is the classic Dial Records 1946 recording of 'Relaxin' At Camarillo' with Charlie Parker's New Stars. Despite being in stellar company he acquits himself well in his solo.

Barney Kessel

The Jazz at the Philharmonic sessions led to recordings with Peterson and many other leading jazz artists. He soon found himself recording as a bandleader. 'Easy Like' and 'To Swing Or Not To Swing' demonstrate his solid tone, intelligent harmonic sense, and lively swing. The winner of many magazine popularity polls, he also recorded a successful series of albums in the guitar/bass/drums format with Ray Brown and Shelly Manne, as The Poll Winners. In so doing he became the most successful guitarist at that point to demonstrate that the jazz guitar did not need a second comping instrument.

Among his many successes as a sideman is the remarkable Julie London debut, *Julie Is Her Name*. Julie was an accurate and expressive vocalist, perhaps more pop than jazz and mainly remembered today for her version of 'Cry Me A River'. On this album she was sensitively accompanied by just Kessel on guitar and Ray Leatherwood on bass. In 1974 Kessel formed The Great Guitars with Herb Ellis and Charlie Byrd, a three-guitar trio that recorded several albums and toured extensively. Byrd was a Latin jazz specialist who played finger-style nylon-string guitar.

Herb Ellis followed Barney Kessel into the Oscar Peterson Trio, where he spent six years touring and recording. His album *Nothing But The Blues* from 1957 demonstrated his blues roots mixed with bebop influence. Wishing to reduce the pressure of touring, he spent many years in Los Angeles television studios as a member of the resident bands of popular shows. In 1971 he began to perform again, notably with Joe Pass, recording two excellent albums, *Seven Come Eleven* and *Two For The Road*. His work from 1974 onwards with The Great Guitars won him a whole new generation of fans.

While the beboppers were inspired by the alto saxophone of Charlie Parker, the next generation of guitarists were influenced by the cool, languid tenor of Lester Young. Johnny Smith claimed not to consider himself a jazz guitarist, yet still managed to produce around 20 albums demonstrating his fluent technique and musical awareness. The most successful of these was *Moonlight In Vermont*, featuring the breathy saxophone of Stan Getz. The title track was a hit, attracting an audience far beyond regular jazz fans and achieving success unusual for instrumental music even in the jazz era.

Tal Farlow is counted among the most technically proficient guitarists of all time, capable of both single-note fireworks and subtle detail. He had an on/off approach to work, music and recording for most of his life, but the late 50s album *The Swinging Guitar Of Tal Farlow* is a good demonstration of his abilities.

Jim Hall, a guitarist noted for his intelligence, sensitivity, and restraint emerged in the late 1950s and has had a long career. Among his most interesting recordings are those he made in a duo with pianist Bill Evans, such as *Undercurrent* from 1959, which sees the pair freely swapping roles as soloist and accompanist, regardless of the lack of bass instrument.

The 1950s were in many ways a golden age for jazz. In concert halls audiences rivalled those for classical music and jazz dominated radio and light entertainment. There were many fine guitarists deserving of a mention in this era, all of whom knew the language of bebop and revoiced it in their own way on guitar; Chuck Wayne, Arv Garrison, Billy Bauer, George Barnes, Jimmy Raney, and Howard Roberts are just some of the names worth checking out.

Jim Hall

The 1960s

Kenny Burrell's early career straddled the 1950s and 1960s. Steeped in both blues and bebop, he is an inventive guitarist with a great sound who has recorded many albums both as leader and side man. In 1958 he recorded *Kenny Burrell And John Coltrane*, a hard bop album with the leading saxophonist of his day and a top-flight rhythm section of Jimmy Cobb on drums, Paul Chambers on bass, and Tommy Flanagan on piano. Kenny is one of the grooviest players around, as can be heard on the 1963 classic *Midnight Blue*, an album that combines cool jazz with the newly emerging soul music and features the tenor sax of Stanley Turrentine. After a long career, Kenny is still recording and has in the last few years devoted himself to teaching.

The early career of Joe Pass was dogged by drug addiction, despite his obvious talent, with the result that he made little progress until the 1960s. After some time in rehab, he emerged as a major influence in the jazz guitar world. Initially, his focus was on long, flowing bebop lines, but Joe was a great chord player too, as can be heard on his 1964 quartet album *For Django*, supported by guitarist John Pisano.

The 1970 album *Intercontinental*, recorded in Europe, also has many standout tracks including 'Joe's Blues', one of many self-penned blues tracks that Pass was to record during his career. In 1972 he recorded the first *Virtuoso* album of entirely solo jazz guitar, followed in 1973 by an album of solo guitar accompanying Ella Fitzgerald on vocals.

Pass subsequently made several more albums under the *Virtuoso* banner and with Ella Fitzgerald, and it is in this area that his legacy to the guitar world is most important. His ability to play walking bass lines while simultaneously comping chords, to comp chords under melody lines, and to improvise the kind of complex arrangement that hitherto had only been found in composed classical guitar music still leaves most guitarists in awe of his amazing technique. He pushed the boundaries of guitar technique more than anyone in his generation.

Wes Montgomery was another leading light of the decade, starting in January 1960 with the classic album *The Incredible Jazz Guitar Of Wes Montgomery*. Wes had a very distinctive right-hand technique, playing only with his thumb and never using a pick as was standard in the jazz guitar world. This gave him a particularly warm tone without the harsh attack that can often be heard with a plectrum (listen to 'Gone With The Wind'). He also had no problem with fast tempos and hard bop, as can be heard on 'Airegin', also from the above album. He was not the first to use octaves when soloing (among others, Django Reinhardt was fond of octaves for emphatic solo passages) but he took their use to a level of fluency never heard before.

Much of Wes's later career involved lush string arrangements and was more pop than jazz, but his early guitar-focused albums, including *Boss Guitar* and *So Much Guitar*, did more than enough to guarantee his position as a major force in the instrument. He is, for example, cited as an important influence on the young Pat Metheny. Sadly Wes was to die of a heart attack in 1968, at the age of just 45.

The irony of the 1960s is that just as jazz guitarists were for the first time at the forefront of jazz, the record companies lost interest in it. After the Beatles-led 'British invasion', rock was more profitable than jazz, which suddenly seemed square, old-hat, and out of touch with its audience. Jazz, as the critic Albert Goodman was to remark, was "talking to itself". Fortunately, a new generation of guitarists arrived, determined to find a new way forward by blending elements of jazz with rock rhythms.

Wes Montgomery

Fusion

Larry Coryell's career began in earnest when he joined vibrophonist Gary Burton's quartet, with whom he recorded two albums. Burton was a jazz-rock pioneer, combining jazz improvisation with rock rhythms and sounds. Coryell's first album as leader was *Lady Coryell* on which he both plays and sings. It is a mixed bag; some tracks sound a little like the British blues/rock band Cream, themselves a fusion between a blues guitarist, Eric Clapton, and a jazz rhythm section. The title track, however, with its multi-layered, distorted guitars and hints of chaos is classic early jazz-rock. Other tracks, such as the jazz standard 'You Don't Know What Love Is' demonstrate Coryell's ability to play 'straight' jazz.

Coryell's career has had many twists and turns and blind alleys and he has a large back-catalogue of work with many of jazz's leading lights. A later jazz-rock outfit, Eleventh House (*Introducing Eleventh House With Larry Coryell*)[9] included Randy Brecker on trumpet and Alphonse Mouzon on percussion and is worth checking out, while for straight jazz his excellent collaboration with bassist Miroslav Vitous is worth hearing. In 1979 he formed The Guitar Trio with Paco de Lucia and John McLaughlin, although he was replaced by Al Di Meola on their outstanding album *Friday Night In San Francisco*.

Larry Coryell

It would be difficult to overstate the importance of English guitarist John McLaughlin on the jazz world. An innovator throughout his career, on both acoustic and electric guitars, he made his recording debut with *Extrapolation* in 1969. With its clean tone and angular phrasing, McLaughlin's playing can be heard as a natural development of earlier free, be-bop, and 1950s jazz styles. However, the overall approach is looser, noisier, and less self-consciously slick than much of the jazz that came before, giving the album a rock vibe. The sudden shifts in tempo and occasional 'free' moments introduce a new sound; these musicians had listened to the latest thing out of the USA and re-worked it their own way.

McLaughlin went on to play with Miles Davis on *In A Silent Way*, *Bitches Brew*, and others before forming the Mahavishnu Orchestra, and subsequently Shakti, both highly

influential bands that combined elements from rock, jazz, and the music of India. Later he worked with Indian percussionist Trilok Gurtu in the John McLaughlin Trio and continues to tour, silver-haired and in his seventies, with his band Fourth Dimension.

Spanish guitarist Paco de Lucia has all the power and dexterity required of a virtuoso flamenco guitarist but also made his mark as effectively the inventor of flamenco jazz, crossing over into the jazz genre particularly through his work in The Guitar Trio with Coryell and McLaughlin. His work is an example of the gradual process during the last 30 years by which jazz has become world music. Jazz has ceased to be about the repertoire of 'standard' songs and more about an approach, or philosophy, that allows music from all over the world to participate.

Not all fusion was 'edgy'. In his youth, George Benson was a fast and fluent player very much in the Wes Montgomery mould, as can be heard on his first quartet album, *It's Uptown* (with the classic hard-bop line-up of guitar, organ, drums, and tenor sax). However, he was to have his greatest commercial success with *Breezin'*, which consisted of laid-back funk grooves with Benson's cool solos often accompanied by scat singing. Jazz fans might know what a fine guitar player he is, but to the general public he was better known as a singer of hit soul songs. There is a direct line from the mostly excellent cool jazz-funk of Benson to the mostly forgettable 'smooth' jazz of the 1990s.

The closer we get to the present day the harder it is to be clear about where jazz is and where it is going. The most influential living, working guitarists are Pat Metheny, John Scofield, and Bill Frissell, each of whom has a distinctive voice, identifiable across a wide range of projects and with a sizeable back catalogue. There are many other fine guitarists from this era whose work deserves a mention but these three are by far the most significant.

Metheny's recording career began auspiciously at the age of 21 with *Bright Size Life*, a trio album featuring the innovative fretless electric bassist Jaco Pastorius and drummer Bob Moses. Metheny had already played with Gary Burton (as had Moses), and the compositions show a remarkable maturity in one so young. He has so far released more than a dozen albums as The Pat Metheny Group, with long-term collaborator Lyle Mays on piano, as well as solo, duo, and trio albums with leading artists such as Jack De Johnette, Charlie Haden, Billy Higgins, Dave Holland and many others. His career total is in excess of 60 albums.

The trio albums, which include *Question And Answer* and *Rejoicing* are good ways to get to know Metheny's jazz playing. He is hard to pin down, as his style seems to incorporate so much of the jazz that has gone before while still sounding fresh and original. Probably the most unique and unlikely ingredient in his writing and improvising is a healthy dose of down-home, wide-open spaces, Missouri country-meets-folk. Even in his blues solos (check out 'Turnaround' from the album *80/81*) you can hear snatches of major pentatonic scale. At the other extreme, *Song X* is his most challenging statement, a free-jazz collaboration with saxophonist Ornette Coleman. His most jazz-rock orientated projects are those with The Pat Metheny Group, such as *Offramp*.

Bill Frisell

John Scofield, like Bill Frisell, is a graduate of the Berklee College of Music in Boston. His debut recording was with Gerry Mulligan and Chet Baker, but more significantly he joined Miles Davis's band for three albums, *Star People*, *You're Under Arrest* and *Decoy*. As a leader, Scofield has recorded in excess of 30 albums; some of the highlights include *Still Warm* from 1985 and *Blue Matter* from 1986, which demonstrate his fluent yet angular post-bop phrasing and jazz/rock/funk influence. Later, more jazz-orientated quartet recordings, with saxophonist Joe Lovano, include *Time On My Hands*, *Meant To Be*, and *What We Do*, all recorded in the 1990s for the Blue Note label.

With *Uberjam* (2002), Scofield returned to a more funk-based groove, with added experimental sounds and samples. *A Go Go* (1997) and *Out Louder* (2006) with

Medeski, Martin, and Wood sought common ground between Scofield's jazz-funk and the trio's avant garde tendencies. All the above CDs are well worth a listen; John Scofield has one of the most distinctive and easily identifiable voices in all of jazz.

Bill Frisell, like Pat Metheny, is also influenced by country music, and most other things too, including rhythm & blues. He uses more electronic effects than most jazz guitarists, particularly a combination of volume pedal and delay unit that allows him to create sounds which sustain infinitely. He is as comfortable with a jazz standard as he is when multitracking on guitar all the vocal parts to Aretha Franklin's 'Chain Of Fools' on *Is That You?* His playing can be textural, ethereal, or downright funky. Nevertheless, there is an underlying jazz awareness in all his playing

Frisell's first album as leader was *In Line* from 1983, which included absorbing guitar solos and duets with bassist Arild Andersen. His catalogue to date exceeds 30 albums. The album *East/West*, from 2005, is a good place to start for anyone seeking to explore this complex and varied player; a double CD of two separate live sets with different bands, recorded in California and New York, it is a fascinating mix of jazz standards and Frisell originals. On *Ghost Town*, from 2000, Frisell accompanies himself on banjo as well as on acoustic and electric guitars and loops; the varied set includes the old time classic 'Wildwood Flower', Hank Williams's 'I'm So Lonesome I Could Cry', and Gershwin's 'My Man's Gone Now'.

Fusion part two

Good technique is a prerequisite of jazz guitar playing, and from the 1980s onwards a new influence came to bear on the jazz-inclined guitarist. A generation of rock players, often called 'shredders', came along, led by Eddie Van Halen, closely followed by Joe Satriani and Steve Vai. They combined intense speed with innovative techniques such as two-handed tapping and expressive use of the vibrato arm. And, of course, their distorted guitar tones were unmistakably rock.

Scott Henderson is a rock-influenced jazz guitarist, forming Tribal Tech with bassist Gary Willis in 1984. They produced nine albums between 1985 and 2000 exploring the boundaries between jazz, rock, and funk. Henderson is a fluent and inventive soloist with a warm, distorted sound combined with expressive effects such as harmonic squeals and vibrato-arm bends. *Thick* is a great example of his work, mixing free-form and varied noise-based improvisation with intense and vibrant melodies over a relentless funk groove.

Other modern fusionistas deserving of a mention are Allan Holdsworth, Mike Stern, Larry Carlton, Lee Ritenour, and Wayne Krantz. These five do not necessarily have anything in common; their music ranges from supersmooth West Coast grooves (Carlton) to angular New York funk (Krantz) to leaping legato melodies and extended harmony (Holdsworth).

John Scofield

Marc Ribot

Kurt Rosenwinkel

21st-century jazz guitar

Frizzell, Metheny and Scofield have continued to dominate the early years of the 21st century, but it would be wrong to leave the 20th century without mentioning British guitarist Derek Bailey, a relentless and determined devotee of guitar-based free improvisation. New York-based Marc Ribot is also determinedly avant garde, though with a background in soul and rhythm and blues and a long list of collaborations.

Guitarists such as Tuck Andress and Martin Taylor are walking in the footsteps of Joe Pass, doing it all on one guitar with no accompaniment necessary. Andress is a particularly innovative guitarist, weaving complex textures using a mixture of conventional picking, tapping, and slapping in the renowned duo Tuck & Patti. Taylor balances basslines, comped chords, and melodies with the skill of a circus juggler. He has also achieved considerable success paying tribute to the music of Django Reinhardt in the band Spirit Of Django.

As for the future, here are a few guitarists from around the world who may prove to be influential in the coming years; in the USA, Kurt Rosenwinkel, Jonathan Kreisberg, Brad Shepik, and Ben Monder; in Europe, Austria's Wolfgang Muthspiel and Holland's Jesse van Ruller; and from Benin in West Africa, Lionel Loueke. Check these players out to hear the latest in jazz guitar. And remember, the starting point for all jazz study is to get out to live gigs and hear it played for real.

PART 1
Making a start

- A guitar for jazz
- Guitar basics
- Beginning with the blues
- Some theory – and all five blues scale shapes
- Intervals and minor blues
- Major pentatonic scales

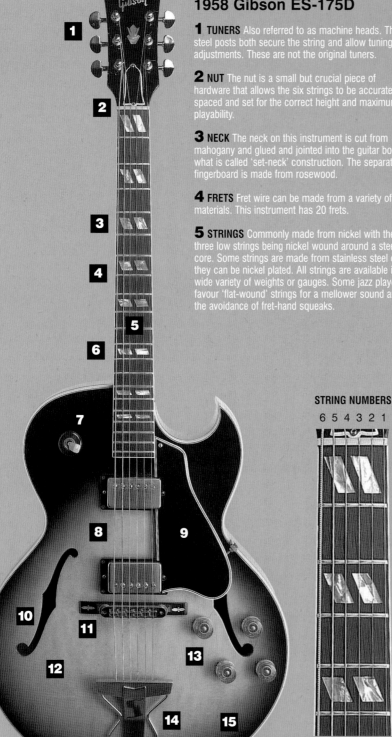

1958 Gibson ES-175D

1 TUNERS Also referred to as machine heads. These steel posts both secure the string and allow tuning adjustments. These are not the original tuners.

2 NUT The nut is a small but crucial piece of hardware that allows the six strings to be accurately spaced and set for the correct height and maximum playability.

3 NECK The neck on this instrument is cut from mahogany and glued and jointed into the guitar body in what is called 'set-neck' construction. The separate fingerboard is made from rosewood.

4 FRETS Fret wire can be made from a variety of materials. This instrument has 20 frets.

5 STRINGS Commonly made from nickel with the three low strings being nickel wound around a steel core. Some strings are made from stainless steel or they can be nickel plated. All strings are available in a wide variety of weights or gauges. Some jazz players favour 'flat-wound' strings for a mellower sound and the avoidance of fret-hand squeaks.

6 POSITION MARKERS These inlayed reference points indicate fret positions to help the players find their way around the guitar's fingerboard. These examples are called block markers and are in a dual parallelogram shape. They are made of mother of pearl.

7 SWITCH The three-way selector switch allows the player to select either pickup or both.

8 PICKUPS Originally produced with a single P90 pickup, the ES-175 acquired humbuckers in 1957. Each pickup sounds different because of its location. The bridge pickup sounds bright and trebly; the neck pickup is full and rounded.

9 PICKGUARD Also known as the scratchplate, this has the function of protecting the body from plectrum strokes and covering the holes cut for the electronics. This scratchplate is made from five-ply laminated plastic.

10 F-HOLES Soundholes play a part in sound production by allowing the guitar's top to vibrate more freely and by permitting sound to emerge from inside the instrument. F-holes were originally used in the violin family and only introduced to the guitar world by Gibson in the 1920s.

11 BRIDGE The bridge supports the strings and transmits their vibrations to the top or soundboard. This is not the original bridge but a later version known as a Tune-O-Matic.

12 BODY The body of this guitar is made from laminated maple, heat-pressed to create the arch-top shape. Before Gibson introduced the technique, the tops of all arch-top guitars had been carved from solid wood. Some still are.

13 CONTROLS The ES-175 features individual tone and volume controls for each pickup.

14 TAILPIECE Arch-top guitars feature floating tailpieces that anchor the strings and sit above the soundboard so as not to inhibit its vibration. This particular design is known as the zigzag style.

15 FINISH This guitar was available in natural or, as here, sunburst finish.

STRING NUMBERS

6 5 4 3 2 1

1
2
3

FRET NUMBERS

4

E A D G B E

TUNING

Section 1

A guitar for jazz

It might be tempting to think you need one of those big fat arch-top guitars for jazz, but in all probability you need look no further than the guitar you already have. Acoustic guitars, whether nylon-strung or steel-strung, can do the job very well. Most solidbody guitars can also be used for jazz, using the neck pickup; the Fender Telecaster, for example, has a surprisingly good jazz tone. If you are starting from scratch, however, or if you feel it's time you gave way to an attack of guitar acquisition syndrome, it might be worthwhile thinking about the ideal jazz guitar.

Instead of just recommending a brand, or a model, we are going to suggest the ingredients and options that might help you to make a good decision. Even the most casual survey of jazz guitar players indicates that they tend to like hollowbodied instruments. Jazz players mostly use clean or only slightly overdriven guitar sounds, because the harmonic complexity of jazz does not sit well with the sort of intense distortion that might work well for a metal band. So jazz guitarists have no particular need to choose a solidbody instrument like a Gibson Les Paul or a Fender Stratocaster, and they are not troubled by the howling feedback that would plague a hollowbody guitar if it were to be played at extreme volume or with intense distortion.

Most solidbody guitars produce overtones that make it difficult to hear the individual notes in complex chord voicings. This is a generalisation, but there is something about the air inside an arch-top, and the arch-top's construction, that seems to suppress certain overtones and allow the individual notes of a chord to be heard more clearly. Arch-tops also have a lean mid-range and a fast decay, which allows rapidly played notes to be distinguished clearly. This means choosing between an acoustic arch-top like an L-5 (with or without an electric pickup), with its acoustic-like response, a pressed/laminate arch-top like an ES-175, with its better feedback rejection, or a semi-solid guitar like an ES-335, which has a solid centre core with hollow wings and which has some of the qualities of both solid and arch-top guitars. We are using Gibson guitars as a guide because they so accurately define the types of guitar available, but there are many other manufacturers including Eastman, Epiphone, Gretsch, Heritage, Hofner, and Ibanez, all making arch-top guitars in a range of styles and budgets. There are also many individual luthiers making specialist instruments to order, and brands from the Far East catering for the cheaper end of the market.

You will probably want a guitar with humbucking pickups, although a fat single-coil pickup like a P90 could be an option. If you are heading for some old-school guitar tones you could try fitting your guitar with flat-wound strings, which are smooth under the fingers and don't give out string squeaks when you're sliding along. They have a mellow and fat sound and are much less zingy than standard round-wound strings.

There is also a type of string known as a half-round, which combines elements of both. Shorter scale-length guitars also tend to have a slightly mellower tone than long-scale guitars. The scale-length on a Gibson ES-175 is 24¾ inches, while on the L-5, like the Epiphone Broadway, it is 25½ inches. Not only is this difference enough to make two similar guitars sound different, if you are trying to stretch short fingers over awkward jazz chords you might prefer the frets to be just a fraction closer together, which they are with a shorter scale-length.

Pretty much everything in a guitar's construction has some effect on its sound. Details such as floating or fixed bridge, wood or tune-o-matic bridge, slim or fat neck — even the weight and style of the tuning pegs — can all bring about subtle differences. For an acoustic arch-top, the choice of wood is fundamental, but it is less so for a laminated guitar. European spruce (*picea abies*) is the most popular choice for an acoustic top, with maple for the back and sides. Mahogany can also be used for the back and sides, but with a different tonal signature. Traditionally, acoustic arch-top guitars have parallel bracing, but as long ago as the 1930s D'Angelico was making arch-tops with X bracing to increase sustain.

Finally, consider whether a deep-bodied jazz box is really for you. Some players find it hard to get comfortable with a deep guitar and as a result prefer thin-bodied or 'thinline' guitars, around one-and-a-half inches deep instead of the usual three or four inches. Clearly, there are many questions a shrewd guitar buyer could ask of a sales person to be sure the instrument is the right one; it is best to get out and play a range of guitars before you make your choice. As for cost, while there are some bargains out there it is fair to say that in the guitar world you get what you pay for. People often say 'buy cheap, buy twice'. Hopefully, these paragraphs of advice will help you to buy the best guitar you can afford.

Whatever type of guitar you play, remember that the way your guitar is set up is a very important part of the playing experience. If the strings are a long way from the fretboard (high action) the guitar will be a struggle to play. If the strings are too low (low action) you will be plagued by fret buzz and the dynamic range of the instrument will be limited. Since jazz is one of the more dynamic styles of music (with a wider range of loud and soft sounds compared to rock, for example) a medium action is preferable. Don't feel you have to have the pickups as close to the strings as possible; a more rounded tone and better string to string balance can be obtained in exchange for a slight loss of output.

Section 2
Guitar basics

This book is not really aimed at the complete beginner, but if you've had just a little experience playing the guitar you should find the first few exercises achievable and be able to progress smoothly from there. I strongly recommend my book *The Electric Guitar Handbook* if you are a complete beginner and are looking for some help with the basics. Cross over to *The Jazz Guitar Handbook* once you are ready and you'll find plenty that looks familiar. Reading music is also covered in more depth in *The Electric Guitar Handbook*.

As much as possible, the exercises in this book are progressive, with each one leading on to the next. But there's nothing to stop you dipping in and out – especially if you are just looking to add some jazz touches to your playing. Occasionally, you may find one exercise harder than the others. Don't lose heart, don't get bogged down, and don't give up. Keep going through the book, but keep returning to anything you had difficulty with. Always practise slowly at first, only bringing up the speed when you can play an exercise correctly at a slow speed. Be patient, persevere, and you'll get there. One possible strategy when using this book is to work on Part One and Part Two simultaneously; Part One deals with single notes and improvisation, while Part Two deals with chords and harmony. The two parts complement each other very well.

Here are some points to get you started:

The hands

For most players the left hand frets the strings on the neck while the right hand plucks the strings down near the bridge. In deference to left-handed players (who often choose to do things the other way around) we shall refer in this book to fretting hand and picking hand. If you are left-handed and have not yet bought a left-handed guitar you might consider learning to play right-handed. After all there is no such thing as a left-handed violin, a left-handed flute or, come to that, a left-handed piano. So there's no reason why one hand should necessarily be better at picking than fretting. The main advantage to learning to play right-handed is that there is a much larger range of right-handed instruments than left-handed instruments. You'll also be able to pick up any guitar at a gig, jam session, or friend's home and play it like your own – a luxury that left-handers often have to forgo.

■ The fretting-hand fingers are numbered 1–4, starting with the index finger, so your pinky is finger 4.

■ The convention (borrowed from classical guitar) for naming the picking-hand fingers, when they are specified, is:

Thumb	=	p
Index	=	i
Middle	=	m
Third finger	=	a

To help you remember, think 'pima', starting with your thumb. The letters come from the Spanish words *pulgar*, *indice*, *media*, and *anular*. The little finger of the picking hand is not often used and has no name in classical guitar, but in flamenco, where it is used for strumming downstrokes, it is called the *menique* and indicated by the letter 'e', so we'll use that where we need it.

Standing

When standing it's important to carry the weight of the guitar on your shoulder and across your back. A good-quality adjustable strap is essential; one that doesn't slip around is best. Don't have the strap too long; a good rule of thumb is that your fretting-hand wrist should be higher than its elbow. This can be a problem, as straps always seem to be made for giants. Check this out before you buy!

Sitting

Practising sitting down is less tiring than practising standing up and will allow you to put in the hours necessary to achieve superhero status. In other words, I recommend it very strongly. Don't use a chair with arms as they will restrict your movements. You could still use a strap to keep the guitar neck up – around a 45 degree angle is ideal, with the headstock about level with your shoulder. Avoid letting the neck dip below the horizontal; not only is the guitar extremely difficult to play with the neck too low, there is also a risk of injury as you strain to get your hands in the right positions when you're playing all those cool jazz chords.

Using the pick

The examples in this book are all intended for the standard six-string electric guitar played with a pick, although some examples are intended for thumb and fingers, otherwise known as 'fingerstyle'. You could also use a steel-string acoustic, or a nylon-string classical guitar – very appropriate for some of the bossa nova examples. Pick technique is a personal matter for every player, but here is some general guidance to get you started. Hold the pick between your thumb and forefinger and point it straight at the guitar strings. If you get it right your thumb will be pointing along the strings and your forefinger pointing straight at the guitar.

Reading the music

The next few pages are a guide to reading the standard guitar notation in this book. For a full course on reading music I humbly recommend my own *How To Read Music* or *The Electric Guitar Handbook*.

Music is written on a stave. The exercises in this book are mostly written on two staves, a notation stave at the top with a tablature stave underneath. The top one has five lines for standard musical notation, or 'dots' as musicians often call it. The tablature (or 'tab') stave has six lines with each one representing a different string of the guitar. The highest sounding string is at the top, the lowest sounding string is at the bottom. The numbers on the lines tell you which frets to play. To avoid cluttering up the music, rhythms are written only in the notation stave.

Fig 1
Staccato, accent and
accented staccato

Fig 2a
Full and 1/2 step bends
Bend and release

Fig 2b
Quarter tone bend
Pre-bend

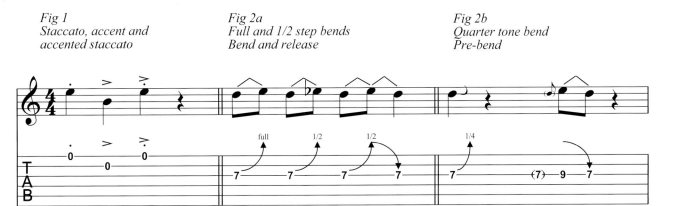

Figures 1, 1a and 2a

Figure 1 above deals with articulation, meaning the volume and duration of notes. A staccato note is cut short of its full duration: 50 per cent is a good guideline. An accented note is played louder or with more attack than others in the phrase. Figures 2a and 2b demonstrate the notation for different types of bends. Bends can be half-step (semitone), whole-step (whole tone) or quarter-step (which is the same as slightly sharp). You can also pre-bend a string before picking it and then release it so that only the descending part of the bend is heard.

THE JAZZ GUITAR HANDBOOK

Fig 3
Glissandos and slides
Slide up or down
Slide to and from 'nowhere'

Fig 4
Hammer-ons and pull-offs
ascending and descending
and linked together

Figures 3 and 4

Slides or glissandos can be both upwards and downwards between specific frets or can have less distinct start and end points. In a hammer-on the first note is picked and the second note is played by hammering a finger of the fretting hand on to the fretboard. In a pull-off the first note is picked and the second note is sounded by pulling off the string with a finger of the fretting hand. Hammer-ons and pull-offs can be chained together – only the first note is picked.

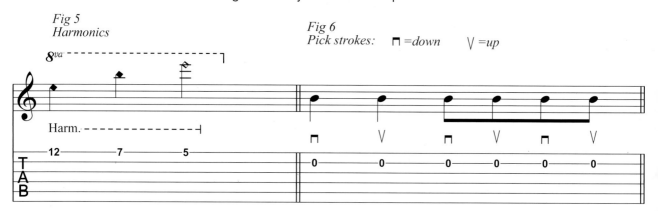

Fig 5
Harmonics

Fig 6
Pick strokes: ⊓ *=down*   ⋁ *=up*

Figures 5 and 6

Harmonics are bell-like sounds that can be sounded above certain frets on the guitar: the string is only touched lightly and not held down in the conventional way. Pick direction can affect the feel of a rhythm: for this reason many of the exercises in the book include instructions on picking.

Fig 7
Repeat from beginning

Fig 8
Repeat between repeat signs

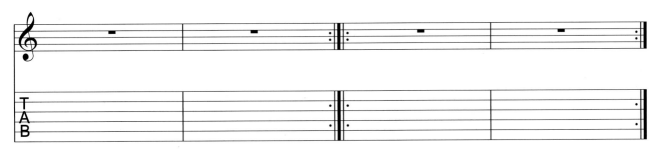

Figures 7 and 8

Repeat symbols show where a section of music is repeated. A double thickness bar-line with two dots appearing at the end of a bar tells you to go back to the beginning (Figure 7). A repeat sign facing right tells you to repeat the music between the two repeat signs (Figure 8).

Fig 9
First and second time bars

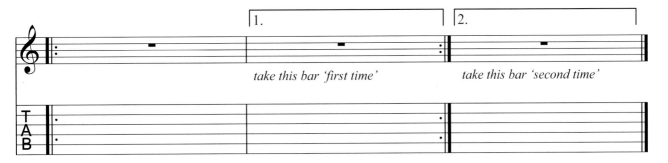

take this bar 'first time'   take this bar 'second time'

Figure 9

A 'first time' or 'second time' bar lets the music have two different endings (Figure 9). Go from the beginning to the first time bar, and on repeating use the second time bar instead.

THE JAZZ GUITAR HANDBOOK

Notes:

16th–note   8th–note   Quarter–note   Half–note   Dotted Half–note   Whole note

Equivalent rests:

Figure 10 Note names and rests

Finally, Figure 10 is a chart showing the names of all the note types coming up in the book. This is just in case you are not a music reader and you see something like "play the three eighth-notes in bar one" – you'll know what type of note to look out for. If you are unsure of the letter names of the notes on the guitar you will find all the information, including fret positions and music notation, in the Appendix at the back of the book.

Getting in tune

No matter what you play on guitar, it won't sound good if you're out of tune. Always start your practice session, rehearsal, or gig by getting in tune: nowadays it's easy with a guitar tuner. Tuners are not expensive and some types clip on to the guitar and don't need to be plugged in, which is great for acoustic. Modern tuners recognise the string you're tuning automatically, and use a system of lights or a needle to show whether the string is sharp (too high) or flat (too low). Sound one string at a time, following it back to its tuning peg so that you know which one to adjust and which way to turn it. There's no need to spend hours on it – 'close enough' will be fine – but it will be worth the effort. If you tune your guitar accurately with a tuner and then find that chords played higher up the neck sound out of tune your guitar may need a setup. Your local guitar tech will adjust the intonation for you so that the guitar stays in tune over the whole neck.

Section 3
Beginning with the blues

B lues and jazz share a common musical heritage, and although jazz has since absorbed many external influences the blues still lives in the heart of jazz. The blues has a simple harmonic form, which is great for learning to improvise, so we are going to start by learning a blues-flavoured piece, which takes its inspiration from a tune called 'Chitlins Con Carne' by the great Detroit-born guitarist Kenny Burrell. You can find this track on his classic *Midnight Blue* album.

Exercise 1.01

Play 'Kenny's Blues' (see over the page) starting with your fretting-hand third finger at the fifth fret on the A-string. You can play the whole thing using just fingers one and three. Your first finger is going down on the third fret, and we count positions on the guitar according to whichever fret your first finger is at, so we would say this piece is in the third position. Alternate picking, or economy picking as it is sometimes known, is the best approach for your picking hand. The pick strokes are included in the first few bars. Basically, each downstroke is followed by an upstroke, except when only playing on the downbeats, as in the lead-in bar or bar four, when it's okay to repeat downstrokes. (By downbeats, we mean one of the main four beats of the bar.)

The whole piece is based on a simple, but nevertheless cool-sounding and very useful scale. It's called a minor pentatonic scale; minor, because it has the minor third, which is found in the minor chord, and pentatonic because it has only five notes. If some of that sentence seemed to be in an alien language, don't worry; in time we will get to grips with intervals and it will all make sense. The scales that we play in rock and jazz are more useful than the technical exercise scales that are found in classical music, because we can use them to make up riffs, licks, and most of all, to improvise solos.

SOUNDS: all the CD tracks in Part One were played using an Ibanez guitar based on the Gibson ES175 design. The pickups have been upgraded to Seymour Duncan Antiquities and the guitar is strung with flat-wound strings. This all-maple laminate guitar has a bright sound and the flat-wounds mellow the tone a little, and only the neck pickup was used, mostly with the tone rolled off to about number eight. The amp was a Fender Deluxe Reverb from the early 1970s, known as 'silverface' to distinguish it from the earlier 'blackface' models. The speaker is not stock, the original having been replaced with a Celestion Blue. The combination produces a rich, clean tone with a wide dynamic range and just a hint of bite when you dig in with the pick.

Exercise 1.01
CD TRACK 1
'Kenny's Blues'

THEORY: there is a metronome mark at the start of the piece, telling us there are 105 quarter-notes per minute. This is usually shortened to BPM, or beats per minute. Also notice the chord symbols which give you the underlying harmony on which the piece is based – we'll cover chords thoroughly starting in Part Two.

TECHNIQUE: avoid elaborate movements with the pick when playing single-note exercises or scales. Aim to keep the pick between the strings at all times; just move it from side to side.

THE JAZZ GUITAR HANDBOOK

G minor pentatonic scale shape 1

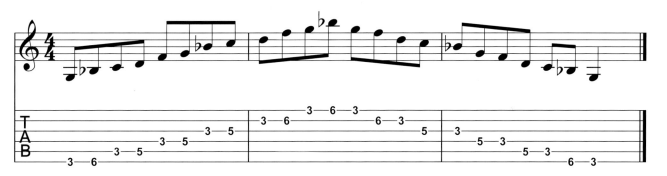

Fingering   **Scale degrees**

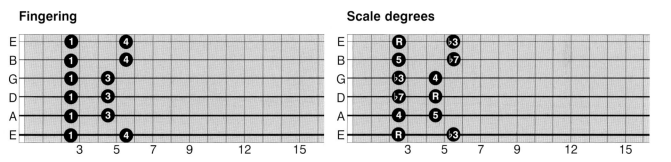

Exercise 1.02

Here is the G minor pentatonic scale, written out to cover the full two octaves that you can reach in the third position on the guitar. Notice that although the scale begins on the root note, G, the highest note is a B-flat; in classical music, scales tend to be played from root note to root note, but in jazz, because we are interested in using the scale for improvisation, we play all the notes we can reach in one position. Follow the fret-hand fingering that is given (on the left), even if you're one of those guitarists who doesn't make much use of your pinky (finger four): now is the time to learn. To play jazz you're going to need all four fretting-hand fingers, and maybe your thumb sometimes too.

TECHNIQUE: when you play scales, make sure you use alternate picking – this is where any notes an eighth-note or shorter are played with a downstroke followed by an upstroke. Start with a downstroke and simply go down-up-down-up all the way across the guitar and back.

You will find that all the notes in 'Kenny's Blues' come from the minor pentatonic scale. Pretty soon, we are going to be using this scale to make up a blues of your own, but first, we need to learn a blues scale.

Exercise 1.02
CD TRACK 2
G minor pentatonic scale shape 1

Exercise 1.03

The blues scale is very like the minor pentatonic scale, but it has one extra note in each octave. In the key of G, the extra note is C-sharp or D-flat (that's the same note by a different name). Just for convenience we call it C-sharp (C♯) for the ascending scale and D-flat (D♭) for the descending part of the scale. Sometimes this extra note is called a 'blue note' as it adds an extra blues twist to the scale. Once again make sure you play it using all four fretting-hand fingers and using alternate picking. The picking is harder on this scale because some strings have two notes and some strings have three. Keep a close eye on your picking hand at first, and when you are confident you can alternate-pick the whole scale, play it without looking at your picking hand. Then play it without looking at either hand; gaze out at your audience, smiling confidently. Seriously though, being able to play without looking at your hands is a useful skill, not least because you'll be able to make eye contact with your fellow band members.

THEORY: in music, terms like 'low' and 'high' always refer to the pitch of the music. So the 'low' end of the guitar is near the nut, on the first few frets where the lowest notes are found. If you read "go up one fret" it means go "one fret higher in pitch". This would mean moving your hand in a downward direction nearer to the floor. It's the same with strings: your low E-string is nearest the ceiling and your high E-string is nearest the floor. Get used to these terms now or you will find some of the coming explanations confusing. Just remember that low and high *always* refer to pitch.

TECHNIQUE: it's up to you what sound to use, but jazz players tend to prefer a clean sound (not too much distortion) so that touch and dynamics can come through. Rock players tend to solo using the bridge pickup – jazzers will frequently use the neck pickup for a fat tone.

G blues scale shape 1

Fingering

Scale degrees

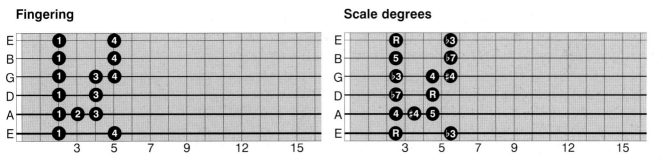

Exercise 1.03
CD TRACK 3
G blues scale shape 1

THE JAZZ GUITAR HANDBOOK

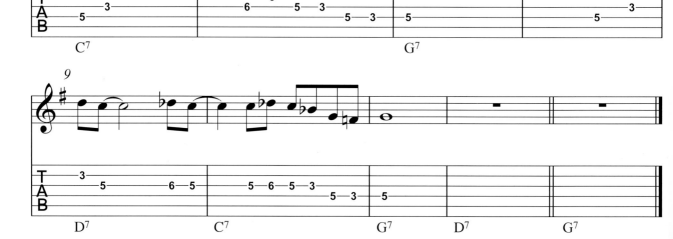

Exercise 1.04

CD TRACK 4

'Blue Note Blues'

Exercise 1.04

'Blue Note Blues', Exercise 1.04, pushes the technique a little more, with some slightly longer eighth-note runs, and also lets you get used to the sound of the blue note in the blues scale on which it is based. It has some things in common with 'Kenny's Blues', Exercise 1.01, which we need to mention. For example, if you exclude the two quarter-notes that make up the lead-in you have a 12-bar structure. This follows a recognised and much-used chord sequence known as a 12-bar blues.

G	G	G	G
C	C	G	G
D	C	G	D

THE JAZZ GUITAR HANDBOOK

These chords are often all played as 'seventh' chords; this gives the music more of a blues flavour:

G7	G7	G7	G7
C7	C7	G7	G7
D7	C7	G7	D7

If you don't know how to play these chords, don't worry – we'll get to that in Part Two. The important point is to understand that there is a common *harmonic structure* to these exercises.

One more point while we're talking about the 12-bar blues: we often add a little interest by moving to the C chord in the second bar, making what is sometimes called a 'quick-change' blues.

G7	C7	G7	G7
C7	C7	G7	G7
D7	C7	G7	D7

We'll use this sequence later and also look at other ways round the 12-bar that make it sound more jazzy.

Another similarity between 1.01 and 1.04 is that they are both constructed using call-and-response, or question-and-answer, phrasing; this is very common in the blues and is a great way of making improvisation seem structured. The lead-in and the first bar are a question, which is answered in the next bar. In bars five and six the question is asked again, in bars seven and eight it is answered again, and so on. It's very important to grasp this question-and-answer idea, as it is a dependable device for building solos. You will need it when you come to make up your own.

TECHNIQUE: once again the whole piece is in the third position. Keep your fretting-hand fingers close to the fingerboard and use one finger for each fret. Also, notice the picking instructions: write in your own in bars 10-12 following the alternate picking principle.

THEORY: jazz can be described as a musical language, but in many ways is a 'dialect' of music, as is 'classical' or 'pop'. As with learning any language, your ears are your most important asset and you should be listening to jazz at every opportunity. If you don't know where to begin, try working your way through the guitarists mentioned in the jazz history section at the start of the book.

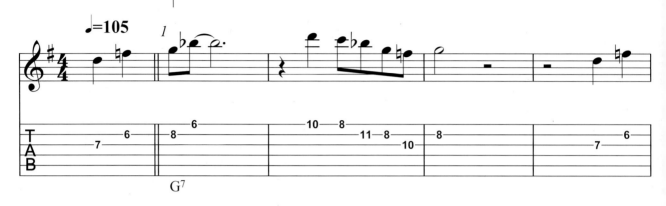

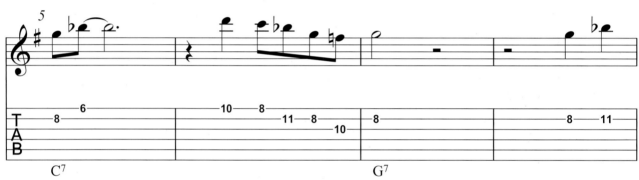

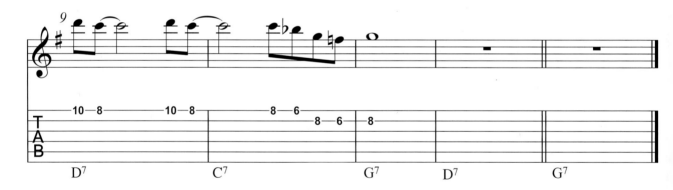

Exercise 1.05

CD TRACK 5

'Kenny's Blues', octave up

Exercise 1.05

Exercise 1.05 is the music of Exercise 1.01 played an octave higher, with a slight change in bar nine to keep things interesting. This exercise pushes the boundaries a little by requiring several position changes. The piece begins with your second finger on the seventh fret of the G-string; that means you're in the sixth (VI) position. The next phrase begins on the note D, at the 10th fret on the top string. It makes sense to play this with your third finger, so you're in the eighth (VIII) position. When making this position change, put your third finger on the top string while your hand is still in the sixth position and use the string as a guide, sliding along without pressing as you move your hand up two frets, taking your thumb with you on the back of the neck.

THE JAZZ GUITAR HANDBOOK

TECHNIQUE: position changes are always easier if you use a string as a guide for the finger you have to put down. If you find it hard to hit the right fret, try looking at the fret you're aiming for rather than watching your hand.

THEORY: the simplest explanation for an octave is "the same note at a different pitch". If you play two notes an octave apart simultaneously you would hear that the notes seem to merge into one; they sound the same, but at different pitch. This is why they can have the same letter name. Musical sounds are waveforms, and waveforms have frequency. Each time the music goes up an octave, the frequency doubles.

Exercise 1.06

All the notes of Exercise 1.05 come from the same minor pentatonic scale as Exercise 1.01, but they are played in higher positions on the neck. If we call the first pentatonic scale we learned shape one, then the notes we are playing in the sixth position will be from shape two, and the notes we are playing in the eighth position will be from shape three. In Exercise 1.06 we see the minor pentatonic scale shapes two and three stretched out all the way across the guitar neck. Note that shape two is in fact played in the fifth position and not the sixth, as some notes in the scale fall on the fifth fret. Take a moment to check out how these two scale shapes were used in Exercise 1.05.

PRO TIP

Just for fun, and for a change, put down your pick and experiment by playing the exercises with your thumb or with the index and middle fingers of your pick hand. You'll produce a different sound and be in good company – Charlie Byrd was a fingerstyle player and the great Wes Montgomery only ever used his thumb.

Exercise 1.06
CD TRACK 6
G minor pentatonic scales shapes 2 and 3

G minor pentatonic shape 2

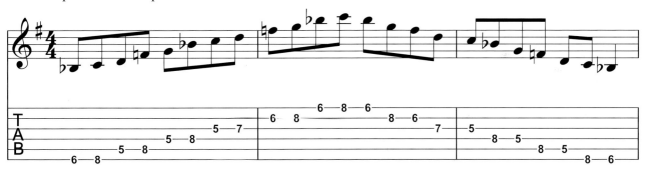

Fingering

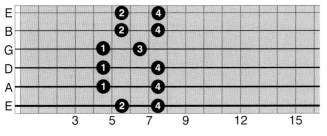

Scale degrees

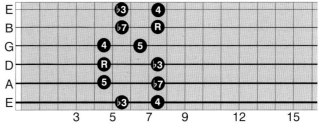

continued over page

THE JAZZ GUITAR HANDBOOK

Exercise 1.06 *continued*

G minor pentatonic shape 3

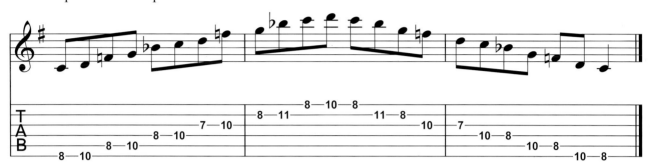

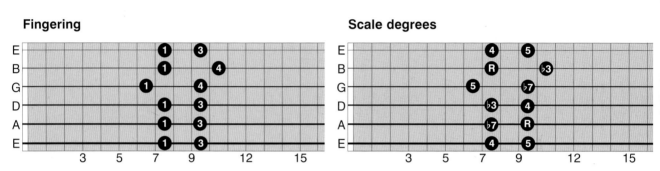

Fingering

Scale degrees

TECHNIQUE: notice that in scale shape three you begin in the eighth position but have to jump down one fret to the seventh position when you come to the G-string.

The important thing about these two new scale shapes is that they don't introduce any new notes. They are made up of the same five-note scale that we saw in Exercise 1.02, but shifted up the guitar neck. There are two reasons why this may be useful. Firstly, the top note of the scale is different, so we have shifted the range of the scale up slightly. Secondly, the way the notes are arranged on the strings has changed. If, for example you wanted to do a slide from a C to D on the G-string it would be best to use shape two, as in shape one these two notes are on different strings.

Exercises 1.07 and 1.08
You can probably guess what we're doing in Exercise 1.07. This is the blue note exercise, Exercise 1.04, taken up an octave, just as we did with Exercise 1.01. As you can see, the fingering is a bit more complex and you also have to deal with the position changes. This exercise is based on blues scale shapes two and three, which can be found in Exercise 1.08 (over the page). Use the fingerings for those shapes and the guide-finger method when changing positions.

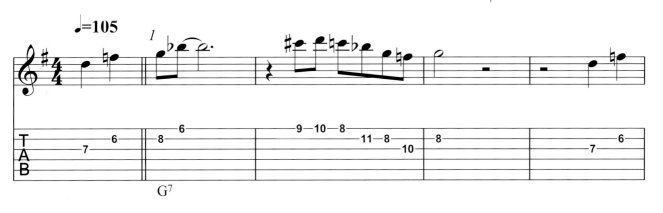

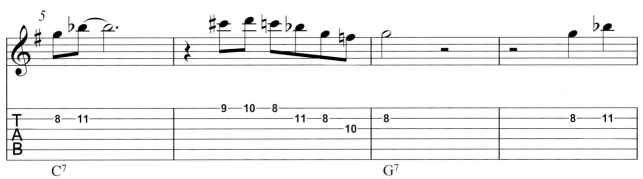

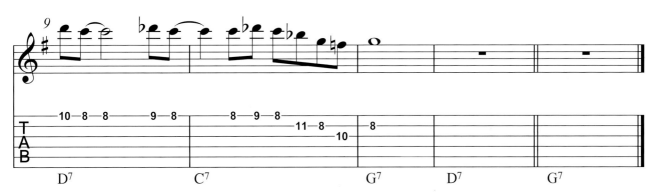

Exercise 1.07
CD TRACK 7
'Blue Note Blues',
octave up

Exercise 1.08 CD TRACK 8 *G blues scales shapes 2 and 3*

G blues scale shape 2

Fingering

Scale degrees

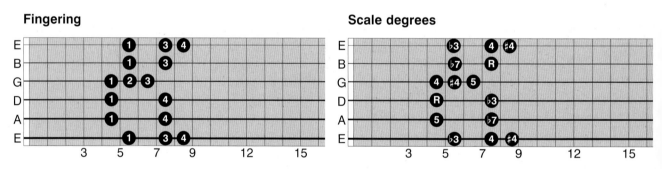

THEORY: notice that we've added some notes at the end of these two scales so they both end on the root note, G. Ending on the root note gives a more satisfactory conclusion to the scale and emphasises the sense of key. One way of explaining what is meant by a key in music is to think of it as being like gravity – the music is always somehow being pulled in the direction of the key-note.

THE JAZZ GUITAR HANDBOOK

Exercise 1.08 *continued*

G blues scale shape 3

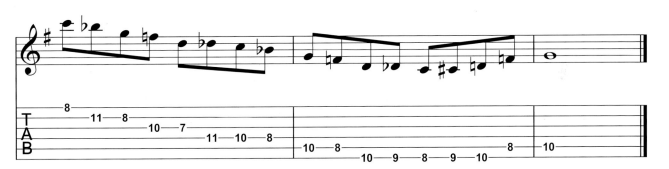

Fingering

Scale degrees

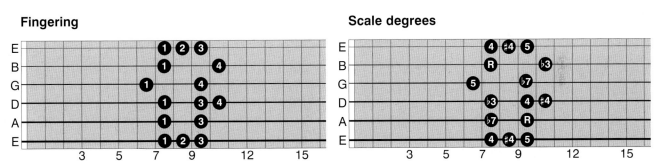

Section 4
Some theory – and all five blues scale shapes

There is a saying among musicians that if you can play jazz you can probably play most things. One reason for this is that to play jazz you need to have a good technical command of your instrument. Another reason is that jazz musicians tend to have – and need – a good grasp of chords and scales and how they relate to each other. Music theory, in other words.

When it comes to learning about music theory, the major scale is the best starting point. It is the major scale that gives us our key system and most of the chords and other scales that are in common use. The simplest major scale begins on the note C, and uses only the 'white notes', so it has no sharps or flats. This gives it a sequence of whole-steps (whole-tones) and half-steps (semitones) that is characteristic of all major scales. It is conventional to number the steps (or degrees) of a scale using Roman numerals.

Exercise 1.09

A major scale consists mostly of whole-steps, but with half-steps between the third and fourth notes and the seventh and eighth notes. To create a major scale starting on a different note – in other words, in a new key – we would need to preserve the same pattern of whole steps and half-steps. For example, if we were to start on G, we would need to add the note F-sharp instead of F, in order to preserve the half-step between the seventh note and the eighth note octave.

Exercise 1.09
CD TRACK 9
C major scale

Exercise 1.10

Play Exercises 1.09 and 1.10 and you will hear the two different major scales starting on different notes, but essentially sounding the same; this is because the pattern of whole-steps and half-steps is the same for both scales. If we were to write a piece of music in the key of G major we could put the F-sharp at the beginning of the piece as

G A B C D E F# G F# E D C B A G

Exercise 1.10
CD TRACK 10
G major scale

a 'key signature' and it would save us having to write a ♯ sign in front of every F in the piece. That is why there is an F-sharp in the key signature at the start of Example 1.10, and an F-sharp at the start of all the preceding blues examples we've played so far; it's like a code to say the music is in G major. It may seem strange that as we are playing the blues and using the blues scale, in which all the Fs are natural rather than sharp, all the Fs in the piece still have to be marked with a natural sign. The blues, however, is a special case, and on balance it is still worthwhile using key signatures when writing jazz and blues.

We can start a major scale on every single letter name, including all of the sharp and flat notes. Each letter name or 'key' would have its own signature of sharps or flats at the beginning of the stave. On the next two pages we have all the key signatures and notes for all of the common keys.

Sharp keys and flat keys

Each letter name occurs once in each major scale. From chart (see over) you can see that D major is D E F♯ G A B C♯ D. F major is F G A B♭ C D E F. As a project, see if you can work out the rest of these scales for yourself. Then play each one on the guitar.

If you are puzzled by E-sharp and C-flat, E-sharp is another name for F and C-flat is another name for B. We need these notes because each letter name is allowed once only in each scale.

Major scales have an important role to play in jazz and we will return to them again shortly, but right now there's one more important thing. We're using chords of G, C, and D to play the blues. Notice that these chords are built on the first, fourth, and fifth notes of a G major scale. We often use Roman numerals to indicate the chords built on the various steps of a scale. In that system, G, C, and D are I, IV, and V of the major scale in G.

Using the Roman numeral method, we could say the chords of a blues are:

I	I	I	I
IV	IV	I	I
V	IV	I	V

THE JAZZ GUITAR HANDBOOK

SOME THEORY – AND ALL FIVE BLUES SCALE SHAPES

Notes of the major keys

Notes of the major keys

SOME THEORY – AND ALL FIVE BLUES SCALE SHAPES

C Major - no flats

F Major - one flat

Bb Major - two flats

Eb Major - three flats

Ab Major - four flats

Db Major - five flats

Gb Major - six flats

This method of using Roman numerals to describe chords is common in jazz and classical music. It is not hard to understand but it does require you to know the notes of your major scales. For example, in C major a blues would be:

C	C	C	C
F	F	C	C
G	F	C	G

We've started on C as I and found that F is IV and G is V. This knowledge lets you work out the blues chord sequence in every key, just by figuring out chords I, IV, and V.

THEORY: the last chord of a blues can be either I or V. Chord I would bring the music to a close, while V would imply that you're going round for another chorus.

Exercise 1.11

The standard layout for a jazz tune is to play the melody or 'head' at the beginning, usually twice through if it's a blues, and then improvise over the underlying harmony. So when jazz players improvise, it is the *form* of the 'head', with its underlying harmony, that is the basis for the improvisation. There are relatively few exceptions to this rule: occasionally jazz composers write a head, and then write a separate set of chords for the solos, but this is rare.

Exercise 1.11
CD TRACKS 11 & 12
(BACKING TRACK)
Blues solo in G

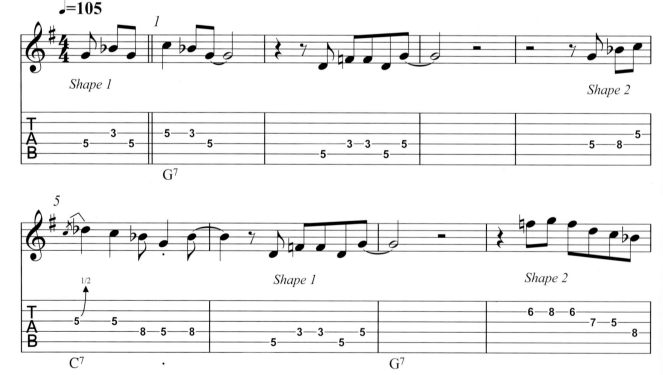

SOME THEORY – AND ALL FIVE BLUES SCALE SHAPES

In Exercise 1.11 (previous page), the playing of the head is left out and we go straight to a solo that is two choruses long. When you've mastered it, play it over the backing track (CD track 12), but also try starting and ending with one of the 'heads' that we have learned already. You could play 1.04 as an intro, then one chorus of the solo, and 1.07 as an outro. Or try any combination of head/solo/head that you fancy. Remember that when you play a blues for real, it's normal to play the head twice at the beginning and then twice at the end. Taking the tune up an octave for the repeat is a great way of maintaining interest.

Taking a closer look at the solo, you'll see that we are drawing attention to the fact that each phrase is based on a scale shape. Aim to use the same fingerings to play the piece as you would use to play the scales we have learned, but feel free to be creative with your fingering – if it works, it's good. In the second chorus you find references to shape four and shape five, which are coming up in the next exercise: the good news is there are only five shapes altogether. Notice the question and answer structure of the whole piece and the use of the entire neck, starting low and ending high; this builds interest and excitement as the solo progresses.

TECHNIQUE: bends are not common in jazz and it's rare for a jazz guitarist to use the wailing bends found in the blues. There's a subtle one at the start of bar five – play the fifth fret with your third finger and push the string across the neck far enough to make it rise a half-step in pitch. Then pull the string back into position in time to play the next note.

THEORY: each of the phrases in this solo could be called a 'riff'. Originally, this term implied a musical phrase that could be repeated again and again, and you could try repeating any of these. Nowadays, the term riff means pretty much 'a musical idea'.

Keep returning to CD track 12 and try making up your own solos to play over this backing track. If you're stuck for inspiration, begin with a 'question' from one of the exercises and then make up your own answer. Stick to notes from the scales we have learnt – they're guaranteed to sound OK over the whole blues progression and help you to become confident with your phrasing. Hold on to the idea of playing three question and answer phrases; you will find that eventually you can improvise your own blues-flavoured solo. You should also try playing all the scale shapes over the backing track as this will help to get the sound of the scales in your head.

Exercises 1.12 and 1.13

Adding the final two scale shapes completes the set and means that we now have the entire neck available in blues scales and minor pentatonics. Start with shape one in the third position in the key of G and play the whole scale across the neck and back. Then play shape two in the same way, beginning on the second note of the scale (B-flat) on the sixth fret of the E-string. Next comes shape three at the eighth fret, starting on C, shape four at the 10th fret starting on D, and shape five at the 13th fret, starting on F,

Exercise 1.12 CD TRACK 13 *G minor pentatonic scale shapes 4 and 5*

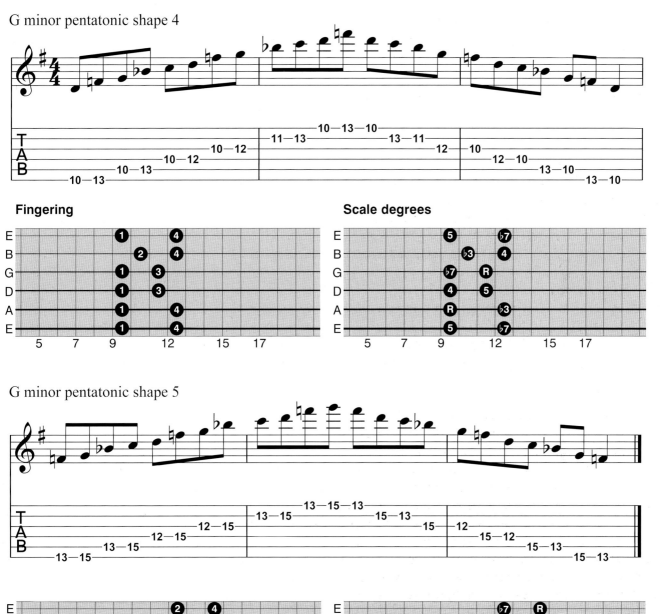

G minor pentatonic shape 4

Fingering

Scale degrees

G minor pentatonic shape 5

SOME THEORY – AND ALL FIVE BLUES SCALE SHAPES

G blues scale shape 4

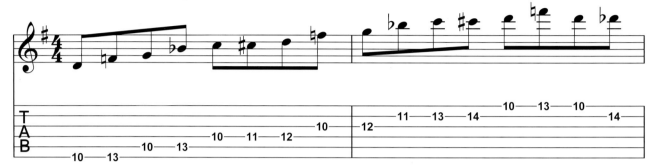

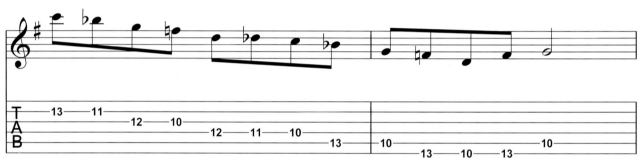

Fingering

Scale degrees

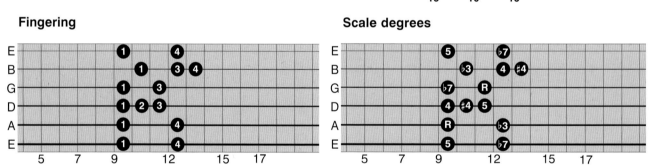

Exercise 1.13
CD TRACK 14
*G blues scale
shapes 4 and 5*

until until you reach the 15th fret, where you will be an octave higher than where you started and can play shape one again. Try using all five shapes to solo over CD track 12; the more you do it the better you'll get at making up your own phrases. As we will see in the coming exercises, you can move these five shapes around the guitar to play in other keys .

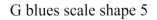

G blues scale shape 5

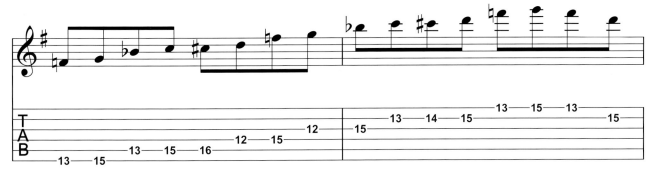

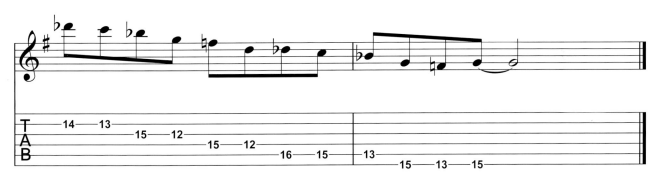

Fingering

Scale degrees

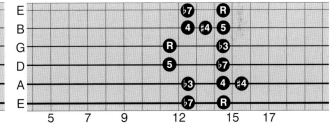

THE JAZZ GUITAR HANDBOOK

Section 5
Intervals and minor blues

In Exercises 1.09 and 1.10 we introduced major scales, and we saw that it is normal to number the steps of the scale. There is a system in music that allows us to use numbers to describe the pitch distance between any two notes; this is known as the interval.

Exercise 1.14

An interval is made up of two elements. Firstly a number describes how far it is from one note to the next. If C is the lowest note of an interval, the gap to D would be called a second, to E a third, to F a fourth and so on. It's quite easy to work out the number part of an interval; treat the lowest note as 'one' and then count up letter

Exercise 1.14
CD TRACK 15
C major in intervals

Simple intervals (intervals within one octave)

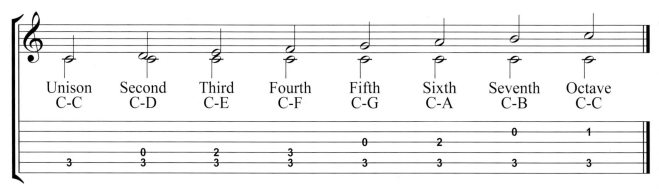

Compound intervals (intervals exceeding one octave)

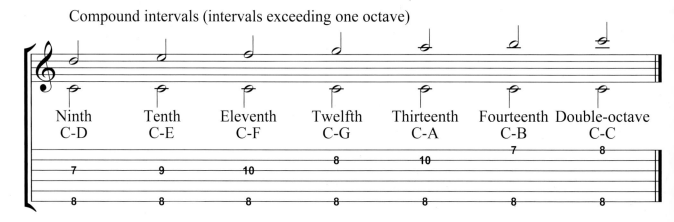

names until you arrive on the highest note. Exercise 1.14 is an illustration showing all of the intervals above C. Notice that you can carry on beyond the eighth note, or octave, to include ninths, tenths, and so on.

Exercises 1.15 and 1.16

The second element in an interval is a word that describes its character. These words are major, minor, perfect, augmented, and diminished. First we will look at how these intervals apply to a major scale:

Exercise 1.15

Interval types, major scale

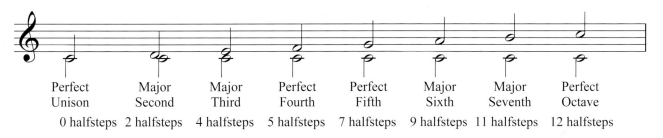

Perfect Unison	Major Second	Major Third	Perfect Fourth	Perfect Fifth	Major Sixth	Major Seventh	Perfect Octave
0 halfsteps	2 halfsteps	4 halfsteps	5 halfsteps	7 halfsteps	9 halfsteps	11 halfsteps	12 halfsteps

This table shows some other intervals that are not in the major scale:

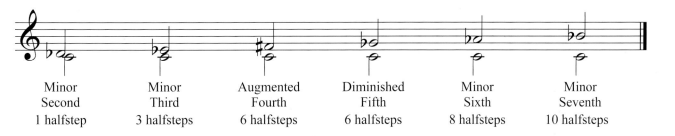

Minor Second	Minor Third	Augmented Fourth	Diminished Fifth	Minor Sixth	Minor Seventh
1 halfstep	3 halfsteps	6 halfsteps	6 halfsteps	8 halfsteps	10 halfsteps

The first table shows that all of the intervals in a major scale are either major or perfect. The second table shows the intervals made with notes not in the major scale, which are all minor, augmented, or diminished.

They say rules are made to be broken. But in the case of intervals, here are some rules that are *never* broken:

Exercise 1.16

CD TRACK 16

Interval types, outside the major scale

- Fourths, fifths. and octaves can only be perfect, augmented, or diminished. They are never major or minor.

- Seconds, thirds, sixths, and sevenths are usually major or minor, but occasionally can be augmented or diminished; they are *never* perfect.

The reason intervals are useful is that they give us a way of describing how two notes played together actually sound. A major third sounds different to a minor third; an augmented fourth sounds different to a perfect fourth. Every melody, riff, or chord is made up of a series of intervals and each interval has its own distinctive sound. With practice you can begin to tell them apart by ear. A knowledge of intervals is also important for understanding chords and how they are constructed.

Exercise 1.17
CD TRACKS 17 & 18
(BACKING TRACK)
F minor blues

HISTORICAL NOTE: the names of intervals go back to the ninth century when monks were formulating music theory in the Christian church. Fourths, fifths, and octaves were called 'perfect' because of their neutral, uncoloured quality, which was heard as the sound of heaven. The earthly, emotional, happy/sad intervals like major

and minor thirds were only worthy of being described in terms of their size; major third = big third (two whole-steps) minor third = small third (one-and-a-half steps).

The diagram shows the difference between the way a major scale sounds and the way the blues scale sounds. Notice that the major scale has only perfect and major intervals whereas the blues scale has two minor intervals and an augmented fourth (which, if the note was D-flat would be called a diminished fifth).

Major scale

Root		Major 2nd		Major 3rd	Perfect 4th		Perfect 5th		Major 6th		Major 7th	Octave
G		A		B	C		D		E		F#	G
G				Bb	C	C#	D			F		G
Root				Minor 3rd	Perfect 4th	Augmented 4th	Perfect 5th			Minor 7th		Octave

Blues scale

Exercise 1.17

So far, we have been using our minor pentatonic scales and blues scales to play over a chord progression consisting entirely of major chords. It is the tension between the minor-sounding scales and the major-sounding harmony that creates the sonic signature of the blues. But it is also possible to use these minor scales over minor chords. The minor blues is less common, but can be found occasionally in jazz, rock, and rhythm & blues. For this exercise we are going to move all the blues scale shapes two frets down the guitar and play in F minor.

THEORY: just to be clear, when playing in F, shape one starts on the first fret. Shape two starts on the fourth fret, shape three the sixth fret, shape four the eighth fret and shape five the eleventh fret. Shape one is then available again an octave up at the thirteenth fret and so on. Practise the scale shapes logically up the neck in this new key.

There are various ways around a minor 12-bar, but this is the chord sequence we are using here, with all chords now minor:

Fm	Fm	Fm	Fm
Bbm	Bbm	Fm	Fm
Cm	Bbm	Fm	Fm

The sequence will also work well using C7 instead of C minor, but the simplest minor blues contains only minor chords.

The first thing you'll notice in this exercise is that the riffs are interspersed with three-

Exercise 1.18 *'Compromise' blues scale shapes in G*

Fingering

Scale degrees

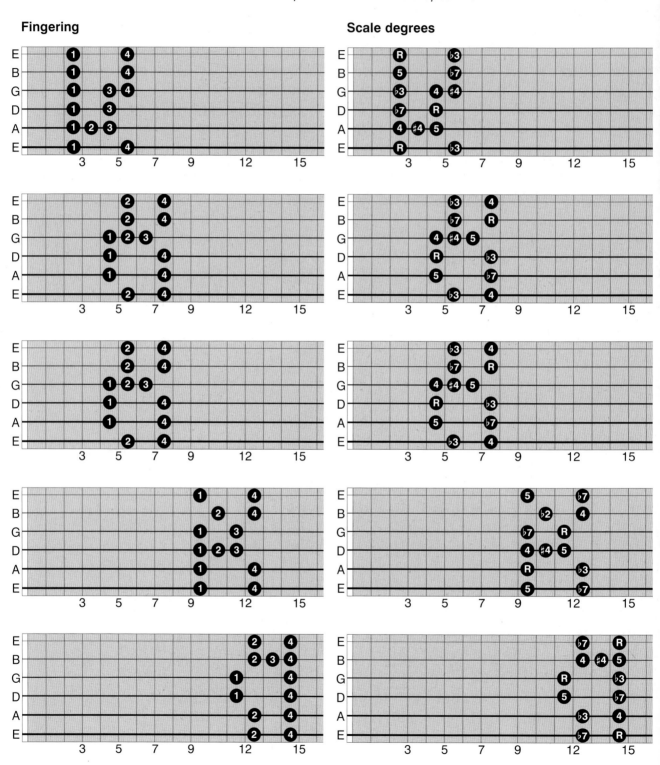

note chords that outline the underlying harmony. This is a cool trick which guitar players do, fooling the listener into thinking they are hearing two things at once by playing a rhythm part 'in the gaps'. If you find it difficult, practise the melody part and the chords separately, and when you can play each part separately try putting them together. Slow the piece down in your practice and gradually work up to full speed when you've got it under your fingers. Don't give up on it or get bogged down. Keep working your way through the book, but also keep returning to any exercises you found difficult.

TECHNIQUE: when you've mastered this exercise play it over the backing track, CD track 18. Then use your blues scales in F to solo over the backing, trying out some of your own ideas as you go.

THEORY: this piece adds repeat signs and first- and second-time bars. Play from the beginning to the first-time bar, then return to the repeat sign at the start of bar one and play the piece through again, this time skipping the first-time bar and going straight to the second time bar to end.

Exercise 1.18

We've already talked about the fact that blues scales and minor pentatonics are very similar; blues scales simply add an extra note per octave. Blue scales sound good but don't fit under the fingers as neatly as minor pentatonics. Some players use a compromise shape, which is based on the minor pentatonic and only adds the blues scale note when it falls under the fingers. Since you have already played the blues scale shapes, you can be aware some notes have been left out and put them back in if you need to. Try using these shapes in your own solos – they're pretty useful.

Section 6
Major pentatonic scales

One of the coolest things about the whole minor pentatonic/blues scale thing is that once you've learnt these scale shapes you find you've got two scales for the price of one. Basically, major pentatonic scales use the same five shapes as the minor pentatonics. Here's how it works:

Here are the notes of the G minor pentatonic scale we've been playing, with the notes of a B-flat major pentatonic scale written underneath:

G	B♭	C	D	F
B♭	C	D	F	G

They are made up of the same five notes, but one scale starts on G while the other starts on B-flat. So B-flat major pentatonic uses the exact same shapes as G minor pentatonic. Another way of saying that is that if we play a minor pentatonic scale starting on the root, nothing has changed. If we play it using the flat third as the root, we will hear a major pentatonic scale.

Exercise 1.19

There are times when a little bit of major pentatonic scale can add a down-home simplicity to your playing. It is a way of escaping the melancholy sound of the blues and substituting a country-flavoured openness. In this example we have changed the underlying key of the backing track to B-flat. We are using the G minor pentatonic shapes but they sound as B-flat major pentatonic scales.

Referring back to our major scales in Exercise 1.11, we can find the B-flat major scale and work out that chords I, IV, and V are B-flat, E-flat, and F. So a basic blues in B-flat is:

B♭7	B♭7	B♭7	B♭7
E♭7	E♭7	B♭7	B♭7
F7	E♭7	B♭7	F7

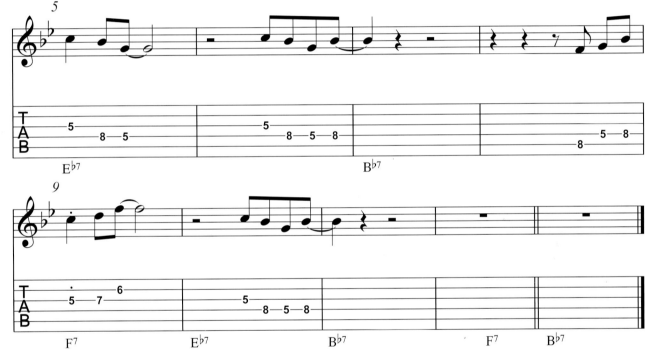

This piece is a quick-change blues, as mentioned above. It is played in the fifth position using shape two; you'll need to use your pinky at the eighth fret. It's cool, laid back, and has a different sound to the exercises that use the blues scale. One possibility for further study is that you also learn the E-flat major pentatonic and switch to that scale for the E-flat chord. (E-flat major pentatonic = C minor pentatonic). There's a backing track on the CD at track 20 for practising over and trying out your own major pentatonic riffs.

Exercise 1.19
CD TRACKS 19 & 20
(BACKING TRACK)
Blues in B-flat with major pentatonic solo

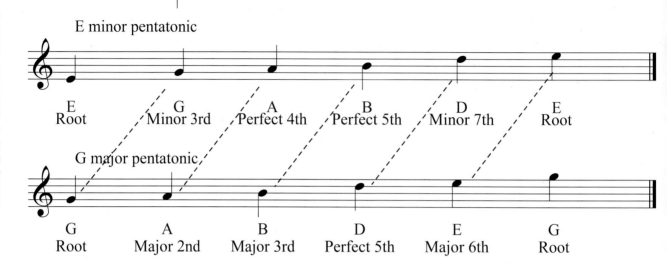

Exercise 1.20

Let's say we want to get away from the blues scale and and play a G major pentatonic scale over CD track 12, the blues backing track in G. We would need to play the minor pentatonic scale that has G as its minor third or second note. Find a G anywhere on the guitar, and go down three frets and you will arrive on the note E. So an E minor pentatonic scale is the same as a G major pentatonic scale. This example shows the two scales one above the other and adds the intervals from which the scales are built; read on to the next exercise for some analysis of how these two scales can work together.

Exercise 1.21

You can mix elements of the major pentatonic, minor pentatonic, and blues scale to create a more sophisticated palette of sound for your solos. This piece uses the shape one G blues scale, mixed with elements of shape two E minor pentatonic, which in this case sounds as G major pentatonic. Both scales begin on the note G, third fret, sixth string and both contain the notes G and D. The major pentatonic adds three new notes, the major second, major third, and major sixth. If you compare this piece to one of the earlier pieces that used just the minor pentatonic, you can hear that these three new notes add a great deal of colour and flavour to the blues. They make it more jazzy, and less like the kind of blues that would be played by a rhythm & blues artist. CD12 is the backing track, so when you are ready you can try your own blues in this extended blues scale style.

THEORY: notice how often the music goes from the blues scale minor third (B-flat) to the major pentatonic major third (B-natural). It's a great jazzy blues sound.

THE JAZZ GUITAR HANDBOOK

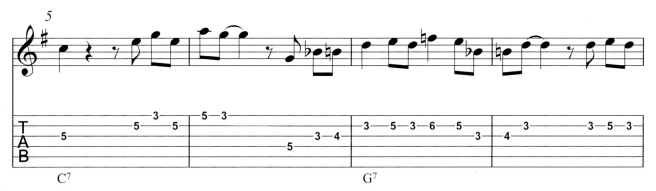

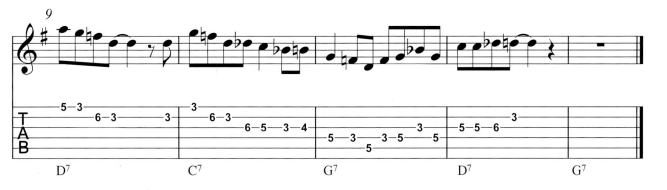

TECHNIQUE: learn the E minor pentatonic scale/G major pentatonic scale using all five shapes – you'll find them three frets down from the G minor pentatonic shapes. Yes, that means shape one begins on the open E string, but you should be able to get your head around that. Solo over the backing track, mixing up elements of the G blues scale and the G major pentatonic scale. Sometimes you will play something that sounds wrong; that's OK, it's part of the learning process. When you play something you like, remember it – add it to your growing library of home-made licks. This is how you develop your ability to improvise.

Exercise 1.21
CD TRACKS 21 & 12
(BACKING TRACK)
Blues in G using major and minor pentatonic scales

THE JAZZ GUITAR HANDBOOK

> **PRACTISE LIKE A PRO**
> The best way to make progress on musical instruments is to practise every day. It does not have to be for hours on end, though that can help, but it does have to be attentive, intelligent, and relaxed. As well as having fun playing over the backing tracks and making up your own solos, you should include some methodical scale practice. For example, you could pick a different key each day and play all the blues scale, minor pentatonic, and major pentatonic shapes in that key. If you really want a challenge, try saying the letter names as you play the scales slowly. Knowing the names of the notes on the guitar is not exactly optional, though there are many guitarists out there who think it is. Also get used to thinking in terms of the intervals that each scale is built from.
>
> Use alternate picking and play with a metronome, which will help you to keep a strict beat and play in time accurately. Keep a note of your speed setting and see if you can bring the speed of your playing up gradually without introducing any unwanted physical tension in your body.

Exercise 1.22

Rock and blues musicians often find themselves playing in guitar-friendly keys like A, D, and E because the open strings make rhythm parts in these keys easier. Jazz guitarists are more likely to find themselves playing in F and B-flat because these are the natural keys for trumpets and saxophones. We have already played major pentatonics over a B-flat blues; the next example adds notes from the blues scale in this more challenging key.

Here is our blues chord sequence in the key of B-flat;

Bb7	Bb7	Bb7	Bb7
Eb7	Eb7	Bb7	Bb7
F7	Eb7	Bb7	F7

For this example we are going to modify this sequence, using the quick-change blues discussed in Exercise 1.04 above. Here's the new sequence for this exercise:

Bb7	Eb7	Bb7	Bb7
Eb7	Eb7	Bb7	Bb7
F7	Eb7	Bb7	F7

There is one other important change in this exercise. All the preceding exercises have been in a 'straight' feel; in other words, the placing of all of the eighth-notes was completely even. This is the first exercise in a 'jazz' or 'swing' feel: the four main beats of the bar stay where they are, but the eighth-notes that fall in between are played later than usual so they seem to lean towards the next downbeat. What is really happening is that we are counting three eighth-notes to each beat, and then playing only on the first and third of each group of three. These three diagrams should make things clearer:

Straight feel

CLAP	1 &	1 &	1 &	1 &
TAP	1	2	3	4

Triplets

CLAP	123	123	123	123
TAP	1	2	3	4

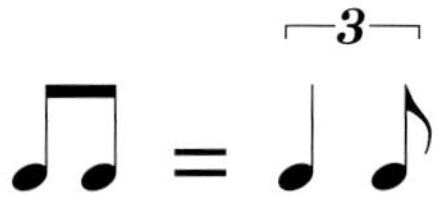

Shuffle feel

CLAP	1 3	1 3	1 3	1 3
TAP	1	2	3	4

THEORY: as you can see from these diagrams, sometimes we play three notes in the time of two, such as three eighth-notes in the time of one quarter-note. These 'three to a beat' eighth-notes are called 'triplets' and in the notation stave are usually beamed together, often, but not always, with a small '3' above the beam.

When we write music with a swing feel it actually looks the same as straight feel. At the beginning of the piece, however, it will often say 'swing' or 'jazz' or sometimes have a sign that looks like this:

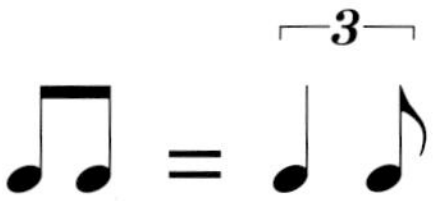

THEORY: you don't always get an instruction like those mentioned above, but jazz is generally played in a swing feel. Latin music, such as Brazilian or Cuban, is an exception to this, tending to have a straight feel. Rock and funk can be based on eighth-notes or 16th-notes and can be swing or straight. We'll look at this later.

THE JAZZ GUITAR HANDBOOK

Kicking off with a rising triplet – three eighth-notes in the time of two – this exercise not only mixes major and minor pentatonics but also introduces more varied phrasing of the type introduced to jazz by bebop. There are some long phrases and some which are much shorter, and there is a sense of the tune unfolding throughout the piece rather than being built from simple two-bar riffs. The small numbers alongside the notes in the music stave are suggested fingerings for your fretting hand. You don't have to stick to them but they should help get the piece under your fingers. This is a more complex piece of music than the earlier exercises and you may need to keep returning to it until you get it right.

The shape one blues scale is now at the sixth fret in the key of B-flat. This means shape five could be played 'behind', starting on fret four, and shape three could be started at the first fret. So as we move shape one up the guitar to play in different keys it makes room for higher shapes to slot in behind. When you solo, you don't always have to start on shape one; to play in B-flat, for example, starting on shape four in the first position would give you more room to gradually work your way up the guitar, building your solo.

TECHNIQUE: you already know the B-flat major pentatonic – it's the same notes as the G minor pentatonic. Practise both scale types in B-flat and use them for soloing over the backing track. From now on you should be working on scales using both straight and swing rhythms.

THE JAZZ METRONOME

Does the metronome swing? If you use it in the conventional way, clicking on every beat, the answer is not really. However, if you can get used to hearing the clicks as beats 'two' and 'four' then it starts to take on the role of the drummer's hi-hat. When you are working on memorising scales, use a metronome and play using both swing and straight feels. Start at an easy tempo and keep your fretting-hand fingers close to the strings. Increase the tempo gradually over a period of time.

When it comes to the jazz feel, the best way to learn it is to listen to jazz from all periods. In early jazz, such as Louis Armstrong's Hot Fives and Hot Sevens, the swing is quite 'dotted', the second eighth-note being delayed as much as possible. In the swing era, artists such as Lester Young and the Count Basie Band introduced a smoother, more triplet-based swing. As fast tempos became more common in the bebop era, swing became smoother still, the second eighth-note still being delayed, but not so obviously triplet-based. Experience, and a good pair of ears, will help you to gauge the appropriate style for any jazz you may play in the future.

MAJOR PENTATONIC SCALES

Exercise 1.22
CD TRACKS 22 & 23
(BACKING TRACK)
'Swing Blues In B-flat'

THE JAZZ GUITAR HANDBOOK

Summing up

Are pentatonics the whole story? These simple five-note scales sound fine played over the blues changes and are an important resource for jazz and blues improvisers, but in other contexts they can sound naïve and ill-informed. As we will see, sometimes the harmony demands something more. For this reason we will need to study more advanced scale/chord relationships in Part Three.

We've come to the end of Part One, and you should be using all five scale shapes to play over the backing tracks on the CD, playing in keys G, F minor, and B-flat and maybe branching out to play in other keys as well. Ideally you should be mixing notes from blues, major, and minor pentatonic scales so that these sounds are in your head. See if you can hum, sing, or whistle a phrase and then play it on your guitar. Remember, the long-term goal is to be able to play the sounds you hear in your head when improvising.

The next section of the book is all about chords, but as you work through, keep returning to the backing tracks in this section and practising your soloing.

These tracks are:

- **CD 12 Blues in G**
- **CD 18 Blues in F Minor**
- **CD 20 Blues in B-flat (straight feel major pentatonic)**
- **CD 23 Blues in B-flat (swing feel major and minor pentatonic)**

PART 2
Chords

■ Open string chords; building triads and sevenths; movable chords

■ Extending beyond the seventh; chords, keys, and modulation; chord voicings

■ Minor harmony; substitutions and inversions

■ Inversions and extensions

Section 1
Open string chords, building triads and sevenths, movable chords.

Eight basic chords

Exercise 2.01 introduces the eight most basic chords in guitar music. If you do not know them already you should learn them thoroughly – and learn their names too. These diagrams, or 'chord shapes' as they are often known, are the building blocks from which we will construct most of the chords that we use to play jazz on the guitar.

Exercise 2.01
Eight open-string chords

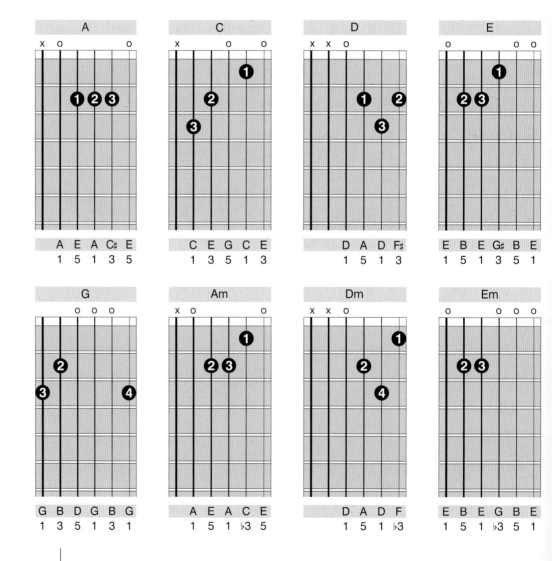

They are known collectively as 'open-string chords', as they all involve open strings as well as fretted notes.

Practise each of these chords in turn, making sure each note is sounding cleanly. In case you've not seen this sort of diagram before, the strings are vertical, the frets horizontal and the double line at the top is the nut. The numbers in the black dots represent your fretting-hand fingers. Do not play strings marked with an X. Open strings, which you must play, are marked with an O. Later on we'll see chords to be played higher up the guitar neck; these diagrams will have no nut, but a fret number alongside them to indicate where on the neck the chord should be held down.

THEORY: notice that at the bottom of each diagram is a line of letters to show the actual notes you are playing. Beneath that are numbers that give you the scale degrees of the notes, relative to the root note of the chord. 1 = root, 3 = major third, ♭3 = minor third and 5 = perfect fifth.

Exercise 2.02

This exercise shows you what the chords should sound like, and also introduces the idea of playing chords as 'arpeggios' – that is, one note at a time. The CD track was played using a Fender Stratocaster, producing a very different sound to all the preceding tracks, which used an archtop ES175-style guitar.

TECHNIQUE: aim to make a clean, buzz-free sound by getting your fretting-hand fingers as close as possible to the frets. Squeeze gently with your thumb on the back of the neck and experiment to find the most comfortable place for the ball of your thumb. You should not be gripping the neck like a handle – the idea is to help your fingers squeeze down on the strings.

THEORY: when we speak about a major chord we usually just say its letter name, so D major would be called just D. With minor chords we always use the full name, A minor or D minor. When writing minor chords it is normal to use the abbreviation 'm', as in Am for A minor and Dm for D minor.

Every guitarist should know these eight shapes, but they don't really sound right for jazz. The prominence of open strings, and their position near the nut, give them a jangly quality more suited to folk music or rock. Also, as we will see, they are based on 'triads' or three-note chords which are not the sort often favoured by jazz players, who tend to extend chords beyond the triad and add sevenths, ninths and other interesting sounds.

OPEN STRING CHORDS, BUILDING TRIADS AND SEVENTHS, MOVABLE CHORDS

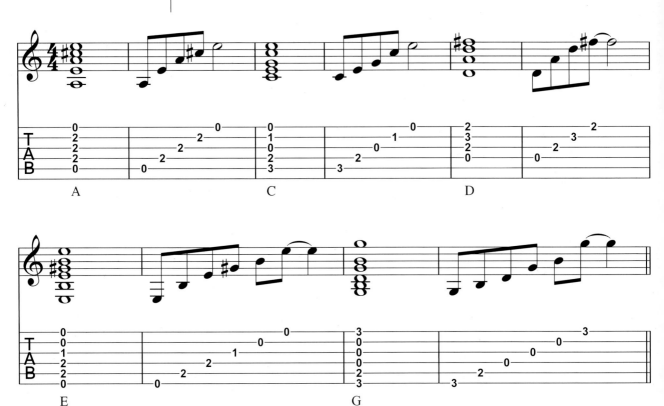

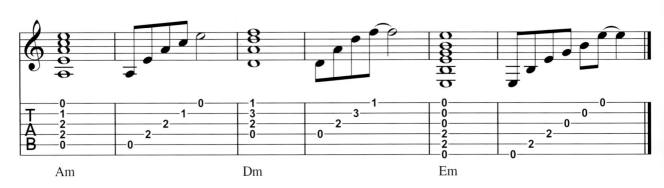

Exercise 2.02
CD TRACK 24
Five majors, three minors

Triads and sevenths

Technically, a chord is any group of notes played at the same time. However, the chords that we use in the sort of music that you hear every day (excluding music that belongs to the avant-garde or contemporary classical tradition) follow a structure that has been established for several hundred years. The most basic chord is a triad, which consists of a root, a third and a fifth. There are only four kinds of triad.

THE JAZZ GUITAR HANDBOOK

■ A major triad consists of a root, major third, and perfect fifth: C major = C E G
Usually written: **C**

■ A minor triad consists of a root, minor third, and perfect fifth: C minor = C E♭ G
Usually written: **Cm**

■ A diminished triad consists of a root, minor third, and diminished fifth: C
diminished = C E♭ G♭
Usually written: **Cdim**

■ An augmented triad consists of a root, major third, and augmented fifth: C
augmented = C E G♯
Usually written: **Caug**

If you have studied the major scales in Part One you will be able to work out the names
of the notes in any triad. For example, D major consists of the root, third, and fifth from
the D major scale: D, F♯, A.

■ To create D minor, flatten the third to produce a minor third: D, F, and A.
■ To create D diminished, also flatten the fifth: D, F, and A♭.
■ To create D augmented, return to the major triad and sharpen the fifth: D, F♯, and A♯.

Notes for common major chords

MAJOR CHORDS

Chord	Root	Third	Fifth
C	C	E	G
D♭	D♭	F	A♭
D	D	F♯	A
E♭	E♭	G	B♭
E	E	G♯	B
F	F	A	C
F♯	F♯	A♯	C♯
G♭	G♭	B♭	D♭
G	G	B	D
A♭	A♭	C	E♭
A	A	C♯	E
B♭	B♭	D	F
B	B	D♯	F♯

Notes for the common minor chords

MINOR CHORDS

Chord	Root	Third	Fifth
Cm	C	E♭	G
C♯m	C♯	E	G♯
Dm	D	F	A
D♯m	D♯	F♯	A♯
E♭m	E♭	G♭	B♭
Em	E	G	B
Fm	F	A♭	C
F♯m	F♯	A	C♯
Gm	G	B♭	D
G♯m	G♯	B	D♯
A♭m	A♭	C♭	E♭
Am	A	C	E
B♭m	B♭	D♭	F
Bm	B	D	F♯

Triads are the most basic kind of chord, with major and minor triads being by far the most common. The four-, five-, and six-note chords from Exercises 2.01 and 2.02 may not seem like three-note triads, but if you analyse the notes being played you will see that there are only three *different* notes in each chord. Also check the numbers beneath the diagrams and you will see that each note is either a root (1), third (3), or fifth (5).

In jazz we are more interested in extending chords beyond the basic triad. Chords are built in thirds; there is a third between the root and the third and another between the third and the fifth. Each time we are counting up three notes. If we want to create a more interesting four-note chord we carry on adding notes in thirds, meaning that the next note would be the seventh.

If you check back to Part One, Section Four, where we studied intervals, you will see we mentioned two kinds of seventh, major seventh and minor seventh. For example, C to B would be a major seventh, whereas C to B-flat would be a minor seventh. One way of making it easier to recognise a seventh is to compare it to the octave. C to B, a major seventh, is one half-step (semitone) away from being a full octave; C to B-flat, a minor seventh, is a whole-step (whole-tone) away from being a full octave.

You can add a major or minor seventh to any triad and you will spice it up and start to hear some of the cool jazz sounds that we are looking for.

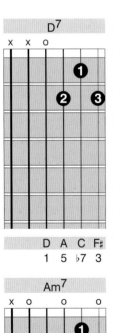

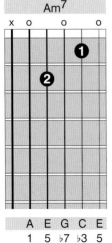

Exercise 2.03

Although we've said that open-string chords are not really the thing for jazz, played in a certain way it is possible to make them work for groovy rhythm parts, and adding some sevenths will make them sound jazzier. In the above chord shapes we've added a minor seventh to both the chords. Starting with an A minor triad and adding a minor seventh creates a chord which we call 'A minor seventh', 'A minor seven', or 'Am7'. Starting with D major and adding a minor seventh creates a chord that we call 'D seventh', 'D seven', or 'D7'. Take a moment to look at the chord shapes (left) and understand which notes are in each chord and why.

This exercise begins with a four-bar intro which outlines the laid-back Latin-inspired groove. At the end of bar four we play a bassline linking the two chords together. Bars five to nine are repeated as bars nine to 12, and at bar 13 we reach the outro with a variation on the previous bassline. The wavy line in front of the final chord tells you to sweep across the notes as a smooth arpeggio from low to high.

If you find moving between the two chord shapes tricky, practise the move separately, and notice that your first finger is in the same place for both chords. There is no need to move it! Watch out for the pick directions, which should help you to get the right feel, and for the two downstroke accents in bar four.

TECHNIQUE: if you are playing a chord accompaniment, it is a nice touch to add a bassline. If you experiment, you will find there are many other notes that can be used to connect these two chords. You can use chord tones, scale tones or chromatic passing notes such as the G-sharp in bar six. (A chromatic scale is a scale that includes every half-step.)

OPEN STRING CHORDS, BUILDING TRIADS AND SEVENTHS, MOVABLE CHORDS

Exercise 2.03 CD TRACK 25 *Am7 D7 groove*

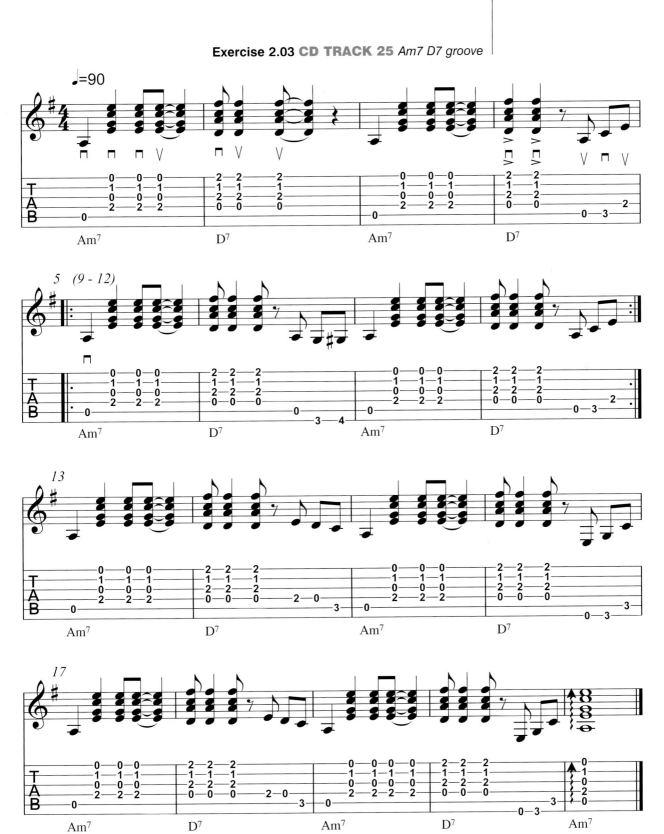

THEORY: this type of two-chord groove is popular with groove-jazz players like George Benson or Earl Klugh and can also be heard in the work of rock players like Carlos Santana. As we will see when we come to analyse chords relative to a key, Am7 is chord ii7 and D7 is chord V7 in the key of G major.

Movable chords

To create the real jazz sounds we are looking for we need to learn to play chords that do not include open strings. Not only do these chords sound more solid and jazzy but they have the advantage of being movable, so that you can learn a shape for a type of chord and then change its root note by moving it up and down the neck.

Exercise 2.04

G major and G minor barre chords formed from the open E major shape

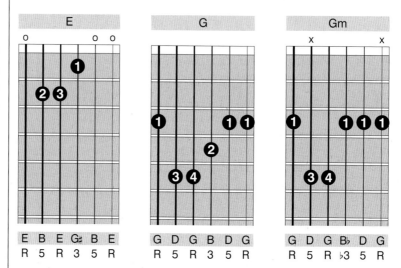

Exercise 2.04

All of the open-string chords in Exercise 2.01 can be turned into movable chords. We are going to start by converting the E major chord into a movable shape. In the G major diagram above (diagram two), the E shape has been moved up three frets and the index finger is making a 'barre', doing the job that was done by the nut in the open-string chord. The rest of the chord has been re-fingered using fingers two, three, and four. As there are now no open strings the chord can be played at any fret.

When we play the E major open-string chord the root note is sounded on the sixth, fourth, and first strings. If we were to play the diagram two barre chord (pronounced 'bar') at the first fret all the root notes would now be on F, giving us an F major chord; one fret higher would be F-sharp major, the third fret would give us G major (as above), and so on.

In the third diagram above we have used the E minor open-string shape as the basis for creating a G minor barre chord at the third fret. This chord also takes its name from whichever note is being held down on the sixth, fourth, or first strings, all of which are the 'root' of the chord.

THEORY: if you are not familiar with the letter names of the notes on the guitar it is time to start learning them. You will find the complete letter names with fret positions and music notation in the appendix at the back of the book. So that you can name this chord shape at every position, begin by learning the notes on the sixth string.

Here are some suggestions for learning the names of the notes on the guitar:

- **Choose a string:** say aloud the name of the note on every fret, beginning with the open string and working your way up to the 12th fret. When going up in pitch, use sharps (E, F, F-sharp, etc). Then work your way from the 12th fret back to the open string using flats (E, E-flat, D, D-flat, etc). There is no need to go further than the 12th fret as the 13th fret is the same letter name as the first fret.
- **Choose a fret:** say aloud the letter names on every string at that fret from the sixth string to the first string.
- **Choose a note at random:** find one example of that note on every string.

If you do each of these exercises every day you will very soon develop a better grasp of the note names on the guitar. Impress your friends!

Exercise 2.05

Exercise 2.05 begins with the G barre chord shape and involves some careful listening. Hold down all six notes, play the full chord and listen closely to what you hear. Barre chords produce a big, but hollowed out and unsatisfying sound. This is because the chord has so many 'doubled' notes. The root occurs three times, the fifth twice, and the third once only. Remember that fifths and octaves are 'perfect' because they have a neutral and uncoloured quality. All that neutrality just makes the chord sound empty.

Compare it to chord shape two. This is still G major, but with some of the doubled notes removed. There is a choice of fingerings for this chord; most players can manage

Exercise 2.05

Seventh chords formed from major barre chords

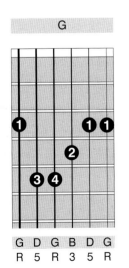

G					
G	D	G	B	D	G
R	5	R	3	5	R

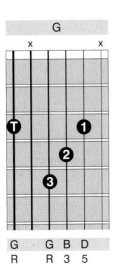

G				
G		G	B	D
R		R	3	5

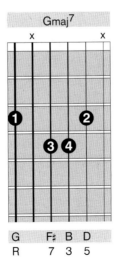

Gmaj⁷			
G	F♯	B	D
R	7	3	5

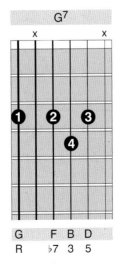

G⁷			
G	F	B	D
R	♭7	3	5

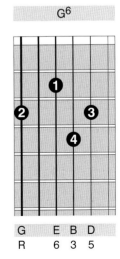

G⁶			
G	E	B	D
R	6	3	5

to use their thumb hooked over on the low E-string, as notated here, but the alternative is finger one on the sixth string and fingers two, three, and four on the other strings. Mute the A-string with the tip of your D-string finger or with your thumb wrapped over. This time you will hear a much more focused and punchy sound – it is a case where fewer notes make a better sound. I'm not saying you can never use the full barre chord shape; it can be pretty handy in a rock context. However, in jazz, we tend to favour chords that avoid doubled notes and give us just the right amount of focused harmonic information.

We are going to use this four-string G major chord shape as the basis for adding sevenths to our basic triads. We still have one doubled note in this chord; the doubled root on the D-string. This note can be moved a half-step lower to become a major seventh. This means the chord has a major triad with a major seventh and is known as a 'major seventh' or 'major seven' chord, in this case, 'G major seventh', containing the notes G B D F♯ (shape three).

THEORY: some jazz composers and arrangers use a small triangle or 'delta' symbol (G△7) in chord notation to show when notes added to a chord are major, but you will also see GM7, Gma7 and Gmaj7, depending on the choice of the writer.

In shape four the major seventh has been moved a half-step lower, producing a major triad with a minor seventh. This chord is known as G7, pronounced 'G seven' or 'G seventh': the notes are G B D F. We saw the same type of chord built on the root note D in Exercise 2.03.

TECHNIQUE: all of the chords in this and the coming exercises require a certain amount of skill in damping unwanted notes. The underside of the first finger near where it joins the hand is often used to damp the top string and prevent it from sounding. Other fingers, including the tip of the first finger, can be allowed to lean very gently away from the vertical in order to mute nearby strings. With the G7 shape, the tip-joint of the index finger mutes the A-string and its base mutes the E first string.

Shape five is not a seventh chord at all but continues the journey down the D-string to the note E-natural, which is the major sixth above the root G. This creates a chord known as G major sixth, usually written G6 and spoken 'G six'.

Exercise 2.06
Like Exercise 2.05, Exercise 2.06 begins with a six-string barre chord (shape one) followed by shape two, a four-note version of the same chord with most of the doubled notes removed and the thumb hooked over the low E-string. In shape three, the doubled root on the D-string has been lowered a half-step to produce a minor triad with a major seventh; this is not a common chord, but it is worth knowing for the rare occasions when it is needed. It is known as 'G minor major seventh' or sometimes 'G minor sharp seventh' (usually written Gm maj7 or Gm△7), with the notes G B♭ D F♯.

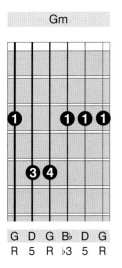

Gm

G	D	G	B♭	D	G
R	5	R	♭3	5	R

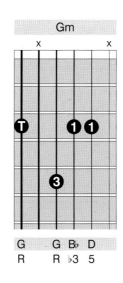

Gm

G		G	B♭	D
R		R	♭3	5

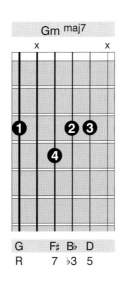

Gm maj7

G		F#	B♭	D
R		7	♭3	5

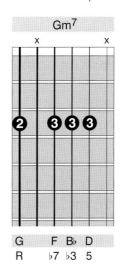

Gm⁷

G		F	B♭	D
R		♭7	♭3	5

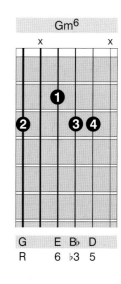

Gm⁶

G		E	B♭	D
R		6	♭3	5

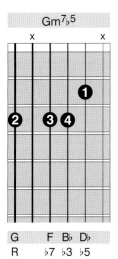

Gm7♭5

G		F	B♭	D♭
R		♭7	♭3	♭5

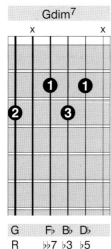

Gdim⁷

G		F♭	B♭	D♭
R		♭♭7	♭3	♭5

Exercise 2.06
*Seventh chords formed
from minor barre chords*

Shape four lowers the note on the D-string one step further producing a minor triad with a minor seventh, named Gm7 or sometimes G-7, pronounced 'G minor seven' or 'G minor seventh' and spelt G B♭ D F. Minor seventh chords are extremely common in jazz; we saw Am7 in Exercise 2.03. Note the given fingering, with the third finger making a barre across the second, third, and fourth strings; if you find this fingering difficult, try using all four fingers with finger one on the low E-string. Other solutions include using the thumb on the low E-string and a three-note barre with the first finger.

THEORY: a dash or minus sign is sometimes used in place of a lower case 'm' to denote a minor chord, for instance G-7, but Gm7 or Gmin7 are more common ways of writing this chord.

In shape five, the note on the D-string is lowered one half-step further to the major

OPEN STRING CHORDS, BUILDING TRIADS AND SEVENTHS, MOVABLE CHORDS

sixth. Combined with a minor triad this produces a chord known as G minor sixth, or Gm6, spelt G B♭ D E.

THEORY: notice that when we add a sixth to a chord it is always the major sixth, whether the chord is major or minor.

In shape six, it is the fifth of the chord that has been lowered a half-step, producing a diminished triad with a minor seventh. The notes are G B♭ D♭ F. This is a common sound in jazz and can be found with two names: 'G minor seventh flat five' (Gm7♭5), because the chord is like a minor seventh with a flat fifth, or 'G half-diminished' (G⌀) because it has a diminished triad with a minor seventh, so only half the chord (the triad) is diminished. Read on – here comes the diminished seventh.

Shape seven then lowers the minor seventh discussed above to produce a diminished seventh with a diminished triad. This is the fully diminished seventh chord, notated with either a small circle (G°7) or the abbreviation 'dim' (Gdim7), pronounced 'G diminished seventh' or sometimes 'G dim seven', and spelt G B♭ D♭ F♭. F♭ is enharmonic for the note E, meaning the same note with a different name.

TECHNIQUE: all of these chord shapes are movable chords and can be moved up and down the guitar neck changing the root note. For example, if played one fret higher, all of these G chords would become A-flat chords; up one fret again would produce A chords, and so on, working your way up the neck. Each time you learn a movable shape it can be rooted on any one of the 12 notes of the scale.

THEORY: as well as understanding and learning these chord shapes it is important to take these chord structures and apply them to other roots. We know that Gmaj7 is G B D F♯, and could probably work out that Cmaj7 is C E G B. How about A♭maj7? The major triad would be A♭ C E♭. The added major seventh would be G-natural (G♮). It will take some time, but in the long run it would be good to use your knowledge of intervals to know which notes go into every chord.

Exercise 2.07

The best way to learn chord shapes is to use them in songs. This exercise uses the chord shapes from 2.05 and 2.06 to produce a turnaround – a two or four bar chord sequence that can be repeated as often as required. 'Blue Moon' and 'I Got Rhythm' are examples of songs based on turnarounds, but there are many others.

Start by memorising the shapes that are shown above and move them to the appropriate fret. Be sure to use the correct fingers and to damp unwanted notes. Use firm downstrokes with your pick, holding the chord after the first stroke and then lightly releasing the chord after the second stroke to create the staccato second and fourth beats characteristic of this kind of swing.

TECHNIQUE: in this piece there is a four-bar intro followed by an eight-bar chord sequence in the style of a jazz standard. The shift from Gmaj7 to Cm6 in bar 11 may need some practice as it is a long way to travel along the neck. Put your second finger on the low E-string as early as possible and use it as a guide. Form the chord shape as much as you can before you arrive at the target fret.

Exercise 2.07
CD TRACK 26
Turnaround in G, rhythm

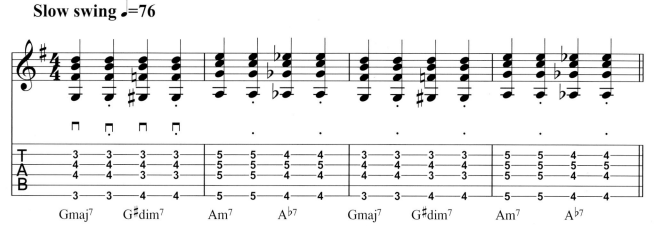

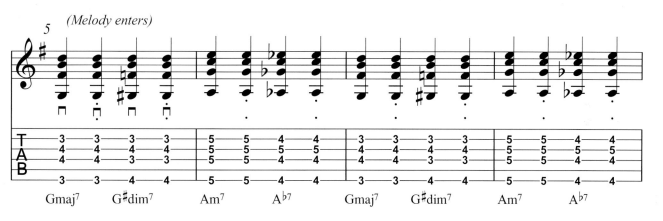

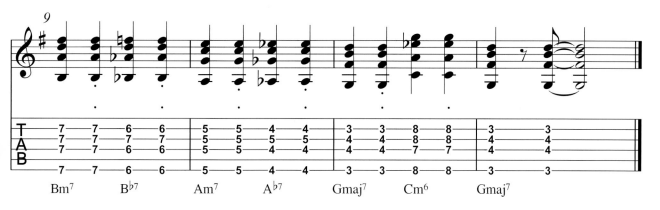

continued over page

THE JAZZ GUITAR HANDBOOK

Exercise 2.07 *(chords)*

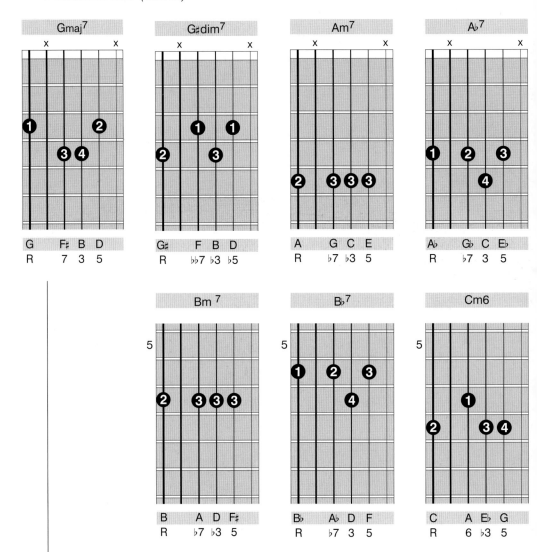

There is a single-note melody part to work on in the next example so that your fretting hand fingers don't seize up from all this chord playing.

THEORY: the A♭7 chord in the above exercise is a substitution for D7, the normal chord that leads to Gmaj7. Chord substitutions are often used by jazz players to create more interesting harmony; we will go into this in more detail in Section Three.

Exercise 2.08
After the four-bar intro, the melody enters, loosely copying the style of a 1930s or 1940s jazz standard. Jazz standards are often built from four eight-bar phrases, with an A section and a B section in the form AABA, making 32 bars in all. While many do not, most jazz songs follow this structure.

THE JAZZ GUITAR HANDBOOK

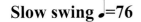

Slow swing ♩=76

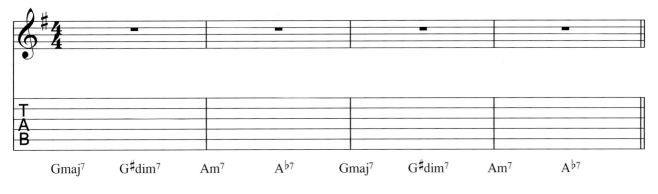

Gmaj7   G#dim7   Am7   A♭7   Gmaj7   G#dim7   Am7   A♭7

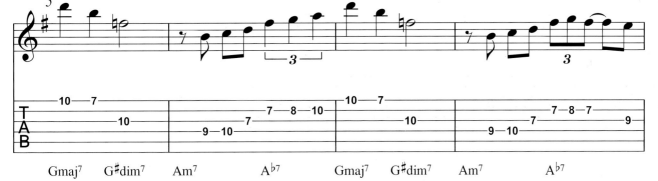

Gmaj7   G#dim7   Am7   A♭7   Gmaj7   G#dim7   Am7   A♭7

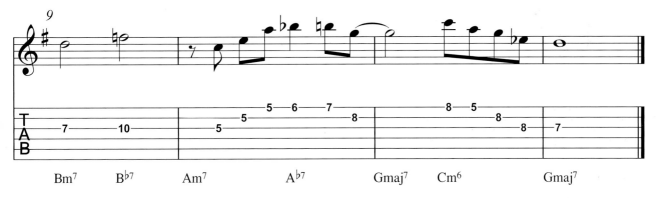

Bm7   B♭7   Am7   A♭7   Gmaj7   Cm6   Gmaj7

The melody here would make a good A section; it is based mainly on notes from the underlying chords mixed with scale passages that are based on a G major scale. All of the eighth-notes should be swung, and also notice in bar six the quarter-note triplet: three quarter-notes in the time of two.

Exercise 2.08 CD
TRACK 26 *Turnaround in G, melody*

THE JAZZ GUITAR HANDBOOK

OPEN STRING CHORDS, BUILDING TRIADS AND SEVENTHS, MOVABLE CHORDS

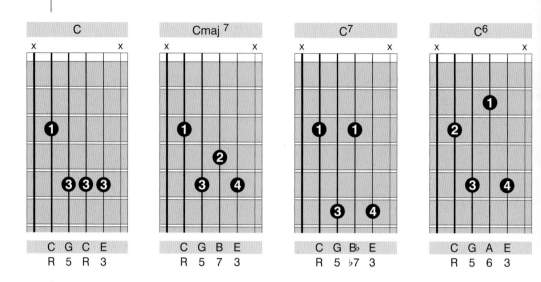

C	Cmaj⁷	C⁷	C⁶
C G C E	C G B E	C G B♭ E	C G A E
R 5 R 3	R 5 7 3	R 5 ♭7 3	R 5 6 3

Exercise 2.09

Major chords with fifth-string roots

Exercise 2.09

All of the chord shapes in Exercise 2.07 had their root on the low E-string. This can be somewhat limiting, as we saw in bar 11, where it was necessary to travel a long way up and down the guitar neck. In Exercise 2.09 we are building chords on the A-string, using the A major open-string shape as a movable chord.

Shape one is the simple four-note major triad with the root doubled on the G-string. It should be possible to see how we arrived at this shape by comparing it to the open A major shape. If you find it hard to make a barre with your third finger, use fingers two, three, and four instead. Use the tip of your index finger to mute the sixth string and its base to mute the first string.

Shape two lowers the doubled root a half-step to B, introducing a major seventh into the chord and creating C major seventh (Cmaj7). Shape three lowers this note a half-step further to B-flat which is a minor seventh, creating C seventh (C7). Shape four lowers this note one half-step further to the major sixth, creating C sixth (C6). This final shape is something of a stretch – if your hands are small it may be best to try it higher up the guitar where the frets are closer together.

TECHNIQUE: notice that none of these chords are really 'barre chords' of the kind that involve so much struggle for beginner guitarists, with the index finger stretched all the way across the neck. These four-note chords are easier to play and have a more focused and effective sound.

Exercise 2.10

Shape one in Exercise 2.10 is a movable chord based on the original A minor open string shape from 2.01. Once again no barre is necessary but it does require some care with damping unwanted notes. Shape two introduces the major seventh, producing a chord of C minor major seventh (Cm maj7). Shape three takes the major seventh down a half-step to the minor seventh and produces a chord of C minor seventh (Cm7). In

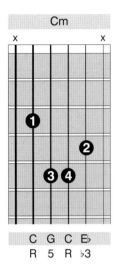

Cm

C G C E♭
R 5 R ♭3

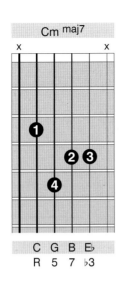

Cm maj7

C G B E♭
R 5 7 ♭3

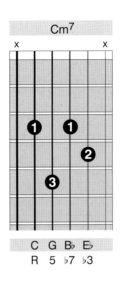

Cm7

C G B♭ E♭
R 5 ♭7 ♭3

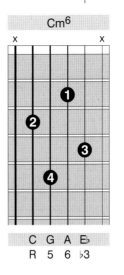

Cm6

C G A E♭
R 5 6 ♭3

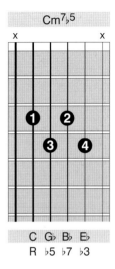

Cm7♭5

C G♭ B♭ E♭
R ♭5 ♭7 ♭3

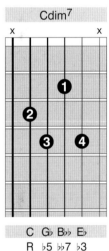

Cdim7

C G♭ B♭♭ E♭
R ♭5 ♭♭7 ♭3

Exercise 2.10
Minor chords with fifth string roots

shape four the minor seventh is lowered again, becoming a major sixth, and producing C minor sixth (Cm6).

Shape five returns to the minor seventh shape, but this time with the flattened fifth that creates C minor seventh flat five, also known as C half-diminished (Cm7♭5 or C∅). Shape six, the final chord in the set, keeps the diminished triad but lowers the seventh to a diminished seventh, producing a C diminished seventh chord (Cdim7 or C○7).

THEORY: notice that the major sixth and the diminished seventh are the same note. However, the major sixth should be called A, whereas the diminished seventh is called B-double-flat (B♭♭).

Exercise 2.11

This exercise is inspired by Duke Ellington's 'In A Sentimental Mood', and features minor chords with a descending inner voice built on A-string and E-string roots. It's a great way to get to grips with all the different minor chords we've been learning and includes selected shapes from all the previous exercises. Check out the fingering in the first two bars carefully; the Dm7 chord is fingered differently from usual to make it easier to reach the Dm6 chord. The G minor chord in bar three is fingered using the fret-hand thumb hooked over the top of the neck at the third fret – note the small T beneath the note in the notation stave. You could use a barre instead if the 'thumb over' method doesn't suit you.

Once again there is an eight-bar A section which in this case is repeated as it would be in a 32-bar jazz standard. A complete song form would then go to a 'middle eight' or B section before the A section returns to complete the form. The tempo is very slow, and as with most jazz tunes in 'ballad' tempo the swing feel is straightened out so that the eighth-notes are not swung. Bars nine to 16 are a slight variation on the first eight bars.

OPEN STRING CHORDS, BUILDING TRIADS AND SEVENTHS, MOVABLE CHORDS

Exercise 2.11 CD TRACK 27 *Minor chords with descending inner voices*

TECHNIQUE: on the CD the track is played using the pick, mostly with downstrokes. However, this could be a good exercise to try out your fingerstyle skills. Remember that your pick hand fingers are labelled p, i, m, and a, starting with the thumb. For example, in the opening bars your thumb (p) would play the root note of the chord, your index finger (i) the note on the D-string, with your middle (m) and third fingers (a) simultaneously playing the two notes on the G- and B-strings. Continue in this way but use i, m, and a for the three-note chord in bar five. Use p, i, m, and a for the four-note chord in bar six and for the arpeggios in bars seven and eight.

Exercise 2.12

In Exercise 2.12 we are converting the open-string C major shape into a movable chord and have moved the shape up to the fifth fret where it produces an F major chord. The F major chord in itself is not particularly easy to hold down, but it can be used to create

Exercise 2.12

F chords derived from an open C major shape

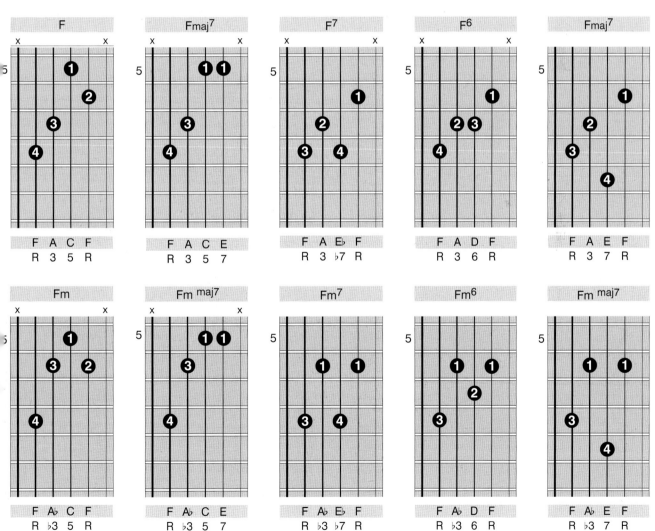

some very useful shapes. In shape two the doubled root on the B-string has been lowered a half-step to create a major seventh chord. In shape three the note on the B-string is back on the root, F, but there is a minor seventh, E-flat, on the G-string, making an F7 chord. In shape four this seventh is flattened to produce a sixth, making an F6 chord. Shape five is a more dissonant-sounding alternative to shape two.

Shape six is the bare minor triad, again, not particularly easy to hold down, and shape seven introduces a major seventh to create a chord of Fm maj7. Shapes eight and nine are the minor seventh and minor sixth. Shape ten is a more dissonant sounding alternative to shape seven.

This exercise demonstrates that the sound of a chord is dependent on both the notes it contains and how they are arranged, something which we call 'voicing'. Shape seven, for example, contains root, third, fifth and seventh, whereas shape ten, the same chord in name, omits the fifth and doubles the root, creating an intense but pleasing dissonance between the root and the major seventh, which are only a half-step apart.

THEORY: it is common in guitar music to leave some notes out of chords and in many of these shapes the fifth has been omitted. The fifth is in many ways the least interesting note in any chord as it is present in both the major and minor. However, a flattened or sharpened fifth is part of the character of a chord and should not normally be omitted.

Section 2

Extending beyond the seventh; chords, keys, and modulation; chord voicings

Exercise 2.13

If we return for a moment to shape three in Exercise 2.12, we can see that both the top and bottom note of this chord are the doubled root. If we continue to build chords in thirds, the next step after the seventh is the ninth. This is the same note as the second, but we call it the ninth to show that we are building chord in thirds: 1, 3, 5, 7, 9, and so on. If we move the F-natural at the top of this chord up two frets it will become a G, which is the ninth, giving us shape one below, F9, pronounced 'F nine' or 'F ninth'.

Ninth chords can be minor too, and in shape two of Exercise 2.13 the major third has been lowered to create Fm9 or F-9, 'F minor ninth'. Shape three brings back the major third but also raises the minor seventh a half-step to produce a major chord with a major seventh and a major ninth; this is known as Fmaj9, F△9, 'F major nine' or 'F major ninth'.

The above chords all used the major ninth, G-natural, but ninths, like thirds and sevenths, can be major or minor. G-flat would be the minor ninth, and this is usually used with the major third and the minor seventh to produce F7♭9, or 'F seventh flat nine'.

The fifth chord in the set, F6/9 or 'F six nine' is often used as a substitute for the major seventh chord or major ninth chord. Essentially it is a major ninth chord with a major six instead of a major seventh.

Exercise 2.13
Ninth chords

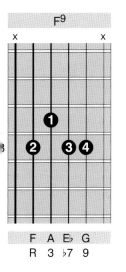

F⁹

F A E♭ G
R 3 ♭7 9

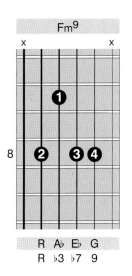

Fm⁹

R A♭ E♭ G
R ♭3 ♭7 9

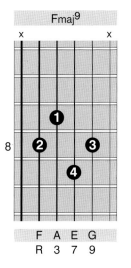

Fmaj⁹

F A E G
R 3 7 9

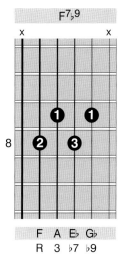

F7♭9

F A E♭ G♭
R 3 ♭7 ♭9

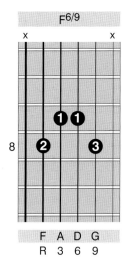

F6/9

F A D G
R 3 6 9

THEORY: it is important to see these chords as belonging to a group or set of ninth chords. In this way, instead of looking at the above exercise and thinking "Oh no, another four chord shapes to learn", we can see that the structure of each chord is identical; starting with the lowest note, they go root, third, seventh and ninth. To 'morph' F9 into Fm9 we need to flatten the third. To morph F9 into Fmaj9, we need to raise the seventh, and so on. In this way, chords on the guitar cease to be abstract shapes that need to be memorised and start to be understood from a point of view of which notes need to be present to create the sounds we are looking for.

Exercise 2.14

For this exercise we need to go back to CD track 1 and listen to the guitar in the rhythm track in the background. Instead of laying down a solid rhythm part that fills up every measure, the chords in this exercise punctuate the gaps in the melody line. This rhythm part can be heard on its own in CD track 12, where it is played three times.

The gaps in the chord part have the advantage of giving us a little more time to get the fingers into position if these shapes are unfamiliar. If they give you trouble, practise each shift in turn, moving backwards and forwards between the two chords, aiming to keep your fingers close to the guitar and making the smallest movements possible. You may need to be patient and practise the changes slowly at first.

Bar five of this exercise introduces the C9 chord, used instead of C7. The sound of jazz is very much dependent upon extending chords beyond the basic triad or seventh. C9 is a good jazz substitution for C7 as it is the same type of chord but with the extended quality we are looking for.

TECHNIQUE: notice the rests between the notes of the chords in bar one, bar three, and so on. Play these silences by releasing the pressure of the fretting-hand fingers so that the strings come off the frets. Do not actually take your fingers off the strings, just release the pressure briefly and then reapply it for the next chord. Remember that the rests (or silences) are as important to a rhythm as the notes you play. Getting the feel of this track also depends to a large extent on following the pick directions.

THEORY: notice that in this track the eighth-notes are straight, not swing.

Straight 8s ♩=105

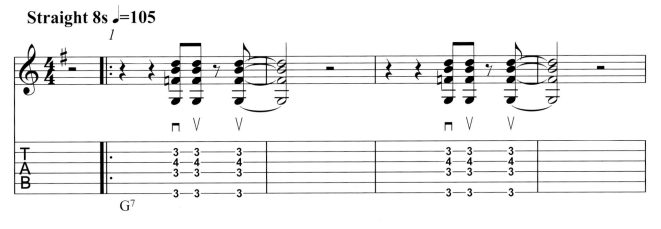

Play X3

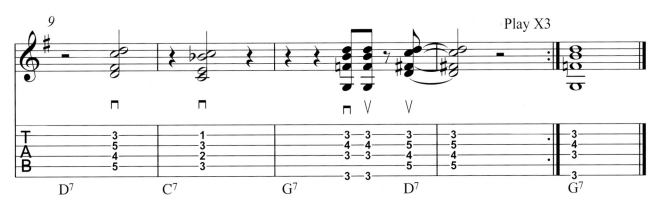

Exercise 2.14
CD TRACK 12
*'Kenny's Blues',
rhythm track*

THE JAZZ GUITAR HANDBOOK

Exercise 2.15

Now that we have a full set of chords with their roots on both the sixth string and the fifth string it might be fun, and of course educational, to see what happens when we use a completely different set of shapes to play the same piece of music. The main difference between this and the previous exercise is that here we have chord IV in the second bar – a common alternative chord sequence in the 12-bar blues. The rhythm is a little looser too, but otherwise it's just a question of choosing to voice the chords differently.

Exercise 2.15
CD TRACK 28
'Kenny's Blues', higher-position chord shapes

THE JAZZ GUITAR HANDBOOK

TECHNIQUE: work out your own way around the sequence and see how much interest you can add to this 12-bar blues by mixing different seventh and ninth chord shapes.

Exercise 2.16

We have looked at how chords are built using roots, thirds, fifths, sevenths and ninths, and we have seen how changing the third, seventh, or ninth from major to minor can create different types of chord. We have also seen that some chords use the flattened or sharpened fifth. Back in Part One we looked at keys and key signatures.

Chords and keys are very closely related, and each major scale or key creates a unique sequence of chords. Let's start with a C major scale, and let each note of the scale be the root note of a chord. Then, using the notes from the scale, add the third and fifth above each root to create a series of triads. We now have a sequence of seven chords all made from notes in the C major scale.

Exercise 2.16 shows two possible fingerings for this sequence of chords; one that uses open strings whenever possible, and one that works its way up the neck keeping to the same three strings. On the CD we've completed the sequence by ending on chord I an octave up. As normal, we have numbered these chords using Roman numerals: chords one (I), four (IV), and five (V) are major chords and are capitalised.

Exercise 2.16
CD TRACK 29
Triads in a key

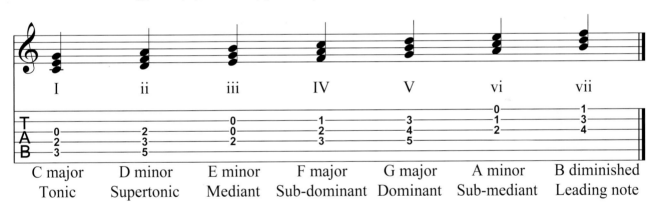

C major	D minor	E minor	F major	G major	A minor	B diminished
Tonic	Supertonic	Mediant	Sub-dominant	Dominant	Sub-mediant	Leading note

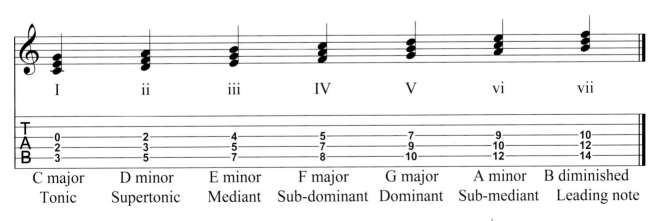

C major	D minor	E minor	F major	G major	A minor	B diminished
Tonic	Supertonic	Mediant	Sub-dominant	Dominant	Sub-mediant	Leading note

THE JAZZ GUITAR HANDBOOK

Chords two (ii), three (iii), and six (vi) are minor and are lower case. Chord seven (vii) is diminished and is also lower case.

Since every major scale has the same structure of whole-steps and half-steps or tones and semitones, this pattern of major, minor, and diminished chords is the same for every major key. If we take G major, for example, we would say the chords in G major are:

■ G, A minor, B minor, C, D, E minor, and F-sharp diminished.

If you know what notes are in the major scales (Fig. 1.11) you should be able to work out what chords are in every key. In a major key, chord I is always major, chord ii always minor and so on. The sequence of seven letter names involved is unique to each key.

In addition to a number, each step of the scale also has a name, as shown above. So we could say the dominant chord in C major is G major, or the sub-dominant chord in C major is F major. You might sometimes hear jazz musicians using these technical terms when describing chord sequences. For example, when playing a blues it may be helpful to clarify whether to go to chord IV in the second bar, which is the same as saying "it goes to the sub-dominant in the second bar".

It is important to learn the sequence of major and minor chords that occurs when a major scale is harmonised. For the sake of looking clued-up rather than ill-informed it would also be a good idea to learn the names of the different degrees of the major scale – just in case you find yourself playing with musicians who use these terms.

Exercise 2.17

Exercise 2.17
CD TRACK 30
C major scale harmonised in seventh chords

It is a small step to go from working out the triads in a key to working out the seventh chords. In 2.17 the seventh has been added to each triad in C major, creating a sequence of chords which goes maj7, m7, m7, maj7, 7, m7, and m7♭5 (half-diminished). These are all chord types that we have come across before, but not in the voicings given above – some of which, particularly the minor seventh and dominant seventh shapes, are virtually unplayable. On the CD these 'impossible' chords are

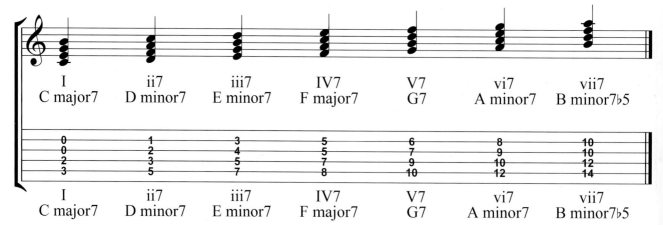

played as arpeggios. The idea is just to get the feel of where the notes are on the guitar when chords are voiced 'in order' from root to seventh.

This type of voicing is relatively rare on the guitar: we are more likely to re-arrange these four-note chords and use a voicing like 'root, fifth, seventh, third' rather than 'root, third, fifth, seventh' as it makes for more playable shapes.

THEORY: there are four different types of seventh chord created when we harmonise a major scale. These are major seventh, minor seventh, dominant seventh and half-diminished. It is possible to add more notes to these chords, such as ninths, elevenths, and thirteenths, without changing their essential character. Most jazz is made using these four basic types of chord, although often with the above extensions.

Exercise 2.18

You should find that you recognise these shapes from those in Exercises 2.09 and 2.10, which all had fifth-string roots. Play these chords in order so you can hear how the chords in a key progress and relate to each other. When you reach the Bm7b5 chord, try resolving the sequence to Cmaj7 an octave up, with its root on the 15th fret. Skip this if your guitar does not have a cutaway!

THEORY: in any major key there are two major seventh chords (I and IV), three minor seventh chords (ii, iii and vi), one minor seven flat five or half diminished (vii), and one 'seventh' chord (V), which is also called a dominant seventh because it is built on the fifth or dominant note of the scale. So if you hear a musician talking about a 'dominant seventh chord', you will know that this means the type of seventh chord found on step five of a major scale: the type with a major triad and a minor seventh, which is notated with the number 7 and nothing else, as in G7 or C7. In classical music analysis you also hear terms like 'supertonic seventh' or 'sub-dominant seventh'. It is good to know what these terms mean, but they are not often used in jazz.

Exercise 2.18
CD TRACK 31
C major in seventh chords, practical voicings

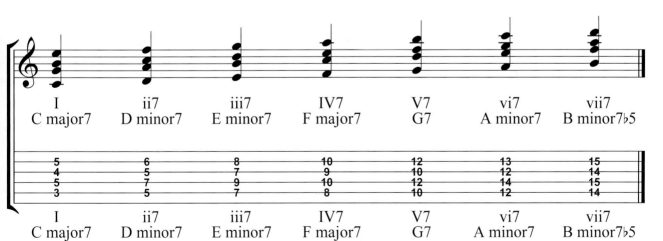

EXTENDING BEYOND THE SEVENTH; CHORDS, KEYS, AND MODULATION; CHORD VOICINGS

Exercise 2.19

Major scales are all made from the same sequence of intervals, and the sequence of triads created by a major scale is the same for every key. This applies to seventh chords too. The seventh chords in G major, for example, would be the same as those in C major, but the root notes would be those of a G major scale:

■ Gmaj7, Am7, Bm7, Cmaj7, D7, Em7, F♯m7♭5

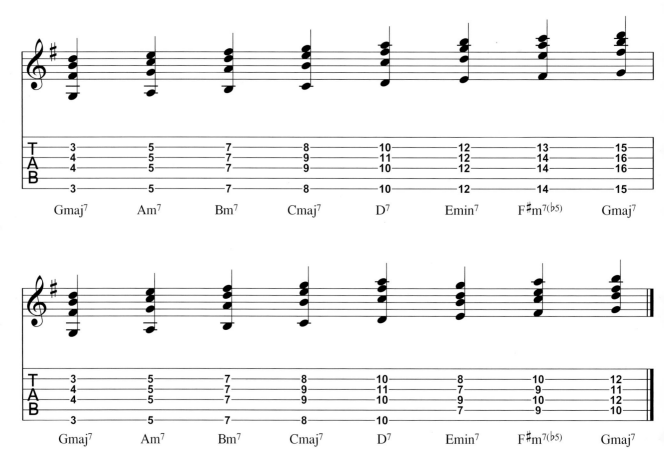

Exercise 2.19
CD TRACK 32
Chords in G major and voice-leading

Exercise 2.19 uses the shapes we know from Exercises 2.05 and 2.06 to play this sequence of chords. There are two examples. The first example uses the above-mentioned shapes and keeps the voicing of the chord consistent through the entire sequence. This has the disadvantage that you end up trying to play four-note chords above the 12th fret, but it is sonically pleasing, in that the voicings are consistent from chord to chord.

The second version of this sequence crosses over to the A-string and uses a different voicing for the Em7, F♯m7♭5, and Gmaj7 chords (taken from Exercise 2.10). This is easier to play but to some extent sacrifices the flow of the notes from one chord to the next; in other words, the 'voice leading' is less satisfactory.

THEORY: voice leading is the term given to the study of how to make the notes of one chord progress smoothly to the notes of the next. The most conspicuous elements of voice leading are the root note of the chord and the top note of the chord. Generally speaking when playing jazz chords on guitar it is best to avoid the jerkiness that we get from large leaps between the root notes of your chords. Equally important, the top notes of the chords are heard as the melody, and again large or erratic leaps can be most unsatisfactory – unless, of course, jerkiness or an unsettling effect is something you are aiming for in your music.

Exercise 2.20

This exercise has the 32-bar structure of a typical AABA jazz standard. It is based loosely on the Duke Ellington song 'Satin Doll'. In addition to practising the 32-bar form, it gives us the opportunity to study the most important relationships between chords in a key. This piece is in C major, and it may be worthwhile at this point to revise the names and numbers of chords in this key:

Cmaj7	Dm7	Em7	Fmaj7	G7	Am7	Bm7♭5
I	ii	iii	IV	V	vi	vii
Tonic	Supertonic	Mediant	Sub-dominant	Dominant	Sub-mediant	Leading note

The most important chord in any key is chord I, the tonic chord, because this chord is 'home'; it is the place to which the music wishes to return. The next most important chord in any key is the dominant, chord V; chord V 'points' in the direction of chord I, so that after chord V we always want to hear chord I. Of course, we don't always get what we want, so in bar three chord V does not lead to a return to chord I; in bar seven however, we finally arrived on chord I and our ears hear the resolution they crave.

The most common way of approaching chord V in jazz is chord ii. The chord sequence ii-V-I is extremely common in jazz, with the unresolved opening move of ii-V even more common. The existence of the ii-V-I opens up the possibility of changing key within even short sections of music. Every time there is a chord ii followed by a chord V it implies, however briefly, movement (the technical term is 'modulation') to the 'chord I' key, whether that chord is actually played or not.

Exercise 2.20 CD TRACK 33 *32-bar jazz standard*

EXTENDING BEYOND THE SEVENTH; CHORDS, KEYS, AND MODULATION; CHORD VOICINGS

Exercise 2.20 *continued*

EXTENDING BEYOND THE SEVENTH; CHORDS, KEYS, AND MODULATION; CHORD VOICINGS

Beneath the stave in the first A section and the B section, you will see an analysis of the chords and the keys that they relate to. You will see that it is possible to travel through several keys in just eight bars. The piece begins with chords ii-V in C major, and in the next two bars we have a ii-V in D major. The next two bars are a ii-V in G major before arriving back on the tonic chord via a ii-V-I.

The B section (or middle eight) begins with a ii-V-I in F major, which is followed by a ii-V in G major, ending with a ii-V in D major which sets up the return to D minor and the start of the final A section. The restlessness that is caused by this continuous changing of key and the chromatic colouring of melodies that we can create as a result are an essential part of jazz; it is the presence of key changes or modulations that is the biggest difference, in harmonic terms, between jazz and rock music, which generally speaking does not modulate.

TECHNIQUE: in this exercise we have separated the bass note from the rest of the chord and have included some arpeggios to create a flowing approach which works well with a walking bassline. When playing chords in this style always finger the chords in the order that you will play the notes; start with the bass note and it will give you half a beat or more to get the rest of the fingers in position.

THEORY: the sliding chord in bars 15 and 19 is not notated separately in the chord symbols as it is just a passing decoration to the main chord of the bar. It is an effective and useful trick to add interest when you have two bars of the same chord. Other points to notice are the frequent substitution of ninth chords for seventh chords and the rhythmic placing of chords on offbeats. Also, the final chord contains both a sixth (A) and a ninth (D) to make C6/9. The third (E) is omitted.

Exercise 2.21

Every major scale or key has a relative minor scale that is built on its sixth step. So the relative minor of C major is A minor; of G major, E minor; and so on. Major keys and the minor keys that share their key signatures can be shown on a chart called the Circle of Fifths. The key signatures (the sharps or flats) are shown around the outside ring, with the name of the major scale in large type. The minor key that shares the same key signature is around the inner ring in smaller type. This chart is useful for showing all the keys and key signatures and which notes are in each scale. As we go from one sharp to two sharps and so on the keynote rises a fifth each time: hence, circle of fifths. It has one other important use, in that it shows important key relationships.

Generally speaking, it is easier to modulate to and from keys which are close together in the cycle of fifths. In Exercise 2.19, we began in C major before taking two steps clockwise to D major, then moving one step back to G major before arriving back on C major. Notice that D major is the dominant chord in G major and G major is the dominant chord in C major. These modulations have been achieved simply by a dominant chord moving naturally to its tonic.

In the middle eight we moved to the key of F major from its dominant C major. All of the modulations in this example are to keys close to the tonic or home key of C major and this contributes to the relative simplicity of this tune. It is also possible within short pieces of music to modulate to quite distant keys; we will return to this later.

THEORY: it is a good idea to memorise the order of sharps and order of flats in key signatures; if you know your key signatures you also know your major scales, and therefore the chords in every key. For sharps, the order is F, C, G, D, A, E, B. Try learning the sentence 'Father Christmas Gave Dad An Electric Blanket'. If you use this sentence, 'Blanket Exploded And Dad Got Cold Feet', you get the order of flats: B, E, A, D, G, C, F.

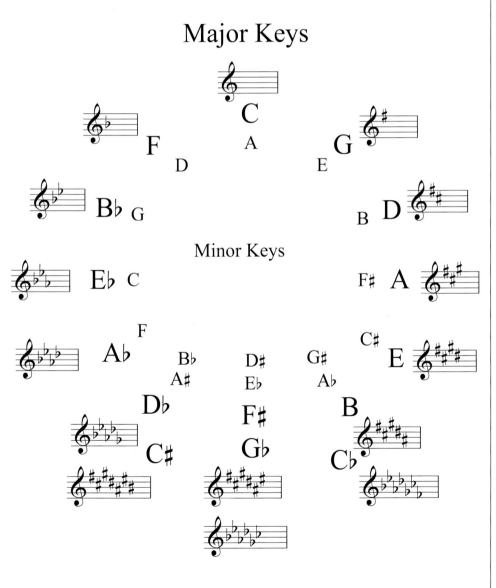

Major Keys

Minor Keys

Exercise 2.21 Circle of Fifths

Major keys are on the outside; their relative minors are inside.

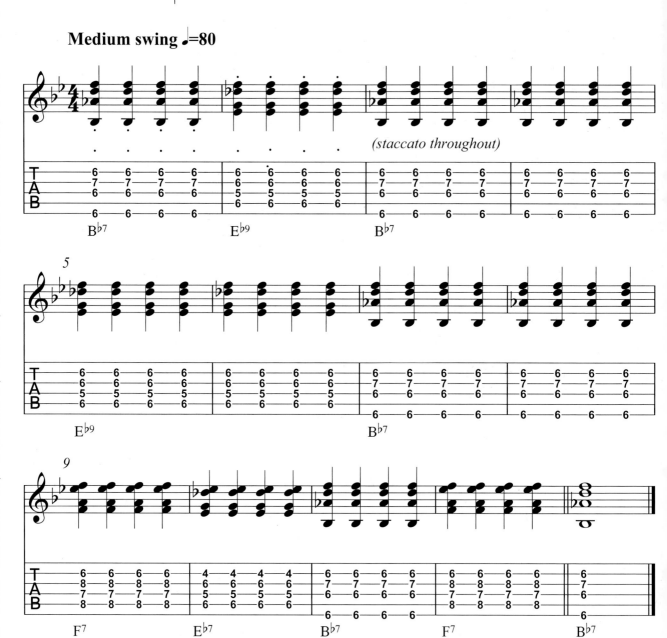

Exercise 2.22
CD TRACK 23
'Swing Blues In B-flat',
rhythm

EXTENDING BEYOND THE SEVENTH; CHORDS, KEYS, AND MODULATION; CHORD VOICINGS

Exercise 2.22

For Exercise 2.22 we are going to return to Part One, Exercise 1.22, 'Swing Blues In B-Flat', and learn the rhythm part that you can hear on the backing track, which is CD track 23. This track showcases the kind of rhythm playing that was popular from the early days of jazz and all through the big band swing era. Sometimes known as 'four on the floor', because it keeps in time with the drummer's kick drum on every quarter-note, it is a solid and propulsive style. Notice that the chords are not played legato, but each chord is separated from the next by allowing the fretting-hand fingers to release the pressure on the strings.

This is, harmonically speaking, the most basic kind of blues. It uses only chords I, IV, and V in B-flat, all played as dominant sevenths. Rhythm & blues and rock'n'roll often use this chord sequence, but as we will see in Exercise 2.23, jazz players like to make the blues chord sequence a little more interesting and challenging. Nevertheless, there are some jazzy touches to this piece, for example, the use of E♭9 instead of E♭7 in bar two and in bars five and six.

TECHNIQUE: the picking for this exercise could not be simpler; just use down strokes.

THEORY: remember that the first four bars of a simple blues can be either four bars of chord I, or can go to chord IV in the second bar.

EXTENDING BEYOND THE SEVENTH; CHORDS, KEYS, AND MODULATION; CHORD VOICINGS

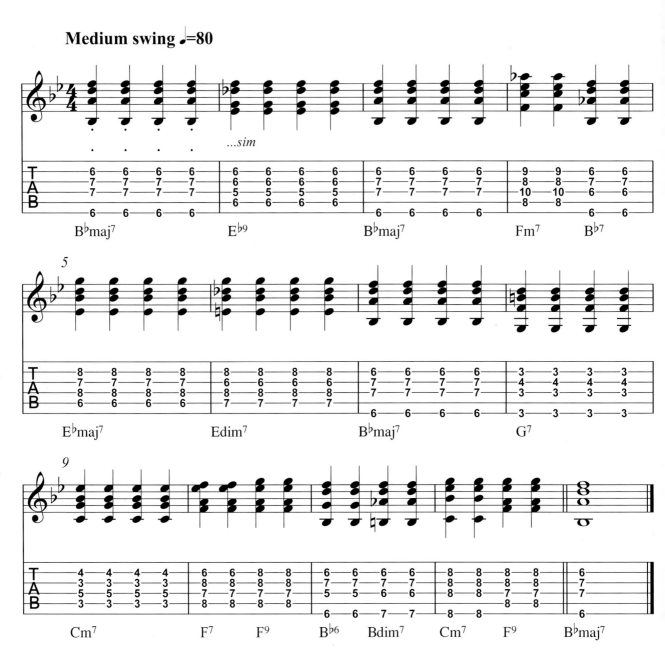

Exercise 2.23
CD TRACK 34
'B-flat Jazzy Blues'

EXTENDING BEYOND THE SEVENTH; CHORDS, KEYS, AND MODULATION; CHORD VOICINGS

Exercise 2.23

All the 12-bar blues sequences that we have been playing up to now have been based on the simplest blues music, using chords I, IV, and V, all as dominant sevenths. When jazz musicians play a 12-bar blues they like to embellish this basic sequence with some more interesting chords, some of which imply a change of key and therefore make the sequence more challenging, but ultimately more rewarding, to play over.

We are staying with the key of B-flat so that this exercise can be compared to Exercise 2.22, and also because jazz is often played in flat keys such as F, B-flat, or E-flat major. These keys are more comfortable for trumpet and saxophone, which are 'transposing instruments'. This means that for a B-flat trumpet a written note C produces the note B-flat. Tenor saxophones are also in B-flat, but alto saxophones are in E-flat. The reason for transposing instruments is to do with the evolution of these instruments and the ease with which a player can 'double', or play more than one variety of the same instrument. Fortunately, guitarists are spared this complexity.

The main difference between this jazzy blues and the more straightforward sequence is the inclusion of ii-V-I chord sequences which modulate, so that the harmony seems more 'stretched' than in the 'all in one key' blues we have seen before. The broad outline of the 12-bar remains the same – we have E-flat at bar five, but this time it is approached by a ii-V-I. There is another ii-V-I in bars 9-11, where we arrive back on the tonic chord. The G7 chord in bar eight has a V-i relationship to the C minor chord in bar nine. (We look at minor key harmony, where chord i is minor, in more depth in Exercise 2.26.) The Edim7 chord in bar six is like a heightened, or more intense version of the E♭7 chord in the preceding bar. At the end we have a turnaround with a ii-V in B-flat in the final bar to take us back to the top or to the end.

THEORY: if we were looking for a simple way of describing what happens to the harmony in this blues we could say that the modulations mean we get deeper into the corners of the harmony. The standard blues never really leaves its home key; this one does some abrupt turns to left and right to pass through several keys on its short journey.

TECHNIQUE: there is a slight loosening of the 'four on the floor' feel in bars 11 and 12, which demonstrates an alternative to the constant staccato chords of Exercise 2.22. At this point the chords on the first and third beats of the bar are held, while those on the second and fourth beats remain staccato. This style of strum was also used in Exercise 2.07.

Exercise 2.24

With a chord sequence that modulates it is possible to write a melody or play an improvisation that gets into the corners of the harmony and contains interesting notes not found in the scale of the original key. Exercise 2.24 hints at the style of the bebop players of the 1940s and uses notes from the underlying chords to produce a melody made up of fragments of arpeggios. Every note is either a root, third, fifth, or seventh from the accompanying chord, yet it still flows, has rhythmic interest and works well as a jazz melody. We'll look at arpeggios in more detail in Part Three.

Here is a bar by bar analysis of this exercise :

- **BAR 1:** D and F are third and fifth of B♭maj7.
- **BAR 2:** D♭ and G are flat seven and third of E♭7 or E♭9.
- **BAR 3:** F, D and B♭ are fifth, third, and root of B♭; the A♭ anticipates the next bar and is the third of Fm7.
- **BAR 4:** the F and A♭ are the root and third of Fm7; the D and B♭ are third and root of B♭7 and the G is the third of E♭9, in the next bar. Alternatively, the first four notes in this bar could be viewed as all belonging to B♭7.
- **BAR 5:** G and E♭ are the third and root of E♭9.
- **BAR 6:** G and E♮ are the third and root of Edim7.
- **BAR 7:** F and D are the fifth and third of B♭maj7; the B♮ anticipates the third of G7 in the next bar.
- **BAR 8:** all the notes in this bar form an arpeggio of G7.
- **BAR 9:** C and E♭ are root and third of Cm.
- **BAR 10:** A, F, and C are from the triad of F7, third, root, and fifth; the D anticipates the third of the B♭ chord in the next bar.
- **BAR 11:** B♭ and B♮ are root notes of the accompanying chords; the D is the third of Bdim; the E♭ is the third of the Cm7 chord in the next bar.
- **BAR 12:** A and F are third and root of F9.
- **BAR 13:** a voicing of B♭maj7 from root to major seventh.

We can see in this analysis a different approach to soloing than that used in Part One. The notes come from arpeggios of the underlying chords and the melody, even if played without accompaniment, outlines the chords and suggests the underlying harmony. This arpeggio-based approach would allow the modern jazz guitarist to play single-note solos over complex harmony even when accompanied only by a bass player.

THEORY: analysing how a melody works against the chords can help you to improvise your own jazz lines. You can take a look back at any preceding exercises with chords and melodies and practise this sort of work for yourself. Also use 2.23 (CD34) as a backing track to try out your own ideas based on this arpeggio-led approach.

TECHNIQUE: always take any phrases you find hard to play out of context and go round and round them in isolation; start at a manageable speed and as you improve you should eventually be able to put them back into context and play the whole piece. The human brain is better at remembering lots of short pieces of information than remembering one long piece, (think, for example, about how we break up phone numbers into short sections) so it makes sense to practise and learn music phrase by phrase.

Exercise 2.24
CD TRACK 35
'B-flat Jazzy Blues',
arpeggio-based blues
melody

THE JAZZ GUITAR HANDBOOK

Section 3

Minor harmony; substitutions and inversions.

Back in Exercise 2.21 we introduced the Circle of Fifths and the idea that each major key has a relative minor that shares its key signature. Minor harmony is subtly different to major harmony and needs to be studied separately, but first we need a better understanding of minor scales.

Exercise 2.25

As usual, we are using the simplest key, C major/A minor, as an example, but everything we say about this key applies to all the other keys. If we simply write out the notes of C major, starting and ending on A, we have a scale of A natural minor. This scale is pleasant enough and has its uses, but if we were to harmonise the scale in the way that we harmonised C major in examples 2.16 and 2.17 we would find that the chords created would be exactly the same seven chords as in C major.

If we were to write a piece in A minor using these chords, every time we arrived on G7 it would point us back towards C major and, harmonically speaking, we would keep ending up in the relative major. What we need is a minor scale that generates a set of harmonies unique to a minor key, where chord V has the same strong relationship to chord I as is found in a major key. The solution to this problem is the harmonic minor scale; as the name implies, it produces good harmony, which we will explore in the next exercise. The harmonic minor is the same as the natural minor except that the seventh step of the scale is raised a half-step; in this example the G has become G-sharp.

There is one more minor scale that we need to consider at this point. The harmonic minor scale may create good harmony, but it does not create good melodies. The

Exercise 2.25
CD TRACK 36
Minor scales

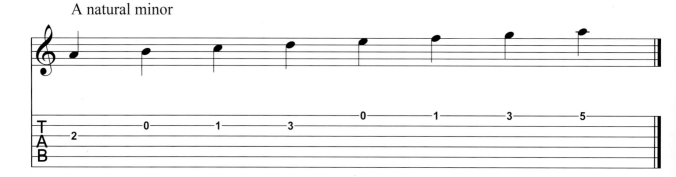

A natural minor

Exercise 2.25 *continued*

A harmonic minor

A melodic minor

augmented second between the sixth and seventh steps of the scale is awkward, and any passage rising stepwise from the fifth to the root or vice versa seems to have an eastern flavour that was disapproved of by composers in the 16th and 17th centuries when the major/minor key system was evolving. The melodic minor was invented to smooth over the lumpiness in the harmonic minor and produce a scale that, as the name implies, creates better melodies.

The melodic minor is unusual in that it ascends with a sharpened sixth step and sharpened seventh (F-sharp and G-sharp in this example), but these two notes are natural when the scale descends. In other words the descending scale is the same as the natural minor. We will return to the natural minor and the melodic minor in Part Three as both these scales can be used for soloing. Right now we are interested in minor key harmony.

Exercise 2.26

This exercise shows the harmonic minor scale harmonised firstly in triads and then in seventh chords. There are four triads that are unchanged by raising G to G-sharp, on step i, ii, iv, and VI. These triads are the same as would be found on the harmonised relative major scale (C) on steps vi, vii, ii, and IV.

Chord III in the harmonic minor is an augmented triad and chord vii is diminished, but the most important change is to chord V. As chord iii in C major it was a minor triad (E minor); it is now a major triad and produces a powerful V-i relationship to the A minor

MINOR HARMONY; SUBSTITUTIONS AND INVERSIONS

chord. Try playing these two triads one after the other to hear this working. The overall effect of changing just this one note of the scale is to produce a set of harmonies unique to minor keys.

A harmonic minor in triads:

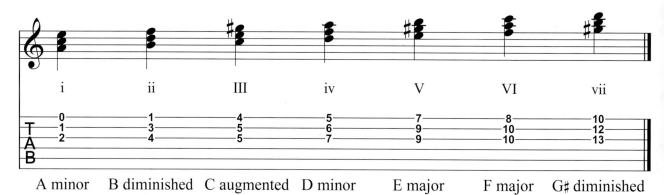

i	ii	III	iv	V	VI	vii
A minor	B diminished	C augmented	D minor	E major	F major	G# diminished

A harmonic minor in seventh chords:

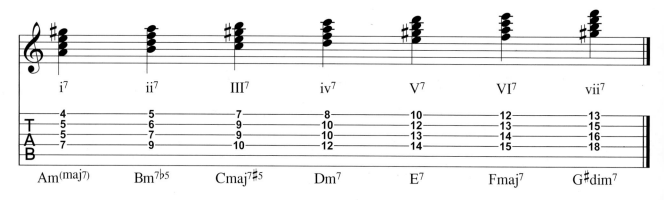

i⁷	ii⁷	III⁷	iv⁷	V⁷	VI⁷	vii⁷
Am(maj7)	Bm7♭5	Cmaj7♯5	Dm7	E7	Fmaj7	G♯dim7

Exercise 2.26
CD TRACK 37

Chords in a minor key: triads and sevenths

Moving on to the seventh chords, we can see that chord I is a minor chord with a major seventh; in fact, this chord is often avoided and just an ordinary minor seventh used in its place. Chord ii is a half-diminished or minor seventh flat five chord. Just as in a major key, chord ii is the most common approach to chord V. Chord V is an E7 chord, with the same structure as the G7 chord that is found as chord V in C major – in other words, a dominant seventh. Using A minor as an example, this means a ii-V-i in a minor key would be:

■ Bm7♭5 – E7 – Am7

Whereas a ii-V-I in a major key (C major) would be:

■ Dm7 – G7 – Cmaj7

THE JAZZ GUITAR HANDBOOK

So we have a fundamental difference between major harmony and minor harmony. When writing in the jazz idiom, composers often use chords ii and V from the minor key and then surprise our ears by arriving in the major key, or vice versa.

THEORY: notice that adding a major seventh to a C augmented triad produces a chord of C major seven with a sharpened fifth. For clarity this should be written as Cmaj7♯5, but the use of a + sign is also sometimes an indicator of a sharpened fifth, as in Cmaj7+.

TECHNIQUE: these chord shapes are cool sounding but not particularly practical; if you don't have a cutaway they are downright impossible. You could try taking the Fmaj7 and G♯dim7 chords down an octave. There are also some very big stretches involved so you should try playing them as arpeggios if stretches are a problem.

Exercise 2.27

Chords are not often played as root, third, fifth and seventh stacked vertically on the guitar. Exercise 2.26 offers a more practical way of playing the seventh chords in A minor from Exercise 2.25. We have used two different approaches; the first set of chords are entirely on the middle four strings with the root on the fifth string. The

Exercise 2.27
CD TRACK 38
Practical shapes for seventh chords in A minor

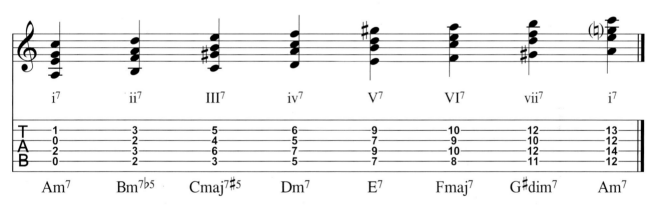

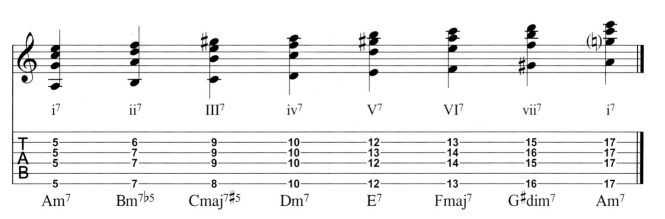

THE JAZZ GUITAR HANDBOOK

second set use the sixth string for the root with the upper notes on strings four, three, and two. Most of the shapes in this exercise should look familiar. We've seen them in the exercises at the start of Part Two when we were learning chord shapes. Now you can see how these chords work together to give music a sense of key, and to allow music to modulate.

THEORY: notice that chord one in these examples is Am7 instead of the more dissonant-sounding Am maj7. You could also try substituting Cmaj7 for the similarly dissonant Cmaj7♯5 for a smoother progression.

Exercise 2.28

This exercise is in the key of C minor and begins on chord i before moving to chord iv. This is then followed by a ii-V-i in C minor over four bars, with another ii-V-I, this time in D-flat major, over the next four bars. The final four bars see a return to C minor with yet another ii-V-i and a ii-V turnaround leading back to the top for the repeat. As discussed above, all of the ii-V-i progressions in C minor have the 'minor' approach chord of Dm7♭5, whereas the D-flat major section has the 'major' approach chord of E♭m7. It is not unusual for the chords of a jazz tune to be essentially a series of ii-V-I progressions.

Exercise 2.28
CD TRACK 39
'Bossa Blue': the ii-V-i progression in C minor

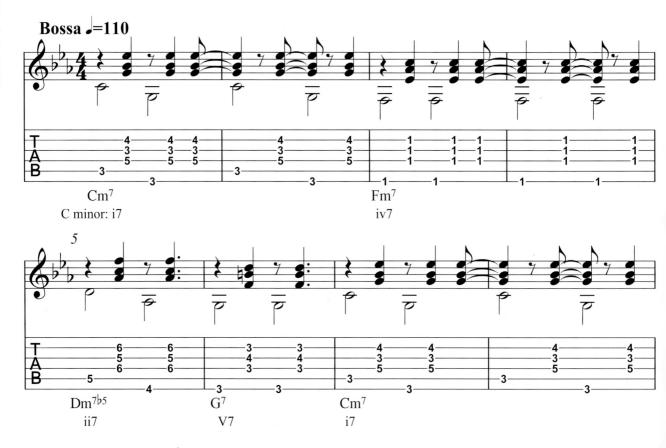

Exercise 2.28 *continued*

TECHNIQUE: this piece should be played fingerstyle, with the picking-hand thumb playing the bassline and the fingers (i, m, and a) playing the three-note chords. Occasionally, the root note of the chord is followed by its fifth, creating a moving, flowing bassline. This 'root and fifth' bass movement is common in this type of music. The style is called 'bossa nova', which originated in Brazil and became very influential on 1960s jazz musicians. The eighth-notes in bossa nova are straight, not swing.

THEORY: classical terminology describes chord progressions at points of harmonic repose in terms of cadences. Chord V to chord I is a perfect cadence; any chord (normally chord ii) progressing to chord V is an imperfect cadence; chord V progressing to chord VI is an interrupted cadence; and chord IV progressing to chord I is a plagal cadence. These are not terms in common use among jazz musicians, but cadences are like punctuation in music, so an awareness of their names in musical analysis could be useful. A perfect cadence is like a full stop, whereas an imperfect or interrupted cadence is more like a comma. Plagal cadences are found mainly in hymns and gospel music; you may have heard one accompanying the word 'amen'.

Exercise 2.29

There's one small detail concerning dominant chords and ii-V-I progressions in minor keys that we need to check out. It involves ninth chords. If we build a ninth chord on the dominant (step V) in C major we get a chord with a G root and A-natural, the major ninth, at the top; we'd call that G9. If we do the same thing in A minor we get a chord with an E root and an F-natural, the minor ninth, at the top; we'd call that E seventh flat nine (E7♭9).

This is shown in Exercise 2.29 and on the CD, demonstrating G9 and E7♭9 in 'piled up' form (with the tab as an arpeggio), together with usable voicings for G9, G7♭9, E9, and E7♭9. We've seen the E7♭9 shapes before, in Exercise 2.13. One interesting feature of the E7♭9 chord is that the upper four notes make a diminished seventh chord built on G-sharp; G♯, B, D, F. This means that a G♯dim7 chord can be used as a substitute for E7♭9. Diminished seventh chords have one other useful feature – they are completely symmetrical, being built entirely from minor thirds. This means that G♯, B, D, and F diminished seventh chords are identical and contain exactly the same four notes. So any one of these four identical chords can be a substitute for E7♭9.

Exercise 2.29
CD TRACK 40

Ninth chords in major and minor keys

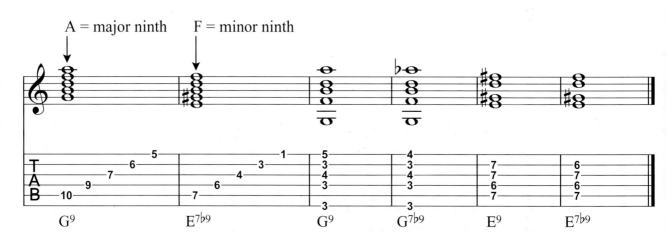

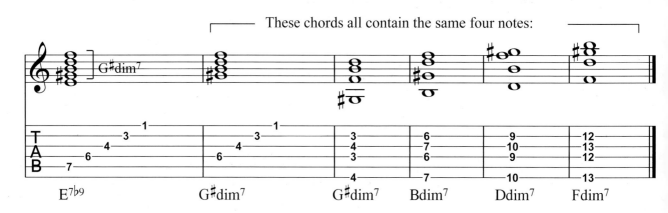

Exercise 2.30

Exercise 2.30 introduces four new chord shapes and contains a succession of ii-V-I or ii-V chord progressions making use of ninth chords. All of these shapes can be seen as extensions of the chord shapes first seen in Exercises 2.13 and 2.05. The Dm9 chord in bar five now has the fifth at the top, and the G7♭9 chord in bar six has the flat nine at the top. In bar seven we have a C6/9 chord, also with the fifth added at the top. Bar 16, the final bar, has the dreamy, mysterious Am6 with an added ninth (B-natural) on the top string.

Exercise 2.30
CD TRACK 41
The ii-V-I with ninth chords

THE JAZZ GUITAR HANDBOOK

continued over page

Exercise 2.30 *continued*

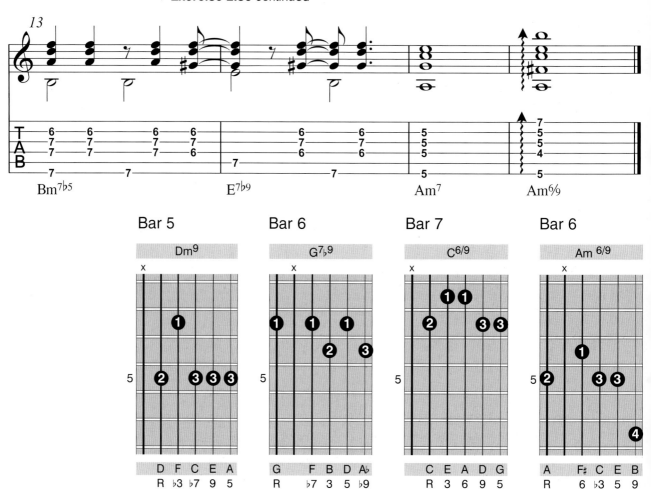

Once again, we are in bossa nova territory, with a steady tempo that should make the moving bassline easier to manage. As before, keep the pick hand thumb for the bassline and use the fingers – sometimes all four, including the 'e' finger, the pinky – to play the chords. The rhythmic pattern covers two bars, with the chord arriving half a beat early in the second bar; be sure to listen closely to the CD track to grasp this classic bossa nova rhythm. Watch out for bar seven, where the high G is allowed to ring throughout the bar while the accompaniment continues underneath.

The first four bars are a ii-V-i in A minor, with another ii-V-I in the next four bars but this time in C major. Notice the 'borrowing' of the dominant G7♭9 from the minor key despite the resolution to a major chord I. In the next four bars, bars nine to 12, we briefly pass through two keys, with a ii-V in E-flat and E majors. If you check back to the circle of fifths, you will see that these keys are a long way from the home key of A minor. However, the music makes a successful return home with a ii-V-i in A minor in the last four bars. This is achieved smoothly because E major, which is the expected next chord after the ii-V, is the dominant chord to A minor.

THE JAZZ GUITAR HANDBOOK

THEORY: do you compose? Many jazz composers begin by writing a chord sequence. If you were to write two complementary eight-bar chord sequences you could make up your own 32-bar jazz standard as in Exercise 2.20, using the form AABA. You could also try composing a 16-bar piece in the style of Exercises 2.28 and 2.30. Establish the keynote firmly at the beginning with a ii-V-I or ii-V and then see if you can move to other keys, returning home to the key chord at the end.

Exercise 2.31

Substituting a chord is a way of making the harmony more interesting without making a change to its underlying function. In this exercise we are going to learn about one of the most useful chord substitutions there is. It is known as 'the tritone substitution', or sometimes 'the flat five substitution'. The terms are interchangeable, because a flat five interval contains three whole-steps, or a tritone. It does not matter if you go up a tritone or down; the tritone is the same distance above as below. If you have listened to jazz at all, you will have heard this sound, and from now on you will know how it is done.

First, we need a little imagination. We know that G7 is the dominant to C major. Let's say we want to make that dominant chord more intense. We could lower the fifth to D-flat, making a chord of G7♭5 or 'G seventh flat five'. The first two bars of Exercise 2.31 have the regular ii-V-I, and the next two bars demonstrate the chromatically altered chord five leading to C6 for a satisfactory voice-leading resolution.

The notes of G7♭5 are: G B D♭ F. That's the exact same four notes found in the chord with its root a flat fifth or tritone away: D♭7♭5. The notes of D♭7♭5 are D♭ F A♭♭ C♭. (You have to allow for renaming A double-flat as G and C-flat as B.)

If the notes are the same, then the two chords are interchangeable, so a ii-V-I in C major could be: Dm7 – D♭7♭5 – Cmaj7, as demonstrated in bars five and six. You do not actually need to flatten the fifth, and Dm7 – D♭7 – Cmaj7 really works just as well (bars seven and eight). Even more impressive, once you have established the principle of the tritone substitution, it turns out that chord ii can be substituted equally well, often with

Exercise 2.31
CD TRACK 42
Chords for the flat five substitution (over page)

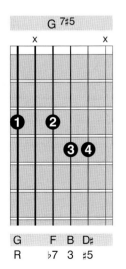

G 7♯5			
G	F	B	D♯
R	♭7	3	♯5

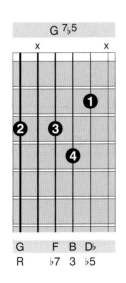

G 7♭5			
G	F	B	D♭
R	♭7	3	♭5

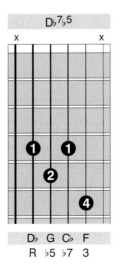

D♭7♭5			
D♭	G	C♭	F
R	♭5	♭7	3

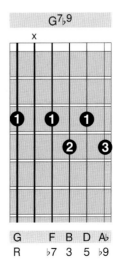

G7♭9			
G	F	B	D A♭
R	♭7	3	5 ♭9

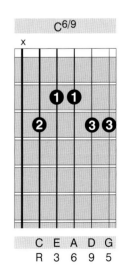

C6/9			
C	E	A	D G
R	3	6	9 5

continued over page

THE JAZZ GUITAR HANDBOOK

Exercise 2.31 *Substitutions in the ii-V-I; the flat five substitution*

the dominant chord whose root is a tritone away (that would be A♭7 in this case) but also with minor sevenths or half-diminished chords: check out bars nine and 10. Bars 11 and 12 show what happens when you 'flat five' both ii and V, giving the sequence A♭7 – D♭7 – Cmaj7.

In all the above examples, chord I could have been Cm7, and chord ii could have been Dm7♭5. Not only is the ii-V-I a tool that allows us to modulate freely to distant major or minor keys, but it can also have a whole range of subtly different characters depending on whether, and how, its component chords are substituted. This also means all sorts of chromatic melodies can be created or harmonised.

THEORY: when you add in other alterations to the chords of the ii-V-I, it turns out there are even more possibilities. Not just flat fives, as in G7♭5, but also sharp fives, as in G7♯5. Then there are the ninths and flat ninths that we have already seen and some others which we have not yet touched on, such as elevenths and thirteenths.

TECHNIQUE: on the CD, track 42 is played using the pick for the bass notes and the m, a, and e fingers for the three-note chords. This is a common technique among jazz players, as it allows all the notes of a four-note chord to be played at once while still holding the pick. If you strum these chords they will always be 'spread' to some extent, as in CD track 43.

Here is a little self-directed study to try out. Play all of the following chord sequences using any suitable chords giving the first two chords (ii-V) a bar each and then two bars on the C chord (chord I). Try major and minor resolutions each time and then try them in other keys.

Dm9	**G7♯5**	**Cmaj9 or Cm9**
Dm9	**D♭9**	**Cmaj9 or Cm9**
Dm9	**D♭7♭9**	**Cmaj9 or Cm9**
Dm7♭5	**G7♭9**	**Cm9 or C6/9**
Dm7♭5	**G7♯5**	**Cm9 or Cma9**
A♭m7	**D♭7**	**Cmaj9 or Cm9**
A♭m7♭5	**G7♯5**	**Cmaj9 or Cm9**
A♭m7♭5	**G7♭5**	**Cmaj9 or Cm9**

THEORY: back in Exercise 2.30 we wondered whether it might be possible for you to use ii-V-I chord sequences to make up your own compositions. Now you can experiment with tritone substitutions in your own chord sequences.

Exercise 2.32

The tritone substitution replaces the expected chord with one that is harmonically more interesting and ambiguous but still has the same function – it is a chord that belongs in a different key but still works in the home key. Too much ambiguity is unsettling, and composers work hard to find the right balance between the expected and the unexpected. When they get it right, we have a satisfying chord sequence. When they get it wrong, it can be either too dull or too restless. Taste and acclimatisation are important elements in this. One listener's restless cacophony is another's fascinating harmony.

The effect of a chord progression on the listener also depends to a large extent on context. If the flat five substitution is used again and again, its effect seems to be reduced, so it is most often used as part of a sequence of normal ii-V progressions to add a surprise at a key moment, as in Exercise 2.32. For this exercise we have used the eight-bar A section of Exercise 2.20, except that in bar six, instead of a ii-V in C major, we have a ii-V in G-flat major, the key that is a flattened fifth or tritone away from the tonic. In bar seven, the music moves to the tonic chord, Cmaj7, as normal.

THEORY: compare 2.20 with 2.31 and listen out for the subtle change in harmony in bar six. Which one do you prefer? Before you make up your mind, maybe you should know that it is the sequence from Exercise 2.31 that Duke Ellington used in the song 'Satin Doll'.

Exercise 2.32
CD TRACK 43
Tritone substitutions in action

TECHNIQUE: on CD track 43 this piece is played entirely with the pick, and you can hear the chords being 'spread' as a result. See if you can play it with pick and fingers too.

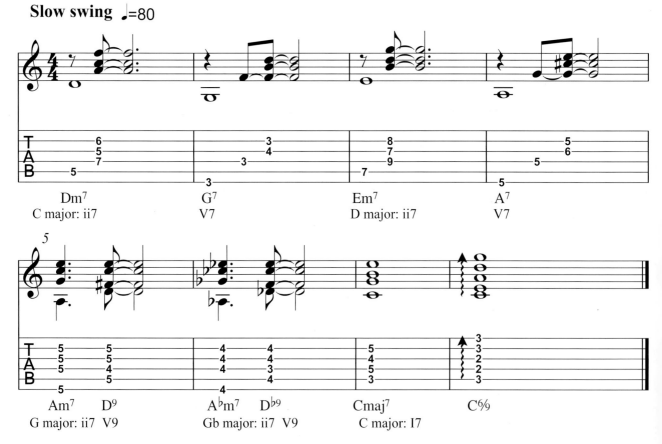

THE JAZZ GUITAR HANDBOOK

Section 4

Inversions and extensions

Exercise 2.33

The chords we have used so far have all had one thing in common. They have been in 'root position'. In other words, up to now the lowest note of every chord has been the root note. If some note of the chord other than the root is the lowest note, we say the chord is 'inverted' or is 'in inversion'. When using Roman numerals to describe inverted chords we use the letter 'a' for root position and b, c, and d for each inversion.

■ If the third of the chord is the lowest note it is in first inversion: (eg, IVb).
■ If the fifth of the chord is the lowest note it is in second inversion: (eg, IVc).
■ If the seventh of the chord is the lowest note it is in third inversion: (eg, IVd).

It is possible to have the ninth of a chord in the bass and have a fourth inversion (IVe),

Exercise 2.33
CD TRACK 44
Inversions of triads and chord position

Major triads

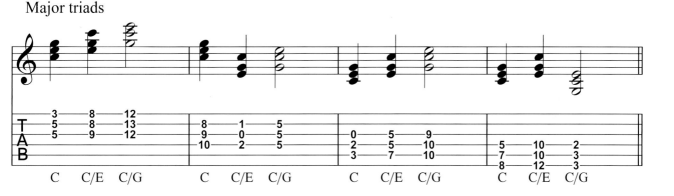

Minor triads

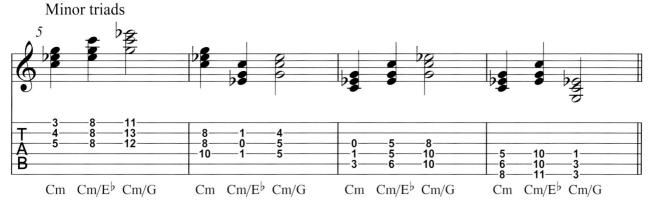

continued over page

THE JAZZ GUITAR HANDBOOK

Exercise 2.33 *continued*

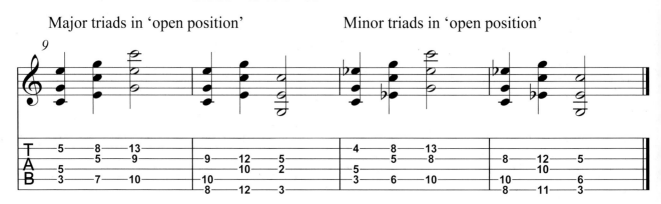

Major triads in 'open position'　　　Minor triads in 'open position'

but anything beyond that would be rare. When a chord is in root position we don't usually bother with the letter 'a' after the Roman numeral. When using chord symbols, we use the chord name followed by a forward slash with the bass note, such as C/E or Cm/G. As a result, this type of chord is often referred to as a 'slash chord'. It is possible for the specified bass note of a slash chord to be a note that is not in the chord, known as a 'foreign' bass note. However, we will deal with that kind of slash chord in Part Four.

A chord that is in inversion has a different quality to a chord that is in root position. In root position a chord is at its most stable and powerful, and chords 'sound best' when in root position. An inverted chord is less stable. Exercise 2.33 demonstrates major and minor triads in all three possible inversions: root position, first inversion, and second inversion.

The first four bars show C major triads in root position, first inversion, and then second inversion. The next four bars show C minor triads in the same way. Because the notes of these triads are as close together as they can possibly be, we say they are in 'closed position'. The last four bars of the exercise show similar root position and inverted triads in 'open position', where the middle note of each triad has been taken up an octave. There are many possible fingerings for these open position triads; the ones illustrated here are intended to make the chord shapes strummable with a pick, with the help of some fret-hand damping.

TECHNIQUE: rock guitarists should get to know these open position triads as they are a great way of adding interest to the straightforward triad-based chord sequences found in most rock and pop music.

Exercises 2.34 and 2.35

After playing Exercise 2.33 you might be thinking that you can use triads to add interest to a chord sequence by moving between the different inversions of the triad on each chord. That would be fine, and if the underlying chord were to be, say, Cmaj7, then you could use any inversion of a C major triad over it. Played with attention to voice leading and in a way which picks out occasional accents in a bar this would be the accompaniment style known as 'comping'. However, as we've mentioned before, triads

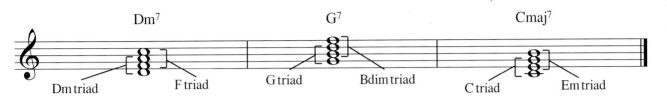

Exercise 2.34 *Seventh chords contain two triads*

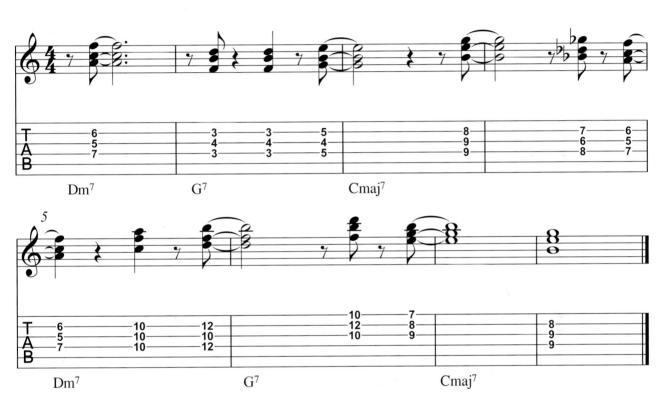

don't really cut it when it comes to jazz. To really use triads intelligently – and they can be great – we need to go into a bit of theory.

Any seventh chord could be viewed as containing two triads, as shown in Exercise 2.34. Let's say we look at the notes of the Dm7 chord in bar one: D F A C. This four note chord contains both a D minor triad (D F A) and an F major triad (F A C). If we were to play different inversions of an F major triad over a walking bassline that outlined the chord of Dm7 we would hear changing positions of a Dm7 chord instead of the bare D minor triad. Harmonically speaking that would be more interesting than using the triad of D minor.

This is demonstrated in Exercise 2.35, where the bassline outlines a ii-V-I in C major:

Exercise 2.35
CD TRACK 45
Comping with triads

‖ **Dm7** | **G7** | **Cmaj7** | **Cmaj7** ‖

THE JAZZ GUITAR HANDBOOK

The guitar part uses the upper notes of a Dm7 chord (F major triad), a G7 chord (B diminished triad) and a Cmaj7 chord (E minor triad) to 'comp' a harmonically alive and rhythmically interesting harmony part over the baseline. This sort of accompaniment would go well under another instrumentalist soloing or playing the 'head', or behind a singer carrying the tune.

THEORY: comping is the standard approach to jazz accompaniment nowadays. Essentially the bass outlines the tonal centre (eg, 'D') and character (eg, 'minor seventh') of the harmony, leaving chordal instruments such as piano or guitar to fill in the details and provide movement in a creative way. Both the bassline and comping are improvised; in other words, in current practice in jazz, everyone is improvising even when accompanying. Believe it or not, the drummer is improvising too.

When done well, comping not only outlines the harmony and provides rhythmic impetus but also inspires, phrases with, and comments on the soloist's performance. Good comping can be the unseen glue that makes a band swing and a performance special. Bad comping can ruin an otherwise excellent rhythm section.

Exercise 2.36
Four-note chords such as sevenths are also very effective when used for comping. There are, for example, four possible positions of a seventh chord; root position, first, second, and third inversion.

There is a technique for working out inversions of chords that is demonstrated in Exercise 2.36. The first bar shows the root-position Cmaj7 chord that we have seen many times before in this book. For the first inversion chord in bar two, each note of the chord has been moved up the guitar to become the next note of the chord. Taking the notes in the order that they come, from low to high, the root note, C, has been moved up the guitar four frets to become the third, E. The fifth, G, has been moved up the D-string to become the seventh, B. The seventh, B, on the G-string, is now the root, C. Finally the third, E, at the top of the chord on the B-string, is now the fifth, G.

This process is then repeated in bars four and five to create second and third inversion chords. In bar three we have an alternative way to play the first inversion chord, in which the root C on the G-string has been moved up two frets to become the ninth, making a shape which is easier to play, though arguably less interesting without the clash between the seventh and root. Technically this chord is Cmaj9(omit root), but you might also recognise it as Em7. This is because the top four notes of any ninth chord will be some kind of seventh chord built on the third. This introduces another possible form of chord substitution; if the underlying harmony is Cmaj7, an Em7 chord will produce a Cmaj9 sound. Em7 is built on the third note of the C major scale, which is the mediant, so this is known as mediant substitution.

The rest of Exercise 2.36 goes through the same process for the other important chord types. Diminished sevenths have been omitted, as all inversions of diminished sevenths are the same shape. Notice that in bar three of the dominant seventh chord

Exercise 2.36 CD TRACK 46 *Seventh chords inverted and a new substitution*

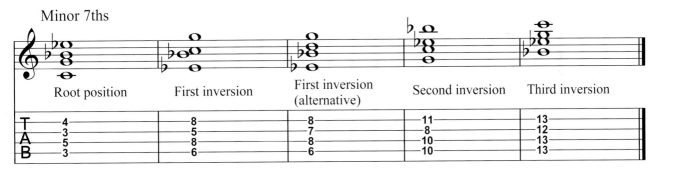

continued over page

INVERSIONS AND EXTENSIONS

Exercise 2.36 *(chords)*

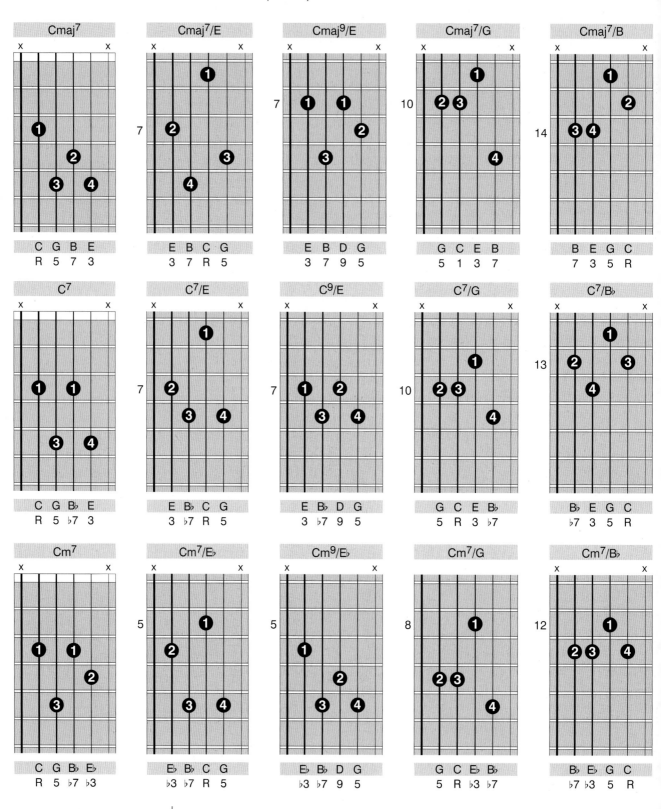

Exercise 2.36 *continued*

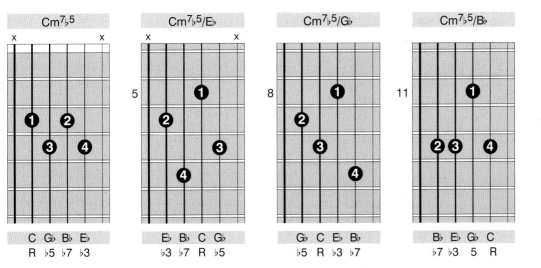

C G♭ B♭ E♭	E♭ B♭ C G♭	G♭ C E♭ B♭	B♭ E♭ G♭ C
R ♭5 ♭7 ♭3	♭3 ♭7 R ♭5	♭5 R ♭3 ♭7	♭7 ♭3 5 R

the root has again been replaced by the ninth, giving a C9 chord with the root omitted. This chord is the same as E half-diminished, meaning that a dominant seventh chord can become a dominant ninth by using the half-diminished chord that is built on the third.

In the minor seventh chords, bar three again contains a ninth chord with no root as an alternative. This chord turns out to be E♭maj7, meaning that a minor seventh chord can be substituted by a major seventh chord built on its minor third.

In the minor seven flat five section there is no chord in bar three because the ninth is not an effective addition to this chord.

THEORY: submediant substitution is also possible; for example, Am7 contains the notes A C E G. Rearranged, these could be C E G A, the notes of C6.

TECHNIQUE: see if you can add a ninth to the second and third inversion shapes for the major seventh, dominant seventh, and minor seventh chords. Simply move the root up two frets from C to D – you will discover some interesting sounds.

Exercise 2.37

To practise comping using four-note chords we are going back to the 12-bar blues, this time in the key of C major. Exercise 2.37 uses examples from 2.36 and other chords that we have seen before, played entirely on the middle four strings of the guitar. The underlying harmony is the same 'jazz blues' as used in Exercise 2.23, but transposed to the new key.

The walking bassline keeps the rhythm flowing while the comped chords outline the harmony and provide rhythmic impetus. Melodic content comes from the voice-leading of the top line. Very often there are two positions of the same chord in the same bar and chords are often anticipated, arriving half a beat early.

There are two choruses, making 24 bars in all; a double barline marks the end of the first chorus. The chord symbols relate to the actual sounds created when the

INVERSIONS AND EXTENSIONS

Exercise 2.37 CD TRACK 47 *Comping with sevenths; a blues in C*

Exercise 2.37 *continued*

F⁹   F♯dim⁷   C⁹   B⁹   B♭⁹   A⁹

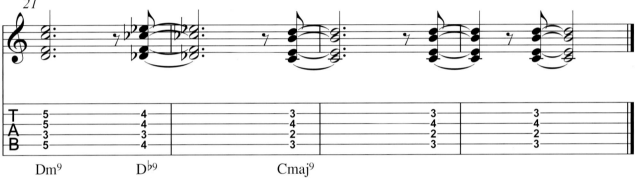

Dm⁹   D♭⁹   Cmaj⁹

bassline is taken into consideration. For example, in bar one, the second chord is Em7♭5, but its function over the bassline is C9. In bars 11 and 12, at the end of the first chorus, we have a turnaround using chords I, vi, ii, and V. In bar 16 the G♭9 chord is a flat five substitution for a C9 chord. Notice in bars 19 and 20 the use of a series of connecting ninth chords between C9 and A9, all of which are m7♭5 chords used as ninth chord substitutions.

THEORY: take some time to analyse the chords in this exercise and get to understand how the inversions and substitutions are being used. For example, a m7♭5 chord used as a substitute for a ninth chord is technically the ninth chord in first inversion with the root omitted. By understanding how the exercise works it should be possible for you to use some of the ideas presented here to comp your own way around a blues in C.

TECHNIQUE: make sure you are keeping your fretting-hand fingers close to the neck and watch out for fingers that are on the same string for consecutive chords. The move will be easier if you glide your finger or fingers along the strings to the new position. Also, remember that your fretting-hand thumb belongs at the back of the neck in whichever position best allows it to do its job of squeezing the tips of the fingers down onto the fingerboard. Keep your elbow relaxed and your thumb position flexible.

THE JAZZ GUITAR HANDBOOK

Exercise 2.38

Exercise 2.38 repeats the process of creating inversions from root-position chords that we saw in 2.36, but this time uses chords that have their root on the sixth string. Mostly, these shapes fall under the fingers well, and easier to play alternatives are not necessary. Start by practising each set of inversions logically up the neck, and as you play each chord take time to register which note is the root, third, fifth, or seventh.

TECHNIQUE: here is a method for practising inversions up and down the neck. Choose a type of chord to practise; let's say, major sevenths. Play the four Gmaj7 shapes, working your way up the neck to the third inversion. Then, using the circle of fifths, work your way back down the neck using Cmaj7 (starting with the first inversion at the 12th fret). Next, go up using F shapes and back down using B-flat shapes and so on until you have completed the cycle of fifths and arrived back on G. Then repeat the process for dominant seventh, minor seventh and so on. It's tough work and requires a lot of concentration, but it's a great way to learn how these chords fit on the neck and progress from one to another.

Exercise 2.38
CD TRACK 48
Inversions of chords with sixth-string roots

Major 7ths

Root position   First inversion   Second inversion   Third inversion

```
T--3----------7----------8----------12---
A--4----------7----------11---------12---
B--4----------5----------9----------12---
   3----------7----------10---------14---
```

Dominant 7ths

Root position   First inversion   Second inversion   Third inversion

```
T--3----------6----------8----------12---
A--4----------7----------10---------12---
B--3----------5----------9----------12---
   3----------7----------10---------13---
```

THE JAZZ GUITAR HANDBOOK

Exercise 2.38 *continued*

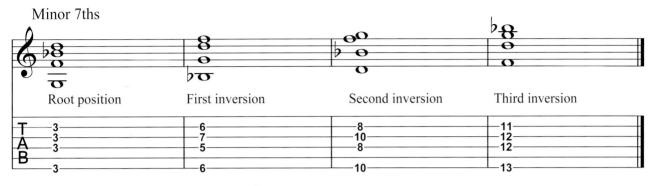

Minor 7ths

Root position · First inversion · Second inversion · Third inversion

Minor 7♭5 or half-diminished

Root position · First inversion · Second inversion · Third inversion

Exercise 2.39

Exercise 2.39 uses the voicings from 2.38 to create an accompaniment to a blues in G. These voicings are 'heavier' than those in Exercise 2.35 because of the low bass note on the sixth string. As a result they are probably more suitable to styles of jazz where there is no bass player, such as in guitar duos or when you are accompanying singers or other instrumentalists. With care, they can be used for comping, but it is usually best to leave the low notes to the bassist and stay off the sixth string when comping.

For the opening bars, the bass note of the chord is played on the beat with the rest of the chord an eighth-note later. By using different inversions, we can hint at a walking bassline – something that can be very effective on the guitar. The strummed chords at bar five continue to make use of inversions to create a bassline, with two positions of the same diminished chord in bar six. We return to the opening eighth-note/dotted quarter-note rhythm in bar nine. In bar 10 the A♭7 chord is a tritone substitution for D7. Notice that tritone substitutions allow us to have two chords in the same bar to maintain movement without changing the underlying harmony. There is a two-bar tag added to the 12-bar form to provide a good ending.

THEORY: the inversions create a bassline that provides forward motion, and the changes of texture add interest. Compare this to Exercise 2.22, which used only

THE JAZZ GUITAR HANDBOOK

Exercise 2.39 CD TRACK 49 *Blues in G: Using sixth-string inversions*

THE JAZZ GUITAR HANDBOOK

downstroke root-position chords. When accompanying a blues you could use the root-position chord approach on the head and then switch to the looser Exercise 2.39 approach for solos.

TECHNIQUE: this one was played only with the pick – could you tell just by listening to the CD track?

Exercise 2.40

Before we leave chords and return to single-note soloing there is one more aspect of music theory that we need to consider. We have added notes to triads to create sixth, seventh, and ninth chords, and there are two further extensions to chords that we have not yet looked at. These are elevenths and thirteenths.

Eleventh chords

An eleventh chord is a 'dominant' type of chord and should in theory include the root, third, fifth, minor seventh, and ninth as well as the eleventh, but in practice it is only the minor seventh, ninth and eleventh which are placed over the root. The major third of the chord is only a half-step away from the eleventh (although theoretically in a different octave) and causes an unwanted dissonance, so is normally omitted. We have already seen that the fifth contributes little to major and minor chords. (See shapes one and two below.)

Exercise 2.40

Dominant eleventh and minor eleventh chords

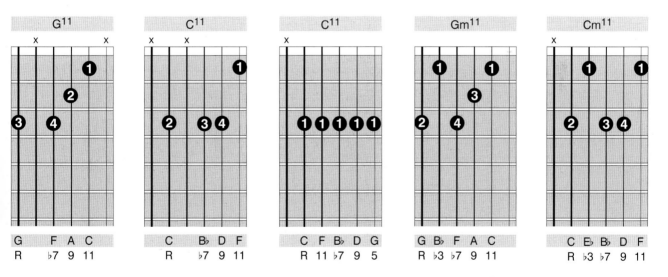

A good voicing can be found by transposing the eleventh down an octave, as in shape three above, which also includes the optional fifth on the top string. Eleventh chords seem to combine elements of chord ii7 and chord V7 as they contain notes found in both of these chords. An eleventh chord built on the dominant can substitute for all of the ii-V section of a ii-V-I.

INVERSIONS AND EXTENSIONS

THEORY: looked at a different way, the G11 chord could be seen as an F major triad with a G bass, and the C11 chord is the same as a B-flat triad with a C bass. In other words, F/G and B♭/C. This slash chord notation (introduced in Exercise 2.33) is sometimes used instead of the eleventh chord symbol and is an example of a slash chord where the specified bass note does not belong in the chord.

The minor eleventh chord needs to have the less dissonant minor third included; two possible fingerings are given in shapes four and five (previous page). These chords can be used as substitutions for minor seventh chords.

Exercise 2.40
Dominant thirteenth and minor thirteenth chords

Thirteenth chords
In theory, a thirteenth chord should also include all the other steps leading up to it – in other words all seven steps of a major scale arranged in thirds. Like the eleventh it is a

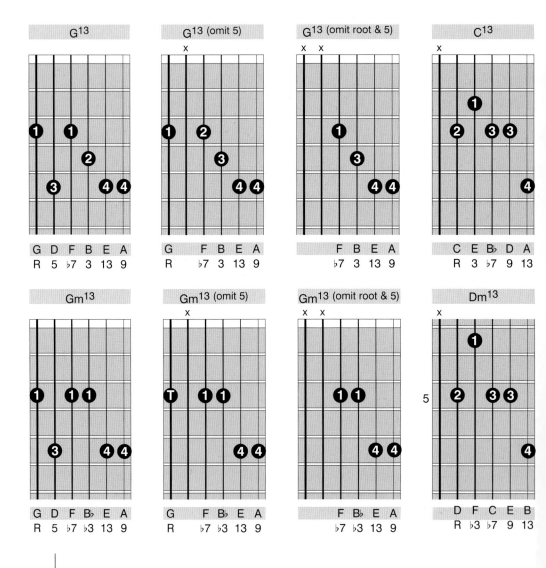

INVERSIONS AND EXTENSIONS

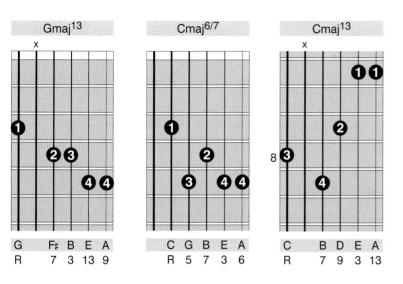

Gmaj13   Cmaj6/7   Cmaj13

G	F♯	B	E	A
R	7	3	13	9

C	G	B	E	A
R	5	7	3	6

C		B	D	E	A
R		7	9	3	13

Exercise 2.40
Major thirteenth chords

dominant type of chord and the root note would be the fifth of the major scale. It is impossible to play seven notes at once on the six string guitar, but in any case the eleventh tends to be omitted because of its clash with the major third. A six string version of G13 is illustrated in shape one (opposite), while shape two is an example that omits the fifth. If you can rely on a bass player or the musical context to give the chord its root (such as when comping) then shape three is an even better compact four-note voicing for this chord, although both root and fifth are omitted along with the eleventh in this example. Another version of a thirteenth chord is shown in shape four, this time with its root on the A-string.

Minor thirteenth (m13) and major thirteenth (maj13) are also used, as shown in examples five to eleven. Flatten the third in any of shapes one to four and you will have a minor thirteenth chord. Shape two can be converted to a minor thirteenth if we use the thumb on the sixth string (see shape six). To make the stretch easier, the minor version of shape four has been moved up two frets to Dm13. The solution lower down the guitar is to omit the root. Shape seven omits the root and is more straightforward.

Raising the seventh and restoring the major third in all the above shapes will create a major thirteenth, as shown in examples nine to eleven. Technically, example ten is Cmaj6/7 rather than Cmaj13, as there is no ninth present, but it has much of the sound of a major thirteenth and with guitar voicings it pays not to be too pedantic. Example eleven is a genuine major thirteenth and sounds great too – experiment with flattening the seventh to make a dominant thirteenth from this chord.

Sus4 chords

The eleventh is the same note as the fourth. In a sus chord the major third of the major triad is raised a half-step, or 'suspended', to become the fourth. The difference between the sus4 chord and the eleventh chord is that an eleventh implies the presence of the seventh and ninth. A sus4 chord has just root, sus4, and fifth, and is common in rock music – listen to the verse of The Who's 'Pinball Wizard' for sus4 chords resolving to

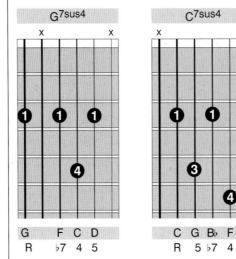

Exercise 2.40
7sus4 chords

major chords. There are also 7sus4 chords, and they are often used in jazz. Two versions of this type of chord can be found above; the G7sus4 chord can be played 'thumb over' if strumming, or as written if fingerpicking.

Exercise 2.41

The thirteenths and elevenths added to the chords in Exercise 2.40 were diatonic extensions (see below) because they are notes which are found in the major scale. It is also possible to add chromatic or non-diatonic extensions to chords by flattening the thirteenth or sharpening the eleventh.

The sharpened eleventh is the same note as the flattened fifth. As before, the seventh and ninth are required for a chord to be described as an eleventh rather than a flat five. Three dominant eleventh examples are shown opposite (shapes one to three), one of which omits the third to obtain a less murky voicing. As the fifth of chord is only a half-step above the sharp eleventh it is always omitted. Flat ninths and sharp ninths are also effective when combined with the sharp eleventh, as shown in shapes 13 and 14.

Major seventh sharp elevenths are also possible; three likely shapes are shown above (shapes four to six). As before, one variant omits the third to avoid murkiness. An alternative voicing can be obtained by using the major sixth instead of the major seventh, creating a 6/9 with a sharp eleventh (shapes seven to eight). If we were to omit the third from these two chords we would have an A major triad with a G bass and a D major triad with a C bass, A/G and D/C.

A flattened thirteenth is the same note as a sharpened fifth, but in a flat thirteenth chord the ninth and seventh should be present, as in shape nine. Flattening the ninth is also very effective as in shape 10. Alternative versions of these two chords, with roots on the A-string, are shown in shapes 11 and 12.

THEORY: diatonic versus chromatic. In jazz, diatonic extensions are those that are

THE JAZZ GUITAR HANDBOOK

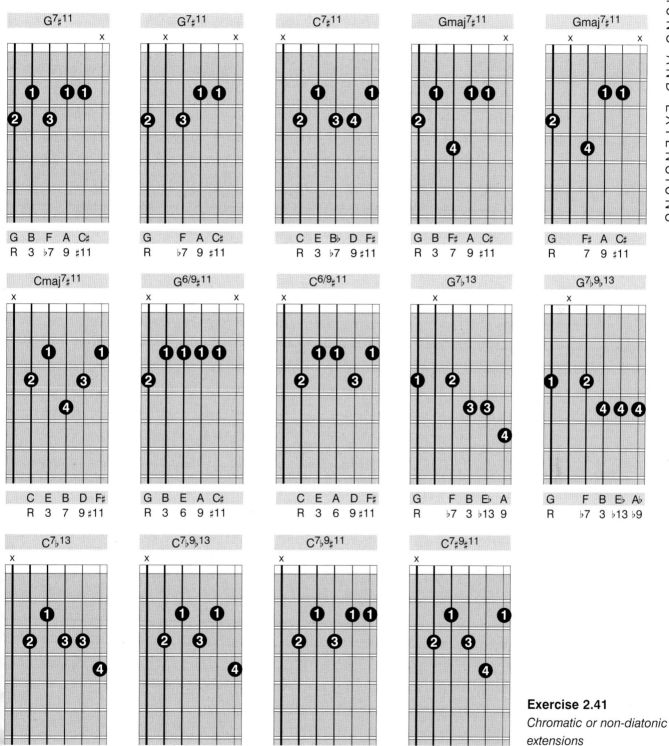

G⁷♯11	G⁷♯11	C⁷♯11	Gmaj⁷♯11	Gmaj⁷♯11
G B F A C♯ R 3 ♭7 9 ♯11	G F A C♯ R ♭7 9 ♯11	C E B♭ D F♯ R 3 ♭7 9 ♯11	G B F♯ A C♯ R 3 7 9 ♯11	G F♯ A C♯ R 7 9 ♯11

Cmaj⁷♯11	G⁶/⁹♯11	C⁶/⁹♯11	G⁷♭13	G⁷♭⁹,13
C E B D F♯ R 3 7 9 ♯11	G B E A C♯ R 3 6 9 ♯11	C E A D F♯ R 3 6 9 ♯11	G F B E♭ A R ♭7 3 ♭13 9	G F B E♭ A♭ R ♭7 3 ♭13 ♭9

C⁷♭13	C⁷♭⁹,13	C⁷♭⁹♯11	C⁷♯⁹♯11
C E B♭ D A♭ R 3 ♭7 9 ♭13	C E B♭ D♭ A♭ R 3 ♭7 ♭9 ♭13	C E B♭ D♭ F♯ R 3 ♭7 ♭9 ♯11	C E B♭ D♯ F♯ R 3 ♭7 ♯9 ♯11

Exercise 2.41
Chromatic or non-diatonic extensions

INVERSIONS AND EXTENSIONS

found in the major key, such as ninths, elevenths and thirteenths. Chromatic extensions include flat nine, sharp nine, sharp eleven and flat thirteen chords; all those which are outside the major key. Even though some of these extensions are found in the harmonic minor, in jazz they are considered to be chromatic. The meaning of these two terms has changed over time and some modern writers consider the extensions found in the minor scale to be diatonic, so it is best to be aware that there can be some confusion as to the exact meaning of diatonic and chromatic in some texts.

Exercise 2.42

The best way to learn chords is to use them in a piece of music. This exercise reworks the 32 bars of Exercise 2.20, using mainly 7sus4 chords for the first eight bars and elevenths and thirteenths for the second eight bars. As you can hear, 7sus4 chords and eleventh chords have a similar function to chord ii and progress smoothly to chord V in the opening bars of these two A sections. At the end of the first A section we use extended chords to create a chromatic sequence from Cmaj6/9♯11 to A7(add13), all of which have an F-sharp at the top. The 'add 13th' means there is a thirteenth but no ninth in the chord.

In the middle-eight or B section we have a series of thirteenth chords followed by a series of eleventh and sharp eleventh chords. The final eight bars feature the juicy

Exercise 2.42
CD TRACK 50
Eleventh chords and sus4
chords in use

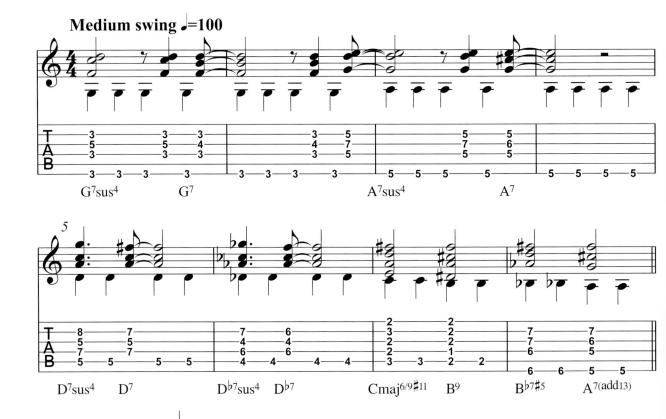

Exercise 2.42 *continued*

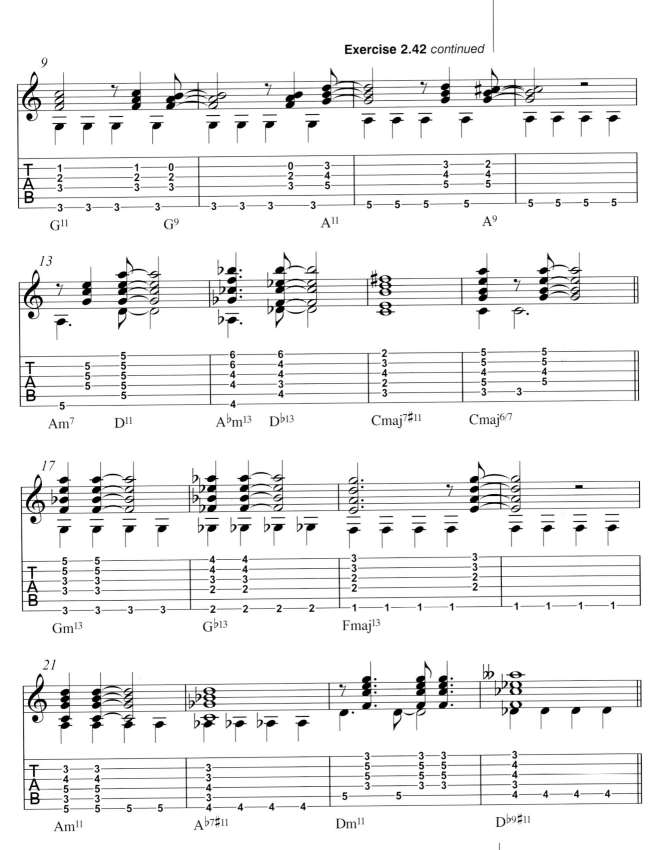

continued over page

THE JAZZ GUITAR HANDBOOK

INVERSIONS AND EXTENSIONS

Exercise 2.42 *continued*

dissonance of the 7♯11 chord. Notice that amongst all this dissonance the Cmaj7♯11 chord in bar 31 seems quite benign; remember that all harmony depends on context.

The piece is in the style of a solo accompaniment and has its own bassline; it is played fingerstyle on the CD, with the thumb reserved for the bass (the note tails point down in the notation staff) and three or four pick-hand fingers playing the upper parts. It is a tough one, so you should expect to have to break it down into sections and to keep returning to it until you've mastered it. Listen back to Exercise 2.20 as well; you will hear that our harmony has come a long way. Better or worse is a matter of taste – but it's certainly different.

THE JAZZ GUITAR HANDBOOK

Exercise 2.43

Sharp-eyed guitarists may have noticed there were a few chords that did not make it into Exercise 2.42. Just to be complete, here are another eight bars using the same A-section chord sequence and the chord shapes that got left out. If you ever have to play the tune 'Satin Doll', or any other tune that involves sequences of ii-V or ii-V-I (and a great many jazz tunes do), feel free to steal the ideas in this exercise, 2.41, or 2.20.

Summing up

In Part Two we have taken an in-depth look at how chords are made and how they are typically used when playing jazz. On the way, we have also considered how chords relate to keys and how they enable us to change key. We will return to chords in Part Four, but first we are going to look at advanced soloing concepts in Part Three: Beyond Pentatonics.

Exercise 2.43
CD TRACK 51
'A Little More'

PART 3
Beyond
pentatonics

- Major scales and modes
- Arpeggios
- The melodic minor scale
- Symmetrical scales – and others

Section 1
Major scales and modes

In Part One we learned minor pentatonic, major pentatonic, and blues scales and found that with five shapes we could play a blues solo over the whole neck in any key. These scales are useful tools for any guitarist dealing with the business of improvisation. They are particularly useful for rock and blues guitar players, and to add a touch of cool blues to jazz solos. But – and it's a very important but – there are many situations in jazz where pentatonic scales just don't cut it.

Major scale

Root		Major 2nd		Major 3rd	Perfect 4th		Perfect 5th		Major 6th		Major 7th	Octave
C		D		E	F		G		A		B	C
C		D		E			G		A			C
Root		Major 2nd		Major 3rd			Perfect 5th		Major 6th			Octave

Major pentatonic scale

If we analyse a major pentatonic scale and compare it to a major scale, we find that two notes are missing, the fourth and the seventh. The fourth and seventh are a tritone apart, giving us the interval of either an augmented fourth or a diminished fifth. This is one of the most dissonant intervals in music, and the major pentatonic scale avoids it. Dissonance in music is not necessarily a bad thing. A dissonant chord tries to find resolution in a consonant chord; without dissonance music is bland, and when played over more complex harmony, the pentatonic scale seems bland because it avoids the more challenging notes. This makes it easy to use, but the downside is that it seems naive and insipid.

Since the chords we are using are built on major scales, major scales can also be used to help us choose notes that sound good when improvising. First we need to learn some major-scale shapes that are movable in the same way as pentatonic shapes and which cover two octaves or more.

Exercise 3.01
To play major scales effectively on the guitar neck we need to be able to spread the fretting-hand fingers over five frets on some strings. The principle here is to stay 'in position', so that having begun in the third position we learn the whole scale across the neck, only changing position where we have to and making sure we return to the third position as soon as possible. We have chosen to start in G because shape one is in a low position on the neck and all the other shapes (yes, there are more) will flow

Shape 1

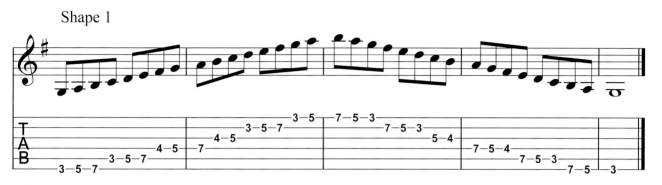

Fingering

Scale degrees

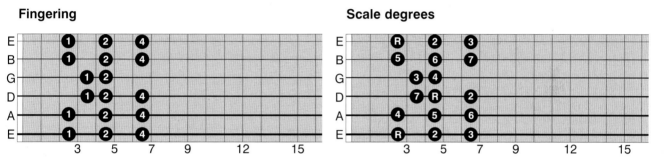

logically up the neck. Also, you may remember that back in Part One we began learning pentatonics in the key of G.

TECHNIQUE: alternate picking is essential to build up speed and fluency with this type of scale. Notice that the whole scale is played with fingers one, two, and four. Do not fix the thumb at the back of the neck but allow it to move back and forth as if making small position changes – this will help with the stretches.

Exercise 3.02

Exercise 3.02 introduces the melodic possibilities of the major scale played over a two-chord groove of G major seventh and C major seventh. The major scale has a pleasing, optimistic but slightly dreamy quality and is very useful when playing over major seventh chords. The four-bar rhythm part is used as an intro, and continues throughout the piece when the guitar solo takes over. Notice that every note comes from the scale shape in Exercise 3.01. As much as possible you should use the same fingerings in the piece as for the scale.

THEORY: the root, third, fifth, and seventh of a G major scale make a G major seventh chord, so it is not surprising that the scale sounds good played over its own major seventh chord. It also sounds good played over C major seventh, which is chord IV in G major. We go into this more deeply in Exercise 3.04, where we look at

Exercise 3.01
CD TRACK 52
G major scale shape 1

THE JAZZ GUITAR HANDBOOK

MAJOR SCALES AND MODES

Exercise 3.02 CD TRACK 53 *Two chord groove, Gmaj7 Cmaj7*

Straight 8s - laid back feel ♩=90

Rhythm part continues...

THE JAZZ GUITAR HANDBOOK

the seven modes of the major scale. First, however, Exercise 3.03 shows all seven shapes that we need to play all over the neck in any key.

Exercise 3.03

As there are seven notes in a major scale there are seven possible shapes, each shape starting on a different note of the scale. For the sake of completeness we include shape one again, with each shape following on, progressing up the neck. Shape one begins

Exercise 3.03
CD TRACK 54
Seven major scale shapes, shown in G major

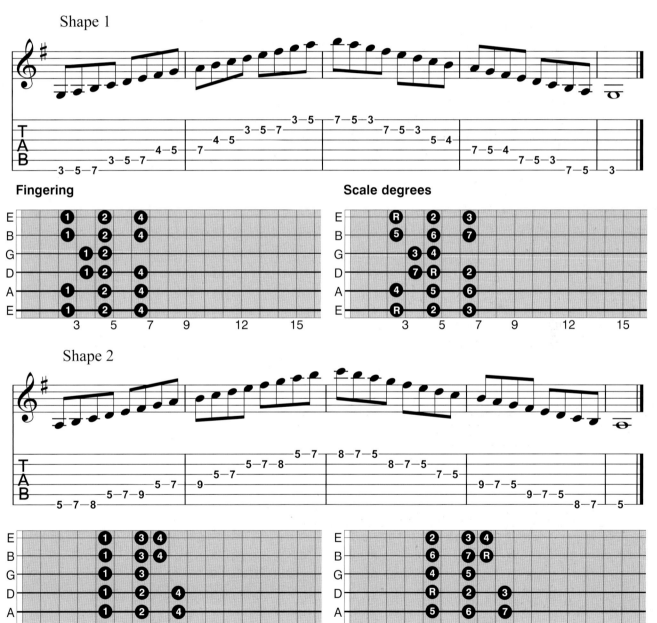

continued over page

THE JAZZ GUITAR HANDBOOK

MAJOR SCALES AND MODES

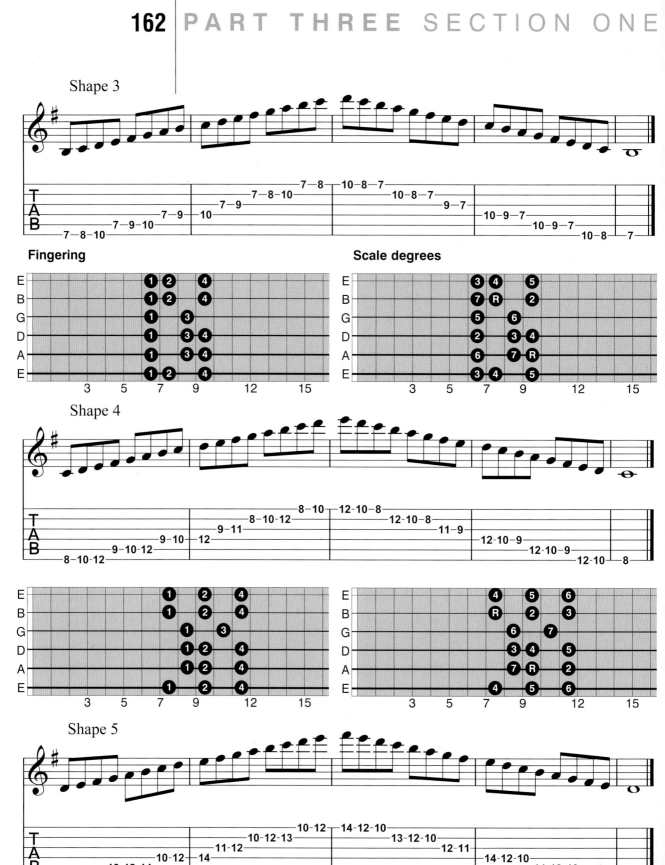

Shape 3

Fingering   **Scale degrees**

Shape 4

Shape 5

Fingering

Scale degrees

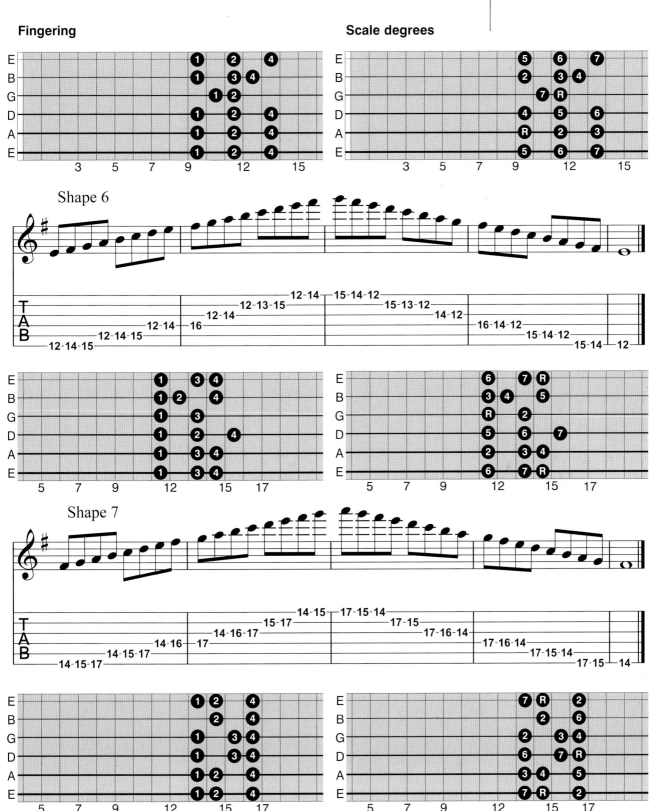

Shape 6

Shape 7

on the root note of the scale (G), shape two begins on the second note of the scale (A), shape three on the third note of the scale (B) and so on.

RECORDING YOUR GUITAR

The most basic computer can be a 'recording studio in a box' nowadays but there are many other useful recording devices, from mobile phones to the old-fashioned cassette tape machine with a built-in mic and speaker. Record yourself playing a few minutes of the four-bar groove that begins Exercise 3.02, then practise soloing over it using the scale we have learned. If you are a computer user you could use audio software to chop out and loop the four-bar intro to provide a suitable backing track. Apple users can use GarageBand, Windows PC users can use the free Audacity audio program or buy an entry-level version of Cubase, Sonar, or any similar recording package. As well as recording your own backing track of Gmaj7 and Cmaj7 and then soloing over it, you could try a backing track in other keys: Cmaj7 to Fmaj7, Fmaj7 to B♭maj7 and so on. Steal soloing ideas from Exercise 3.02 and make up your own riffs too. Move the scale shape to the new key too; eventually you could have a backing track for practising major scales in every key.

TECHNIQUE: start by learning the scale shapes methodically up the neck – the best way is to play them every day. When you have learnt all seven shapes, begin working your way around the Circle of Fifths, playing them in every other key. As well as learning the shapes, try to be aware of what notes you are playing too, so that you continue to develop an awareness of which notes are in which keys.

THEORY: notice that shape seven can be played starting at the second fret or the 14th fret.

Exercise 3.04

In Part One we discovered that inside every minor pentatonic scale there is a major pentatonic scale. A similar process takes place within major scales, except that with major scales we can start a new scale (known as a mode) on every note. Exercise 3.04 shows the notes of a G major scale written out seven times, each time starting on a new note. In other words, the seven modes of the G major scale. We have also given the interval created between each note and the mode's root note. Each mode is made up of a unique set of intervals.

   The modes have names that were given to them by music theorists in the Middle Ages. They are derived from the names of ancient Greek tribes, which may seem strange, but we have to call them something, so jazz musicians tend to go along with that. Each mode will sound good played over the chord that is outlined by its root, third, fifth, and seventh, so in this exercise the chord is played first. Among the modes there are two modes with a major seventh flavour and three with a minor seventh flavour, so there are some interesting choices to be made when it comes to choosing a mode for soloing over these chords. There are also one mode each for dominant seventh chords and half-diminished chords. Here are the modes in order, along with some pointers as to how we use these modes in jazz.

Ionian (major) The terms major and Ionian tend to be used interchangeably by jazz musicians. As we have seen, this mode sounds good played over major seventh type chords and their diatonic extensions.

Ionian (major) mode on G

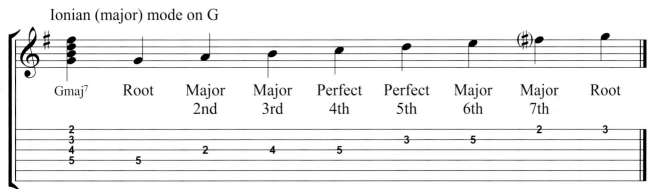

Dorian The Dorian mode has a minor flavour because it has a minor third. The minor seventh means that it suits minor seventh chords, and the major sixth gives it a cool, jazzy vibe. It tends to be the first choice mode for soloing over minor seventh chords and their extensions.

Dorian mode on A

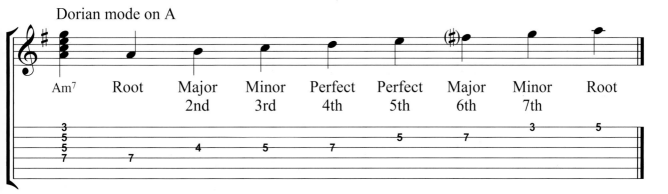

Phrygian In the Phrygian mode every possible interval is minor. Its most distinguishing feature is the minor second. It is often referred to as the 'Spanish' mode, as the Phrygian is commonplace in flamenco. Jazz musicians tend to use this mode if they are trying to evoke the sounds of Spain.

Exercise 3.04
CD TRACK 55
The seven modes of the major scale

MAJOR SCALES AND MODES

Phrygian mode on B

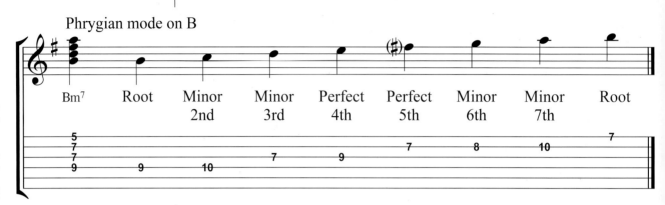

Bm7 — Root — Minor 2nd — Minor 3rd — Perfect 4th — Perfect 5th — Minor 6th — Minor 7th — Root

Lydian The Lydian mode is a major scale with an augmented fourth. It sounds great over major seventh chords but is particularly suited to maj#11 chords. In many ways it sounds like an ultra-jazz version of the major scale. C Lydian would be used for soloing over Cmaj7 and its extensions. In Exercise 3.02 we heard the sound of a Lydian mode when the G major scale was being played over Cmaj7.

Lydian mode on C

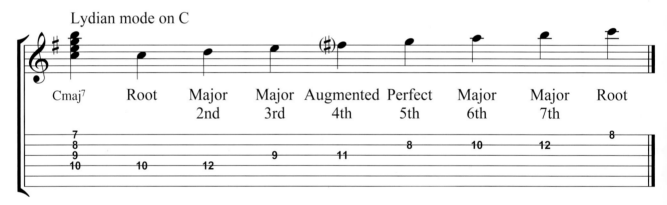

Cmaj7 — Root — Major 2nd — Major 3rd — Augmented 4th — Perfect 5th — Major 6th — Major 7th — Root

Mixolydian The Mixolydian is a major scale with a minor seventh. A dominant seventh chord is outlined on steps one, three, five and seven of this mode and as a result this D Mixolydian mode would be perfect for soloing over a D7 chord. However, the major ninth and thirteenth might make it less suitable if the dominant seventh were to be

Mixolydian mode on D

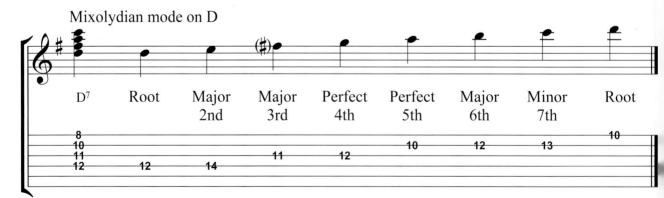

D7 — Root — Major 2nd — Major 3rd — Perfect 4th — Perfect 5th — Major 6th — Minor 7th — Root

THE JAZZ GUITAR HANDBOOK

chord V in a minor key, with its flat ninth and flat thirteenth. We will find some scales that are suitable for a minor key dominant later.

Aeolian (natural minor) The Aeolian mode sounds a little darker than the Dorian mode because of the minor sixth; in other respects the two modes are the same. The minor sixth can sometimes give this mode a Gothic or mediaeval quality, but it is nevertheless useful for soloing over minor and minor seventh chords. This E Aeolian would be used for soloing over E minor seventh.

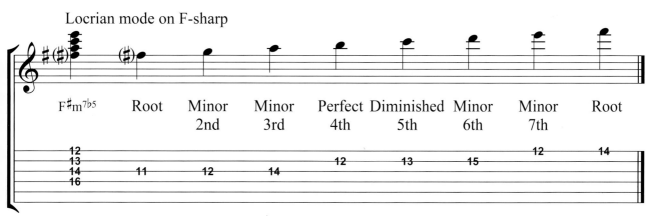

Locrian The Locrian mode has only minor intervals, and in addition has a diminished fifth. As such, it is the darkest sounding of all the modes, yet it perfectly suits the m7♭5 chord that is contained within it. F-sharp Locrian would be used over F♯m7♭5 (F♯ half-diminished).

THEORY: the easiest way to understand modes (or other scales) is to compare them to the major scale and then just describe the differences. The Dorian, for example, has a minor third and a minor seventh. The Lydian has a raised fourth, while the Mixolydian has a minor seventh and so on.

We have already seen that jazz is commonly based on four essential chord types, and we now have one or more modes to fit each type of chord.

■ Major seventh chords and their extensions: use either Ionian or Lydian.

■ Minor seventh chords and their extensions: use either Dorian or more rarely, Aeolian.

■ Dominant seventh chords and their extensions: use the Mixolydian, but a better solution may be available for dominant seventh chords in a minor key. More on this later.

■ Half-diminished or m7♭5 chords: use the Locrian mode.

Before we begin using modes to play over chords, however, we are going to get familiar with the sound of each mode. The best way to get to know the modes is to play each one over a suitable modal groove. Over the next few exercises we shall work our way through the most useful modes trying them out over appropriate backing tracks.

MODAL JAZZ
In the late 1950s Miles Davis (trumpet), with the help of Bill Evans (piano), began to experiment with a new kind of jazz. Chord progressions, like the ii-V-I sequences that we examined in Part Two, were replaced by extended passages based on a mode. In many ways modal jazz is like any other kind of jazz but with the chord changes slowed down to the point where one chord might last for anything from four to 16 bars. Occasionally whole tunes ('Freedom Jazz Dance', from the *Miles Smiles* album, for example) are played on just one chord or one mode.

The breakthrough album for this type of jazz was *Kind Of Blue*, which revolutionised jazz and jazz composition and is reported to be the biggest-selling jazz album of all time. In the hands of artists like John Coltrane (*Impressions*) and Wayne Shorter (*Footprints*) modal jazz was significant throughout the succeeding decades.

Exercise 3.05

Exercise 3.05 relies on a classic ride-cymbal rhythm, a walking bassline, and comped accompanying chords to create a cool swing feel. Clean jazz-guitar sounds come from a Gibson ES-175 neck pickup played through a Fender Deluxe Reverb. The walking bassline emphasises A Dorian; the root note is placed on the first beat of every two bars and the other notes come from the mode. Occasional chromatic connecting notes are welcome if they do not disturb the overall Dorian tonality. The harmony is supplied

Exercise 3.05 CD TRACK 56 *Dorian groove, solo*

Cool modal swing ♩=105

THE JAZZ GUITAR HANDBOOK

by guitar two, and we'll take a closer look at these 'modal' chords in Exercise 3.06, but suffice to say that these chords are also built from the Dorian mode.

The solo mostly uses shapes one, two, and three from Exercise 3.04. Notice the repeated use of a rising seven-note motif in bars one and three. A motif is a short, memorable, and recognisable phrase that can be transposed, lengthened or shortened without losing its essential character. Beginning a series of phrases with a recognisable motif is a great way to emphasise structure, particularly at the beginning of a solo. If you have established a good phrase to begin with there is no need to throw in new idea after new idea; it is far better to develop the material you started with. Also notice that the phrasing goes across the bar lines; novice improvisers often start every phrase on the first beat of the bar. Remember that you don't have to start or end your phrases on the note A – the strongly stated A Dorian harmony establishes the tonal centre, so that the G major scale is *heard* as the Dorian mode on A. However, the final note of the solo is an A – providing a strong conclusion on the keynote; this is followed by a chord constructed from the eleventh, minor seventh, minor third and major sixth (low to high) over the A bass note, which could be called Am11/13.

THEORY: although musicians have kept the mediaeval names for the modes we are using, ancient music theorists would have been very puzzled by what we are doing. Imagine a world where there were only white notes – no black notes and therefore no flats or sharps. The Ionian mode would have been the seven notes starting on C. The Dorian mode would have been the seven notes starting on D, the Phrygian the seven notes starting on E, and so on. There was no major scale system, and therefore these starting points were fixed and modes were not transposable to other keys.

In jazz, a Dorian mode is any major scale played as if its second note were the root. So our modes are transposable and every major scale has its own Dorian mode built on step two. As we mentioned above, you don't actually have to start each phrase that you play on the root note of the mode, just think of the second note of the major scale as if it were 'home'. Of course, it might create a satisfactory phrase ending if you end a phrase on the root, as at the end of 3.05.

Exercise 3.06

Exercise 3.06 provides us with an opportunity to learn the modal chords from 3.05 and also provides a backing track for you to practise your soloing using A Dorian. The backing track chords are voiced mainly in fourths, although the interval between the top two notes is a third. Taken on its own, the first chord appears to be a C major triad in second inversion with a D bass (C/D). However, this ignores the importance of the bass line, which emphasises the keynote A. Adding the root note A to the above notes produces a chord of Am11. The modal chord shape is moved progressively up the guitar in bars one to eight, being altered when necessary to ensure that all of the notes remain within the mode. In bar nine a new voicing is used and is again used modally up and down the neck. At the end of bar 16 there is a one-fret slide to arrive

PRO TIP

Playing over a backing track, whether one you have made yourself or one that is on a CD, is a great way to practise your soloing. The most famous jazz 'play-alongs' are those recorded by Jamey Aebersold. They include basic theoretical material, such as tracks for practising ii-V-I progressions, and backing track CDs of work by major jazz artists such as Miles Davis and Duke Ellington.

Exercise 3.06 CD TRACK 57 *Dorian groove, backing track*

Cool modal swing ♩=105

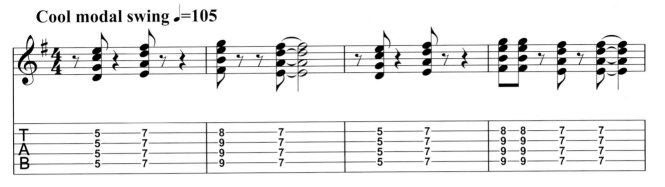

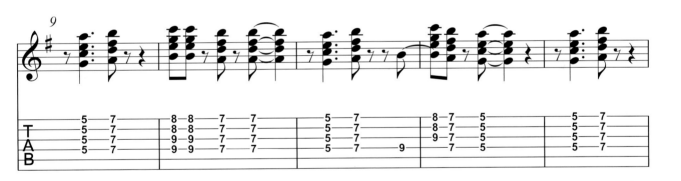

chromatically on an A minor seventh chord. This kind of chromatic chord can be used in modal playing as a source of tension moving to resolution.

Exercise 3.07

For Exercise 3.07 we have adopted a 'fusion'-style rhythm track with a floating bossa nova groove and a legato solo. (Legato means 'smooth' or 'joined up'.) The Lydian chord accompaniment forms Exercise 3.08; it combines with the C-centred bassline to emphasise both the tonal centre and the Lydian tonality.

There is a distinctive opening motif based on quarter-note triplets in the first two bars, which is repeated at a higher pitch and extended in bars three and four. Motivic ideas can be very important in this open style of soloing, as a distinctive motif can tie an entire solo together and make it coherent. Notice how bars five to eight are one long answering phrase, but bars nine, ten, and eleven all make reference to the opening pattern of rising and falling notes, this time with eighth-note triplets. We are using the scale patterns from Exercise 3.03; work out which scale shape is being used where, and choose appropriate fingerings and pick strokes.

In shooting for a more modern, fusion vibe we've switched to a 20W Marshall combo, adding a smooth overdrive from the pre-amp and a little movement from a Uni-Vibe type pedal. The guitar is still the ES175, neck pickup.

TECHNIQUE: any long note should be given gentle vibrato by rhythmically moving the string sideways across the neck. Some players pull the string towards the floor, moving the G-string towards the B-string and back. Others prefer to push the G-string towards the D-string. Some push and pull. Experiment, and decide what works best for you.

There are many slides, slurs and grace notes, all of which contribute to the legato style. A grace note is a note written smaller in size than a regular note; it is also sometimes known as an ornament. It is played in place of the regular note that it precedes with the regular note following immediately after. Slurs and slides are commonly used when playing grace notes on guitar. Examples can be found in bars two, seven and 15 in this piece – in each case the grace note is followed by a slide to the regular note.

THEORY: there is often confusion about the relationship between scale shapes and the different modes. In some books, scale shape two is called the Dorian mode, and shape three is called the Phrygian mode and so on. While this is not actually wrong, it is not the full story. You can play a Dorian mode using shapes one, two, three or any other shape. Playing the G major shapes from Exercise 3.04 you simply have to treat the note A as the root and you'll have a Dorian mode. Similarly, if you treat the note C as the root, you will have a Lydian mode. So the modes are not fixed to any one shape, and the seven shapes will give you every mode over the entire neck.

Exercise 3.07 CD TRACK 58 *Lydian groove, solo*

C Lydian throughout...

Exercise 3.08

This exercise begins with a Lydian version of a Cmaj7 chord, in which the sharpened fourth (F-sharp) has replaced the fifth (G). This four-note voicing is unusual in that the middle two notes are a major second apart. In the same way as for the Dorian backing track, this chord is then moved around the guitar and altered so that the notes stay in the C Lydian scale.

Exercise 3.08
CD TRACK 59
Lydian groove,
backing track

TECHNIQUE: these voicings will be unfamiliar at first but they are very effective and colourful. If you can, experiment with chorus, tremolo, and delay effects to duplicate the dreamy and swooshy effect of this track.

Dreamy bossa ♩=119

With chorus, tremolo and delay...

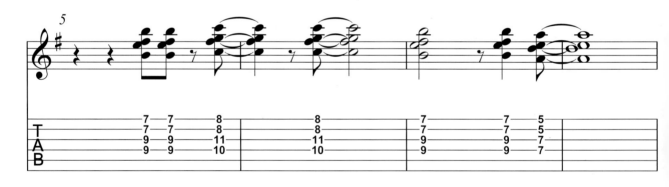

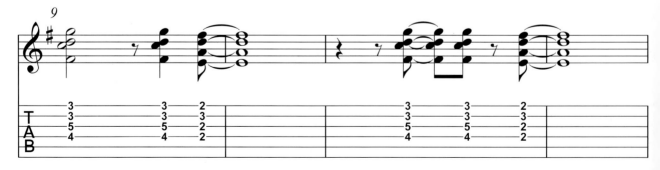

THE JAZZ GUITAR HANDBOOK

Exercise 3.08 *continued*

Exercise 3.09

This part of the book is entitled 'Beyond pentatonics' and you would be right in expecting it to be mostly about scales and soloing, but it would be a shame to leave these modal chords without a little further explanation. All chords should be analysed in context, and this is particularly true with modal chords.

For Exercise 3.09 we have moved to the simplest key, C major, and every note in this exercise is entirely inside the key (no sharps or flats). Starting with a pile of fourths built on the note A the shape is moved up the guitar with B, C, D, etc, in the bass, each time being altered when necessary to keep the notes within the C major scale. The first part of the exercise keeps to the middle four strings of the guitar, with the second part switching to the top four strings. Each one of these chords taken on its own would be difficult to name, but taken in context we can see that collectively they belong to one

Exercise 3.09
CD TRACK 60
Modal chords in C

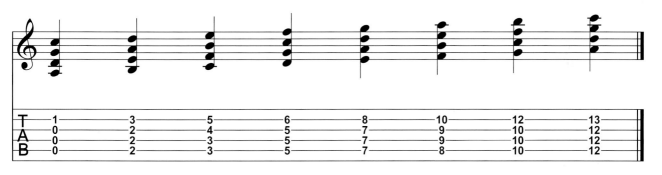

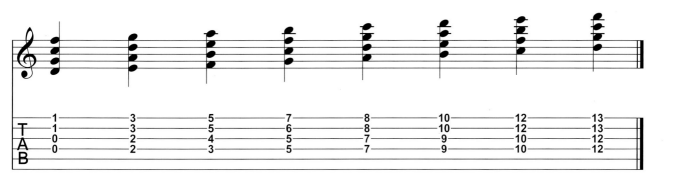

MAJOR SCALES AND MODES

scale. Played over a C bass, these chords would suggest C Ionian; over a D bass, they would suggest D Dorian; over an F bass, F Lydian and so on.

THEORY: over the past few exercises we have experienced several different shapes of modal chord. Revisit Exercises 3.06 and 3.08 and see if you can extend the range of the modal chords used in those exercises to a complete octave, as in Exercise 3.09.

Exercise 3.10

Exercise 3.10 takes its inspiration from funky jazz tracks like John Scofield's 'A Go Go' and other tracks from the album of the same name, but you can trace the roots of this funky style to the James Brown band back in the 1960s. Check out 'Sex Machine' for some funky rhythm guitar, for example.

The guitar part here can be viewed as having two eight-bar sections. The first eight bars use a call and response structure, the call part being the rising whole-step figure that is played four times, with the response part being the mostly falling phrases that follow. These strongly structured first eight bars act as a launch pad for bars nine to 16, which demonstrate a more open and free style of soloing. Bar 17 concludes the piece by hinting at the opening rising whole-step motif. The phrasing in the second section is strong and clear, although the phrase lengths are more broken up and less predictable. When you work on this exercise, remember it's always easier to learn music phrase-by-phrase.

Exercise 3.10
CD TRACK 61
Mixolydian groove, solo

Funky swing 16s ♩=82

D⁹ *(D mixolydian throughout)*

Exercise 3.10 *continued*

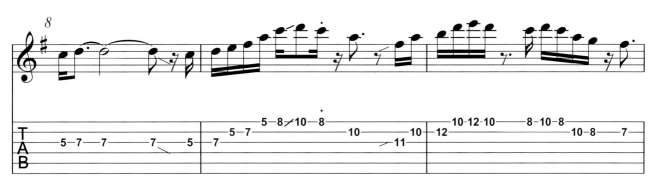

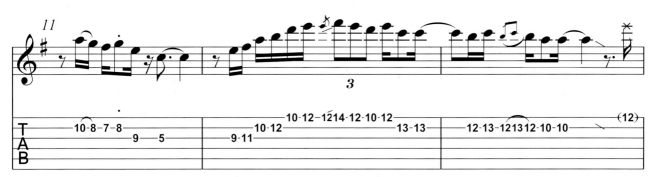

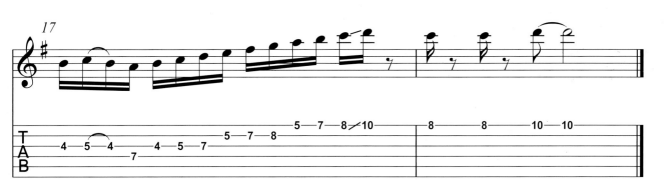

MAJOR SCALES AND MODES

PRO TIP
Now that you have a funky guitar rhythm and a bassline you can record yourself playing Exercise 3.10 in some other keys (or maybe all 12) and practise your Mixolydian soloing.

The underlying feel is swing 16th-notes, so although the 16th-notes are notated straight they are played swing, as illustrated here:

THEORY: the notes come from the D Mixolydian mode, although here and there you will find the sharpened fourth, G-sharp, most often used as a passing note between G and A. We've seen this note before as the sharp fourth that turns the minor pentatonic into a blues scale; it is also the note that distinguishes a Lydian mode from a major (Ionian mode) scale.

TECHNIQUE: there are many expressive devices used in this example. The opening note is staccato and followed by a rising slur or hammer-on to a held note with subtle vibrato. The opening 'response' phrases tend to be staccato, whereas in the second half legato phrasing dominates. Notice the frequent use of muted notes, which can be very effective in a funky environment.

Exercise 3.11
The backing is a repeated two-bar funky guitar part with an accompanying bassline. The rhythm guitar part is shown in Exercise 3.11. The 'x' notes are muted by touching the strings with the fretting-hand fingers but not pressing them down. On the notation stave the pitches are shown by the location of the 'x' signs; they are given in parenthesis on the tab stave. Keep your picking-hand moving in 16th-notes and feel free to develop the rhythm by lightly dropping in a few extra muted notes as the backing track proceeds – it's part of the funky guitar style.

Exercise 3.11
CD TRACK 62
Mixolydian groove, backing track

Funky swing 16s ♩=82

Play 8 times

Exercise 3.12

The repeated two-bar bassline is arranged for guitar in Exercise 3.12, which means transposing it up one octave. It outlines a D7 chord and includes most of the notes of a D Mixolydian mode. Notice the use of the sixth as a passing note when descending and the non-mode sharpened fourth when ascending.

Exercise 3.13

We have already seen that the Dorian mode is first choice for jazz soloing over minor seventh chords. However, the Aeolian mode can be very useful for soloing over chord i and iv in a minor key, such as the chord sequence from Exercise 2.28, CD track 39. The melody of the inspiration for this track, 'Blue Bossa' by Kenny Dorham, uses only notes from the Aeolian mode for the first eight and last four bars. The original track can be heard on the Joe Henderson album *Page One*.

Up to now, we have been using modes that are related to the key of G major, which would give us E Aeolian if played starting on the sixth step. To solo over 3.13 (over the page) we are looking for an Aeolian mode starting on C. One way to work this out is to think which major scale has C as its sixth note; the answer is E-flat major. An E-flat major scale played with C as the root will produce a C Aeolian mode. It may help to remember that the Aeolian mode is the same as the natural minor scale, which is built on the keynote of the relative minor, the sixth step of the major scale.

Played over a C minor chord, the notes of E-flat major will produce a C Aeolian mode. Played over F minor, they will produce an F Dorian mode. Played over Dm7♭5 they will produce a D Locrian mode, perfect for a half-diminished chord. Can we get away with the same notes played over G7? It worked for Kenny Dorham and it seems to work here. This is because the B-flat and A-flat that occur in C Aeolian make a sharp nine and a flat nine over the G7 chord – interesting!

There is a four-bar middle section in this tune, made up of a ii-V-I in D-flat major.

‖ E♭m7 | A♭7 | D♭maj7 | D♭maj7 ‖

Exercise 3.12
CD TRACK 62
Mixolydian groove, bassline

MAJOR SCALES AND MODES

Exercise 3.13 CD TRACKS 63 & 39 (BACKING TRACK) *'Bossa Blue' solo, Aeolian and Locrian modes*

THE JAZZ GUITAR HANDBOOK

Exercise 3.13 *continued*

THE JAZZ GUITAR HANDBOOK

We have used an E-flat Dorian mode for chord ii, an A-flat Mixolydian mode for chord V and D-flat major or Ionian for the D♭maj7 chord. These last three scales are all made from the same seven notes, but by thinking of the appropriate mode we will ensure that we get in the corners of the harmony and emphasise the underlying chord changes.

TECHNIQUE: the piece is played mostly around the eighth position, using scale shape six. The exceptions are bars 16 to 18, where we explore the lower end of C Aeolian using shape three. For the two sections in D-flat major we switch to shape seven in D-flat, again played around the eighth position. Practise these scale shapes to familiarise yourself with the notes and get them 'under the fingers'. Then solo over the backing track (CD track 39) using your own riffs and licks.

THEORY: finding a scale that will fit a four- or eight-bar sequence of chords is great for playing in a linear, melodic way. The first 16 bars echo the phrasing of 'Blue Bossa' in the style of an opening melodic statement or 'head'. The second 16 bars are much more expansive, in the style of a solo, with more complex rhythms and phrases of varying lengths played across the bar line.

Section 2
Arpeggios

As we saw in Part Two, an arpeggio is a chord played one note at a time. In Exercise 2.23 we touched on the idea that arpeggios can be used for soloing. Now that we have become more familiar with the chords and scales that jazz musicians use, it is time to take another look at arpeggios and their uses in improvising. What we need are usable arpeggio shapes that can be learned in the same way as the seven major scale shapes in Exercise 3.03.

Exercise 3.14

This exercise begins with scale shape one from Exercise 3.03, just in case you have yet to learn it. Then there are seven arpeggios all built from the notes of this scale shape. Think of it like this: there are seven chords in a major key, and a two-octave major scale will allow you to play a two-octave arpeggio of every chord. As jazz musicians are interested in extending chords beyond the simple triad, each arpeggio is played here as a seventh chord. Notice that only the first arpeggio actually starts on the root; we could say that most of these arpeggios are inverted in the same way that we learned to invert chords in Part Two. The idea is to start on the lowest possible chord tone and progress to the highest possible chord tone, playing only notes from the chord and staying within the scale shape.

TECHNIQUE: fingering should be self-explanatory; as much as possible use the same fingers as you would for playing the scale. Occasionally, you will need to be creative to find good fingerings that avoid awkward jumps with the same finger. When you listen to the CD track you may notice that the quavers are played in a swing feel – using different feels is one way to keep things interesting when you are practising all your scales and arpeggios.

Exercise 3.14
CD TRACK 64
Seven arpeggios on G major scale shape 1

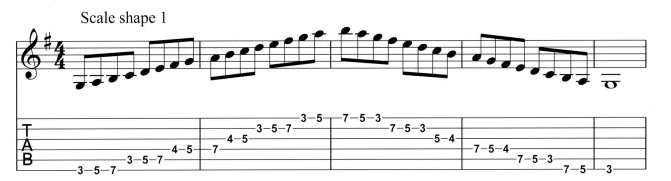

continued over page

Exercise 3.14 *continued*

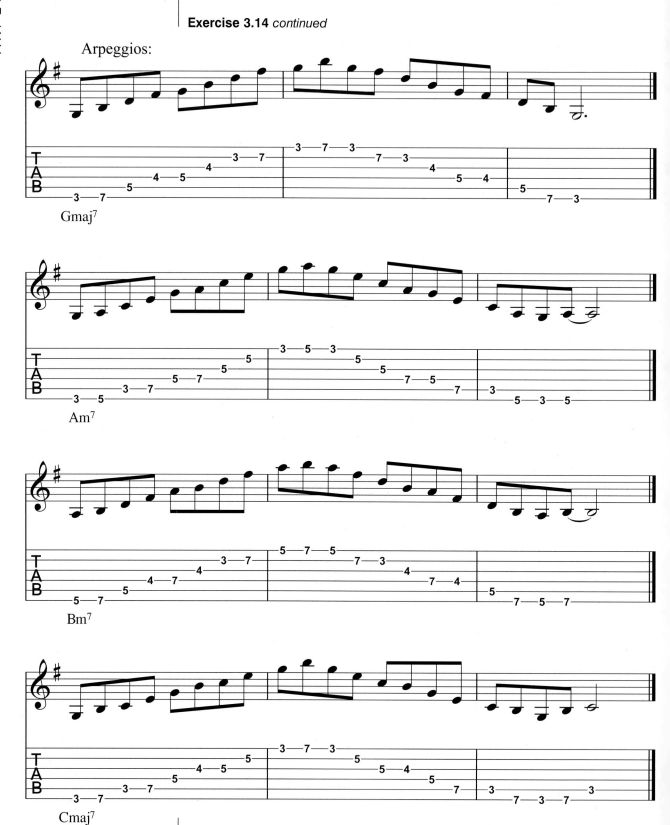

Exercise 3.14 *continued*

D⁷

Em⁷

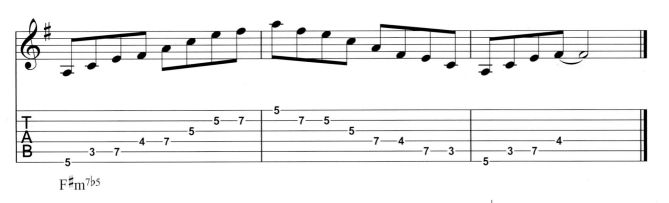

F♯m⁷♭⁵

THEORY: the main thing to take away from this exercise is the idea that arpeggios are contained within major scales. Every one of the two-octave major scale shapes from Exercise 3.03 can produce a series of arpeggios, in the same way as this exercise.

Exercise 3.15

We are not going to work our way through all seven scale shapes; this is a great opportunity for self-study and taking up a great many pages of this book duplicating

THE JAZZ GUITAR HANDBOOK

Exercise 3.15 *Seven arpeggios on scale shape 7*

Scale shape 7

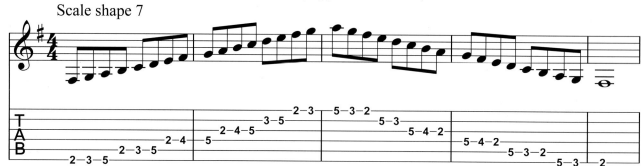

Arpeggios:

Gmaj⁷

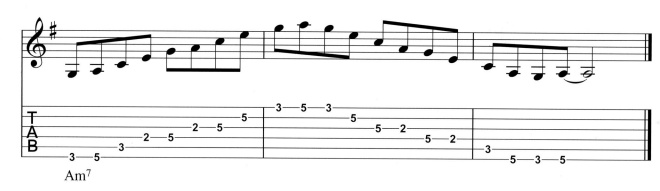

Am⁷

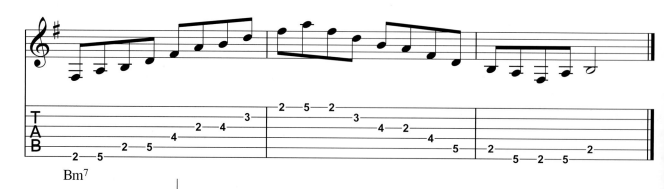

Bm⁷

Exercise 3.15 *continued*

Cmaj⁷

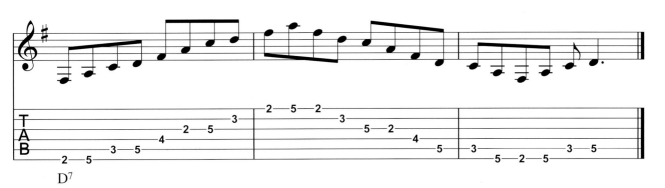

D⁷

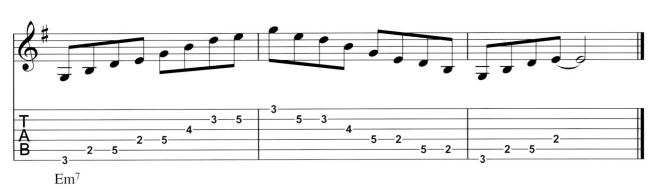

Em⁷

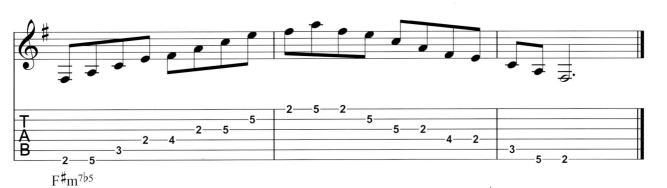

F♯m⁷♭⁵

THE JAZZ GUITAR HANDBOOK

the process from Exercise 3.14 with every scale shape is hard to justify. However, Exercise 3.15 takes scale shape seven, starting at the second fret (we know it can also be started at the 14th fret) and produces an arpeggio shape for every chord in G major. These shapes are, if anything, more useful than those from scale shape one, in that they fall under the fingers very well. This one is not on the CD – you should be OK figuring it out without needing any audio.

THEORY: arpeggios are like chords in that they can be played as inversions. All of these chords contain four notes, so there should be four possible arpeggio shapes for any chord: Gmaj7, for example, could be played starting on G on the third fret of the sixth string; or on the seventh fret, on B; or on the 10th fret, on D; or on the 13th fret, on F. In fact, because of the nature of the guitar and the fact that the same note can be found in more than one place, there are all kinds of optional fingerings for arpeggios. This scale-based approach is a good way of getting to grips with most of them.

Exercise 3.16

In Exercise 3.16 we are using the arpeggio shapes for Gmaj7 and Cmaj7 described in Exercises 3.14 and 3.15 to create a melody over the backing track to Exercise 3.02, which consists of those same two chords.

Apart from bars 10 and 13, which contain brief scale fragments, every note in this exercise comes from the arpeggio of the underlying chord. Occasionally, for example at the end of bar four, the coming chord is anticipated slightly – which can be a very effective device for adding a little tension. Gmaj7 is G, B, D, and F-sharp; Cmaj7 is C, E, G, and B-natural. Work your way through the piece, figuring out where the notes have come from; for example, starting in bar one, we have the seventh, root, third, fifth, and seventh again of Gmaj7. In bar two, we have the fifth and third of Cmaj7.

THEORY: arpeggios can sound exciting because they cover a large amount of ground on the guitar very quickly; this is because, compared to scales, they are made up of 'jumps' rather than 'steps'.

TECHNIQUE: this track was played using alternate picking. Some players prefer to use 'sweep picking', where consecutive notes on adjacent strings are played with either continuous downstrokes when ascending (the music rising in pitch) or continuous upstrokes when descending. For example, the rising figure in bar one could be played using a 'sweep' down stroke, and the falling three-note figure in bar nine could be played with an upstroke. Try it both ways.

PRO TIP
Try mentally linking each of the arpeggio shapes to the nearest chord of the same name – this may help you learn the shape.

Exercise 3.16 CD TRACK 65 *Gmaj7 and Cmaj7 groove with arpeggio-based solo*

Exercise 3.17

The notes of a typical jazz melody, whether composed or improvised, tend to come from three sources: the underlying chord, the scale that is associated with the underlying chord, or chromatic 'tension' notes that are outside the chord or scale and need to be treated with care in terms of how they are approached and quitted. For the sake of simplicity, we regard the essential chord tones as the root, third, fifth, and seventh and ignore any extensions (such as ninths or thirteenths) that are present in the chord.

**Exercise 3.17
CD TRACKS 66 & 62
(BACKING TRACK)**
*Chromatic decoration of
arpeggios*

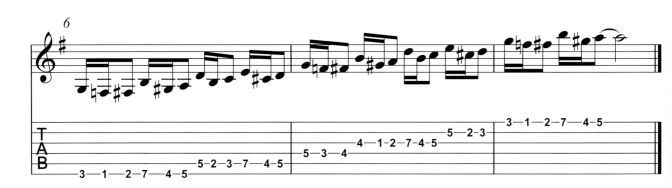

Approaching arpeggio notes chromatically is an effective way of introducing and resolving chromatic tension notes into a solo. This may sound complicated but as Exercise 3.17 demonstrates, it is not that hard to do. The first two bars take the D7 arpeggio from Exercise 3.15 and approach every note from the half-step below. Try playing a descending arpeggio in the same way. It can also be interesting to begin a 16th-note earlier, so that the arpeggio notes are on the strong beat, with the chromatic notes on the weak beat. These two bars were played using only fretting-hand fingers one and two.

Bars three to five have a descending arpeggio of D7, this time with each note being approached by two consecutive half-steps. Try playing the ascending pattern too and also try changing the rhythm; played as continuous 16th-notes the three-note groupings would add an interesting complexity against the underlying 4/4 rhythm. Each three-note figure was played starting with finger one, followed logically with fingers two and three.

The final three bars have a rising arpeggio in a similar rhythmic pattern to bars three to five. This time, we have the diatonic note above, the chromatic note below and then the arpeggio note. Once again you should try playing this as constant 16th-notes and also work out the descending version. Where the diatonic note was a whole step above the chord note we started each three-note pattern on finger four; where it was a half-step, we started on finger three.

THEORY: there are many possibilities for this kind of chromatic decoration of arpeggios, for instance using whole-steps where we have used half-steps or descending to the chord tone where we have ascended. Experiment and find some of your own and then try them on different chord types. Also try leaving out the seventh and just using the triad – some patterns work well and may even be preferable without the seventh. This is particularly true when playing over the major seventh chords, as the major seventh interval is already only a half-step from the root of the chord.

Exercise 3.18

In Exercise 3.18 we have a series of D7 arpeggios played two notes per string. Compare this approach to the D7 shapes used in Exercises 3.14 and 3.15, which stay in one position.

The first bar of the exercise shows an arpeggio starting on the major third, F-sharp, and climbing, using two notes per string, to the root note on the 10th fret of the top string. Bar two has the descending pattern for the same arpeggio. When playing the ascending arpeggio, the first finger of the fretting hand always leads, followed by finger three or four as appropriate. When descending it is slightly trickier, as we have to remember whether to put down finger three or finger four each time we arrive on a new string.

Bars three and four demonstrate the D7 arpeggio but this time starting on the fifth of the chord, A, and climbing to the third. You can play all of this shape using only

Exercise 3.18 CD TRACKS 67 & 62 (BACKING TRACK) *More D7 arpeggios: two notes per string*

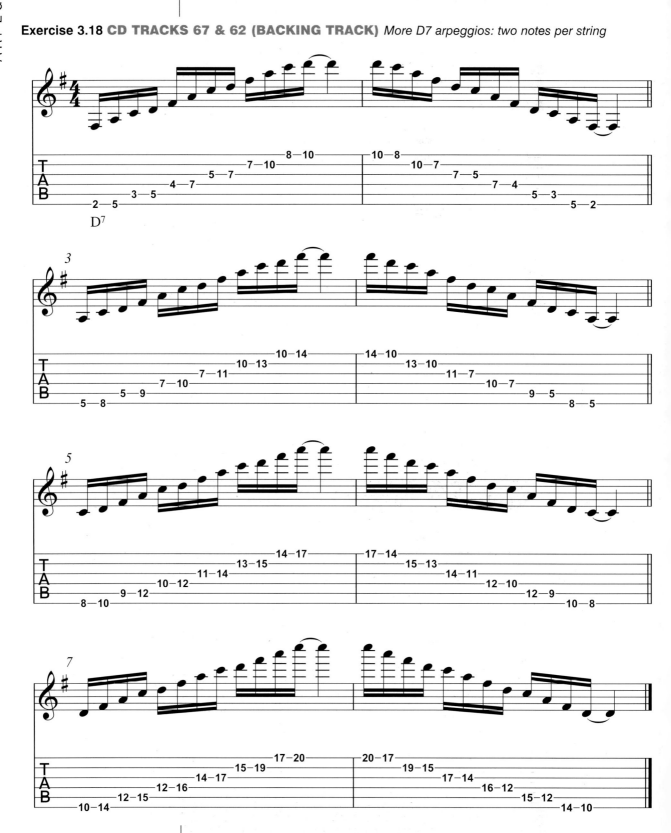

fingers one and four. Bars five and six show the arpeggio beginning on C, the seventh. Begin with fingers one and three on the sixth string, then use one and four on the fifth string and so on. Bars seven and eight show the arpeggio in root position starting on the 10th fret. Like the second example, this should be played using fingers one and four.

TECHNIQUE: if you find the continuous 16th-note rhythm hard to sustain, try switching to playing eighth-notes over the backing track. When you can manage a group of four 16th-notes in time, play them on the first beat and sustain the last note, playing the next pattern on the third beat, gradually working your way up to playing 16th-notes right across the neck. As you have probably guessed, we are using alternate picking for this exercise.

THEORY: each of these arpeggio shapes has a range of almost three octaves, confirming, as mentioned before, that arpeggios are useful for covering large areas of the guitar very quickly. To put that in a more musical context, they allow the improviser to create melodies with a wide range from lowest note to highest note.

Exercise 3.19

Once you have mastered the dominant seven arpeggios in Exercise 3.18 you can modify each shape in turn to produce the arpeggio of a different chord. For example, in bars one and two of Exercise 3.19, all of the F-sharps from bars one and two of 3.18 have been turned into F-naturals, producing a Dm7 chord.

Bars three and four take this same chord and additionally flatten all the A-naturals to A-flat, producing an arpeggio of Dm7♭5.

Bars five and six then alter the half-diminished chord by additionally changing the minor seventh C to C-flat, producing an arpeggio Ddim7.

Finally, bars seven and eight have restored all of these flattened notes to their original condition but added a C-sharp, producing an arpeggio of Dmaj7.

TECHNIQUE: this exercise uses bars one and two from Exercise 3.18 to create four different chord arpeggios from what was originally a dominant seventh. Once you have got to grips with this concept you should perform the same exercise with the other three shapes in Exercise 3.18, enabling you to play the entire neck with the arpeggio of each of these five basic chord types. The next step would be to choose a different key (perhaps working around the circle of fifths) and play all the shapes in each key in turn.

There are a great many ways to play arpeggios on the guitar, particularly when you ornament or decorate them as in Exercise 3.17. Using arpeggios when developing a solo usually sounds more ambitious and mature than just using scales, though that is not to say that scales are not useful. In the long run, if you are seeking to play jazz guitar really well, you will want to be able to play the arpeggio and the related scale of any chord everywhere on the guitar.

Exercise 3.19 CD TRACK 68 *Four more arpeggios*

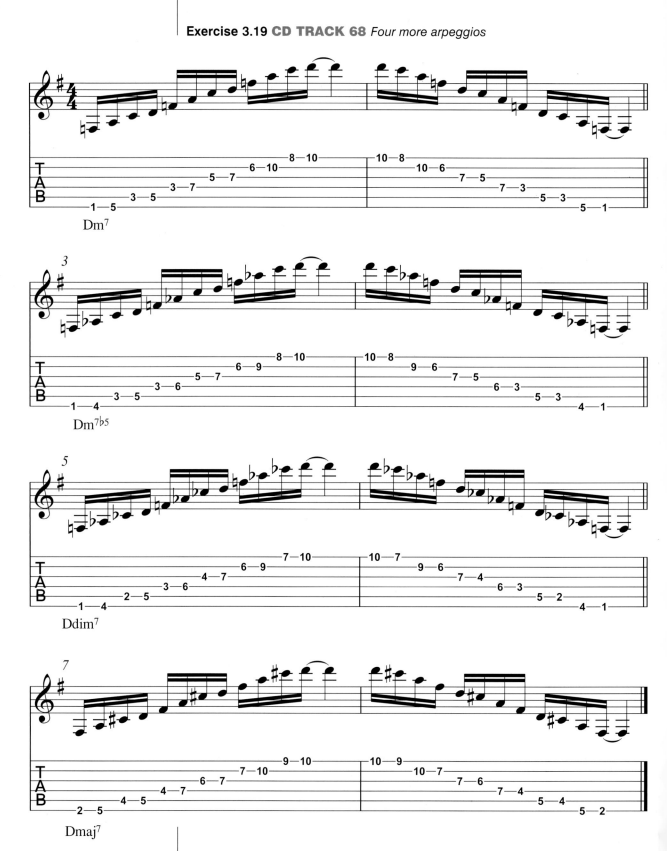

Section 3
The melodic minor scale

In Part Two we learned about the melodic minor scale. This scale is different from the natural minor or Aeolian mode in that when ascending it has a major sixth and major seventh. The descending version of the scale is the same as the natural minor or Aeolian. Another way of looking at this ascending scale is that it is like a major scale but with a minor third.

Exercise 3.20

This example compares a C major scale with a C melodic minor ascending scale. There is only one note difference; the melodic minor has a minor third, E-flat, and the major scale has a major third, E natural. Notice that the first stave has no sharps or flats for the C major key signature and the second stave has three flats for C minor.

From now on we shall refer to the ascending melodic minor scale as just the melodic minor, as we already have a name for the descending melodic minor scale – either Aeolian mode or natural minor. It is the ascending scale that is the most interesting to the improvising jazz musician.

Exercise 3.20
CD TRACK 69
C major versus C melodic minor ascending

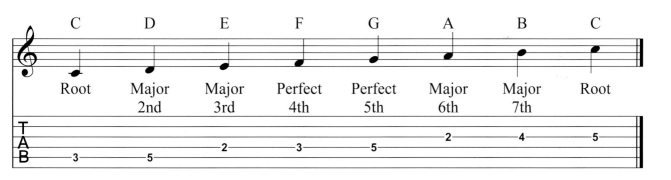

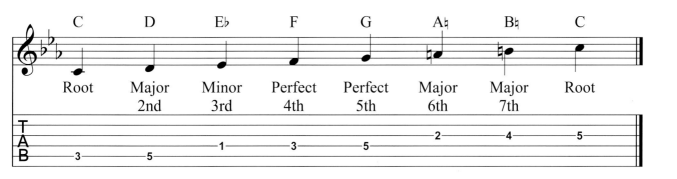

Exercise 3.21

Just like the major scale, we can 'mode' the melodic minor. It is easiest to describe these modes as variations of the major scale modes we have already encountered. Even though there is only one note difference between a major scale and the melodic minor, the effect of the 'major scale with a minor third' is enough to create a completely new set of sounds, some of which are extremely useful, and some less so.

For this exercise we have written out the modes of G melodic minor; this makes it easier to compare them to Exercise 3.04, the modes of G major.

Mode one: Dorian ♯7 The first melodic minor mode is the same as a Dorian mode from root to sixth but then has a major seventh instead of the usual minor seventh. This 'Dorian with major seventh' mode would be suitable for playing over a minor chord with an added major seventh, or Gm maj7 in this case.

Mode two: Dorian ♭2 The second melodic minor mode also resembles a Dorian mode, but this time with a flattened second. The minor second does little to improve a Dorian mode when used over the Am7 chord that is built on its root. Some jazz theorists, however, suggest that this mode might be useful for playing over dominant chords, because its upper range is the same as a Mixolydian, and its lower range includes a minor second and minor third, which are the same as the flat ninth and the sharp ninth.

Mode three: Lydian augmented The third melodic minor mode, in this example starting on B-flat, is like a Lydian scale with the sharpened fourth but also a sharpened fifth. It sounds great over major seventh chords with sharp elevenths or sharp fifths or both.

Mode four: Mixolydian ♯4 The fourth melodic minor mode combines the augmented fourth of the Lydian mode with the minor seventh of the Mixolydian mode to produce a mode known as the Mixolydian ♯4. It implies a dominant chord with a sharp eleventh, but in fact works well over diatonic extensions of the dominant chord too.

Exercise 3.21
CD TRACK 70
Modes on G melodic minor

Mode five: Mixolydian ♭6 The fifth mode resembles a Mixolydian mode with a flattened sixth. While this mode might appear suitable for playing over dominant chords

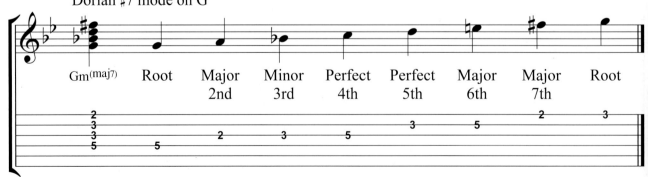

Dorian ♯7 mode on G

Dorian ♭2 mode on A

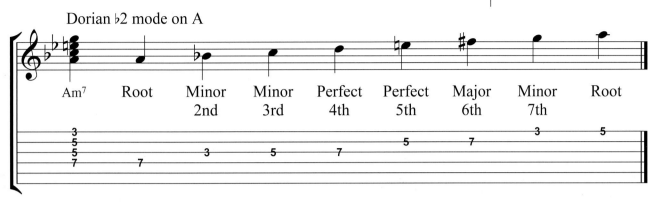

Lydian augmented mode on B♭

Mixoydian ♯4 mode on C

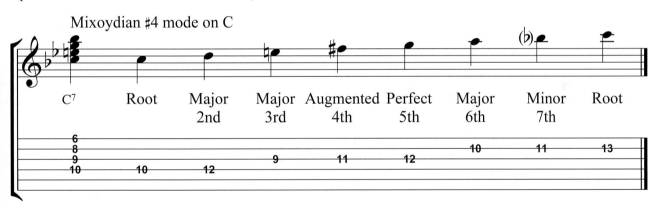

Mixolydian ♭6 mode on D

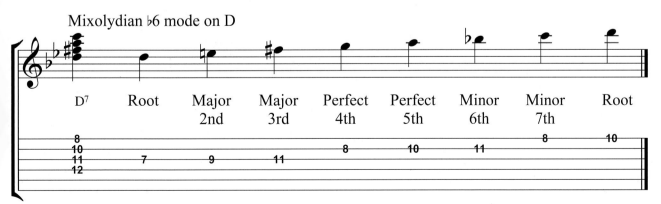

continued over page

THE JAZZ GUITAR HANDBOOK

Exercise 3.21 *continued*

Locrian ♮2 mode on E

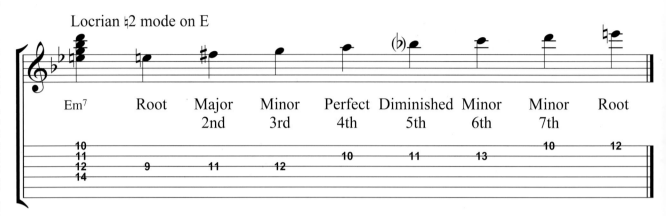

| | Em⁷ | Root | Major 2nd | Minor 3rd | Perfect 4th | Diminished 5th | Minor 6th | Minor 7th | Root |

Altered or Diminished/whole tone scale on F-sharp

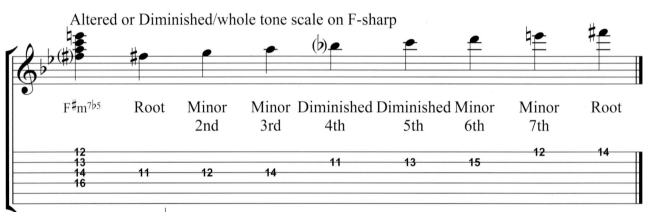

| | F♯m⁷♭⁵ | Root | Minor 2nd | Minor 3rd | Diminished 4th | Diminished 5th | Minor 6th | Minor 7th | Root |

that include the flat thirteenth, it is seldom used because, as we shall see when we come to mode seven, there is a better option.

Mode six: Locrian natural 2 (♮2) The sixth mode is essentially a Locrian mode but with a major second. This mode can be a useful alternative to the standard Locrian when playing over minor seventh flat five (half-diminished) chords as the major second has a brighter quality than the normally sombre and Phrygian-like minor second.

Mode seven: Altered scale or diminished/whole tone The seventh mode at first sight also seems to be useful for playing over minor seventh flat five chords, in that it resembles a Locrian with a diminished fourth. However, the diminished fourth is the same as the major third (in this case B-flat is the same as A-sharp over the root note F-sharp). This means that this mode, played over a dominant chord, includes all of the non-diatonic extensions together with the major third and the minor seventh. The minor second and minor third supply the flat ninth and sharp ninth. The diminished fifth is the same as the sharp eleventh and the minor sixth is the same as the flat thirteenth.

For this reason this mode is often referred to as the 'Altered scale', as it includes all the altered notes that are commonly added to dominant chords. It is also sometimes

THE JAZZ GUITAR HANDBOOK

known as the diminished/whole-tone scale because it begins like a diminished scale and ends with a series of whole-tones. Yet another name for the scale is the 'super Locrian', drawing on the above-mentioned connection to the Locrian mode. As we have not yet studied diminished scales or whole-tone scales and use it for playing over altered dominant chords we will refer to it as the Altered scale, but bear in mind that this is a scale which can have more than one name.

Exercise 3.22

We have seen that the modes of the major scale are very useful for soloing in a great many contexts. The modes of the melodic minor are a little more esoteric – perhaps a

Exercise 3.22
CD TRACK 71
Seven melodic minor scale shapes, shown in G minor

Shape 1

Shape 2

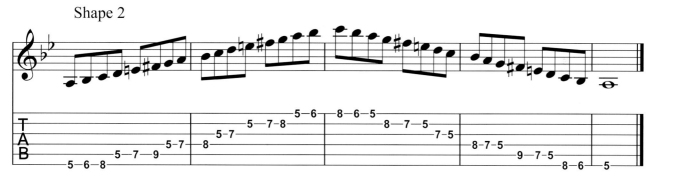

Shape 3

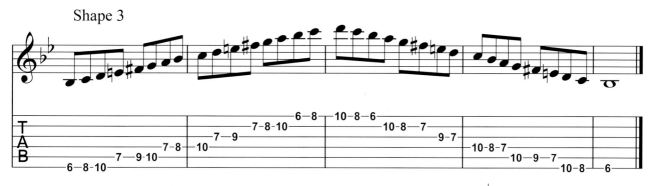

continued over page

THE JAZZ GUITAR HANDBOOK

little 'out there' and modern, but still useful. The easiest way to learn these scale shapes is to take the major scales that we know already and flatten the third each time it comes around, as in Exercise 3.22. For the most part this method produces scale shapes that fit under the fingers very well, but feel free to modify any fingerings that you wish. Shape six, for example, can be improved by moving the B-flat on the 11th fret of the B-string to the 15th fret of the G-string.

TECHNIQUE: if you have already learnt the seven major shapes from Exercise 3.03 it should not be too hard to get to grips with these seven new shapes; remember, only one note has changed in each octave. Begin learning them in the key as written and then work your way around the Circle of Fifths. The most useful modes are numbers one, three, four, six, and seven, so concentrate on these; your long-term goal is to be able to play these in all keys.

Exercise 3.22 *continued*

Shape 4

Shape 5

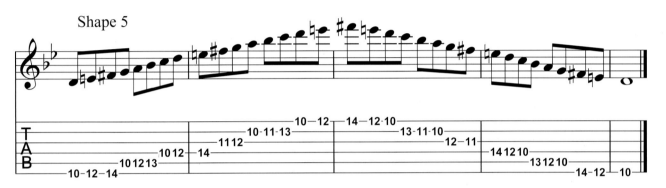

Shape 6

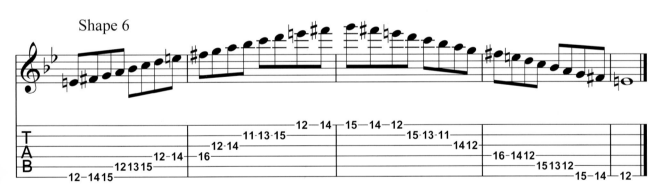

Shape 7

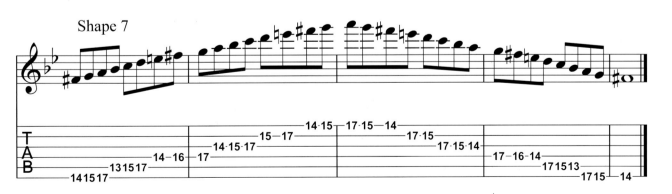

Exercise 3.23

Exercise 3.23 is based on a four-bar groove made up of two bars each of Gm maj7 and C9♯11. This is effectively a ii-V in the key of F major using extended chords. The Gm maj7 chord is clearly stated at the start of each four-bar cycle; the focus here is on rhythmic placement of the chord followed by the colourful addition of notes from the arpeggio of the first inversion. The C9♯11 chord is never played in root position, the close-voiced structures emphasising the innate dissonance of the sharp eleventh sound. The essentially clean guitar sound is given a little additional life and movement by the addition of a flange effect, and the four-bar groove is played four times making 16 bars in all.

TECHNIQUE: although we learned some shapes for minor major seventh chords back in Part Two, we have not made much use of them up until now. Keep your fingers on their tips for these Gm maj7 chords – avoid using a barre – and you will be able to mute the A string and play the chord with a downstroke from the pick.

Exercise 3.24 *(over the page)*

Exercise 3.24 is a solo over the rhythm track of Exercise 3.23. The perfect scale for soloing over Gm maj7 is G melodic minor (mode one), because it has the minor third and jazzy major six from the Dorian, combined with the major seventh that is present in the chord.

Mode four of G melodic minor is C Mixolydian with a sharp eleventh. This would be perfect for playing over C9♯11. So our G melodic minor scale will fit perfectly over the two chords that make up Exercise 3.23.

The solo begins with two short 'question' phrases in bars one and two, which are 'answered' by a longer phrase in bars three and four. This type of phrasing is a great way to get started in a solo, as it not only provides material that can be elaborated later but also establishes a sense of structure. All the notes come from the G melodic minor mode but are often played as fragments of arpeggios mixed with fragments of scales.

As is common in modern jazz, some of the phrases are long and travel freely across bar lines; in early types of jazz, phrasing tended to be much more square. This track was recorded using a Fender Deluxe Reverb amp and ES175 through a vintage fuzz pedal clone. A rotary speaker emulator provides some additional movement to the sound across the stereo image. We're shooting for a modern sound here, leaving behind the clean, fat vintage tones of the 1950s and 60s.

THEORY: analyse the solo, working out how the notes fit against the underlying chord. For example, the opening bar goes 3, 1, 3, 4, 7 in terms of scale steps of the G melodic minor. Bar three goes 3, 2, 1, 7, 5, 7, 1 over C7♯11. Also try recording your own solo over the backing track and transcribe it (write it down), performing the same analysis. There's no better way to get inside your own playing.

Exercise 3.23 CD TRACK 72 *ii-V G melodic minor modes, rhythm*

Laid back, swing 16s ♩=75

THE MELODIC MINOR ASCENDING

Exercise 3.24 CD TRACK 73 *ii-V G melodic minor modes, lead*

Exercise 3.24 *continued*

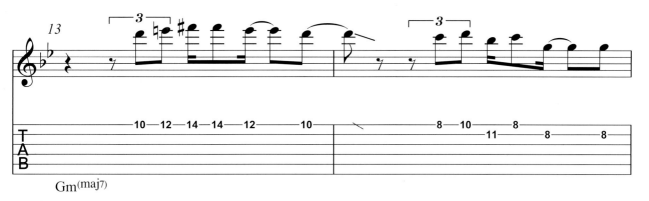

Gm(maj7)

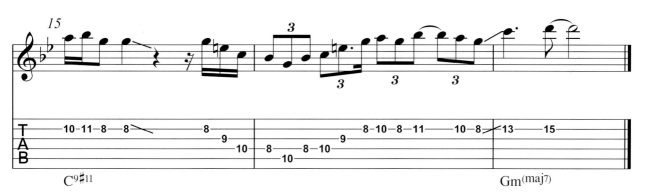

C9♯11   Gm(maj7)

THE JAZZ GUITAR HANDBOOK

Exercise 3.25

For Exercise 3.25 we have reworked the original C Lydian Exercise 3.07, changing everything except the drum part. The bass has been changed to emphasise the sharp fourth and fifth, and in keeping with the edgy, contemporary vibe it is played on a synth (transcribed for guitar in Exercise 3.27). As we will see in Exercise 3.26, the rhythm guitar part has also been altered to emphasise chords with a sharpened fourth and fifth. The G melodic minor scale explored in Exercise 3.21 gives us a Lydian augmented mode on B-flat, but in this exercise we have moved the scale shapes up two frets to A melodic minor, producing a scale of C Lydian augmented so that we are in the same key as Exercise 3.07.

Notice the long pause before the lead guitar enters: don't be afraid to leave gaps when you are soloing, or feel you have to burst in right at the start of a solo. Wind instrument players have to breathe, which encourages them to play phrases, whereas guitarists can (and sadly, often do) widdle away endlessly. Learn the scale shapes and learn the solo, playing it over the backing track. Then experiment with your own solo over the backing track.

The first two short phrases are very similar, the second being at a higher pitch. When a melodic figure is echoed at a different pitch in this way it is known in music as a sequence. We would say, for example, that the melody 'moves sequentially', although in this case the melody merely hints at a sequence. The third phrase, starting in bar five, also appears to be about to repeat the sequence, but instead develops into a long answering phrase over the next four measures.

TECHNIQUE: there is some very fast playing in bar 13, but it is simply a scale played three notes per string. On the CD every note is picked, using alternate picking. If your pick hand is not up to this, try picking the first note on each string and hammering on to play the next two notes.

THEORY: this exercise is written without a key signature, so we are treating the music as if it is in C major. Back when we looked at Exercise 3.07, we regarded the Lydian mode as being derived from the G major scale, and so used the G major key signature of one sharp (F-sharp). Which is correct? My personal belief is that the key signature should reflect the tonic key of the music, not the key from which a mode is derived, and therefore the approach used in 3.25 is to be preferred. However, this is one area where the jury is still out, and you will come across both of these approaches in modal music.

Exercise 3.25 CD TRACK 74 *Lydian augmented scale, solo*

C Lydian Augmented throughout

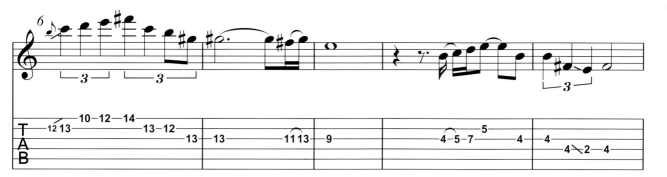

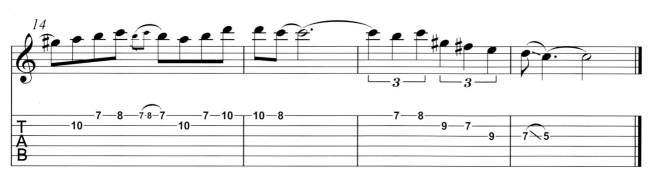

Exercise 3.26 CD TRACK 75 *Lydian augmented scale, backing track*

THE MELODIC MINOR ASCENDING

C Lydian Augmented throughout

Exercise 3.26

The opening chord of Exercise 3.26 is Cmaj7♯5 in its third inversion. That means C E G♯ B with B in the bass. This chord is then 'moded', working its way down the neck to produce a succession of shapes, all of which are built from the Lydian augmented scale. The whole piece only uses five shapes.

TECHNIQUE: mostly, Exercise 3.26 is played using the pick and fingers of the picking hand. This useful technique has been mentioned before. It allows the notes of a four-note chord to be played simultaneously rather than successively as happens when using the pick. The pick plays the note on the D string with a downstroke while the middle, ring, and pinky make an upstroke on the top three strings. This can be tricky at first, but it is a technique well worth acquiring.

SOUND: in keeping with the contemporary vibe on this track we've switched to a Telecaster guitar, both pick-ups on, with tremolo, ping-pong delay, and Uni-Vibe clone.

Exercise 3.27

Exercise 3.27 shows the bassline to Exercises 3.25 and 3.26, transposed for guitar. Notice that it focuses on the essential notes of C Lydian augmented. The first part of the riff uses the tonic, the major seventh, major second and major third. The second part again emphasises the tonic and major seventh but continues down to the sharpened fifth and sharpened fourth.

PRO TIP

if you are serious about getting these more exotic scales together you need to record your own backing tracks. You could play the chords of Exercise 3.26 in a new key and then add the bassline (using a bass, a keyboard or if necessary, your guitar) in the same key. Gradually, you would build up a library of varied backing tracks and improve your ability to play in all keys.

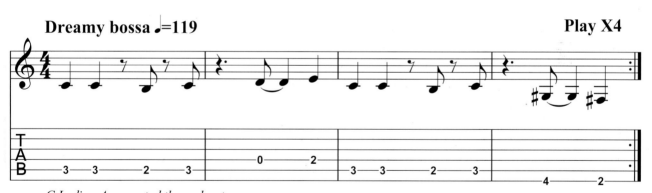

Dreamy bossa ♩=119 — Play X4

C Lydian Augmented throughout

Exercise 3.27
CD TRACK 75
Lydian augmented scale, bassline

Exercise 3.28

Exercise 3.28 is the backing track for Exercise 3.29, in which we take a look at using the sixth and seventh modes of the melodic minor scale, the Locrian ♮2 and the Altered scale. The music is inspired by the A section of the Duke Ellington standard 'Caravan'. Like much Latin-inspired music, it has a strong 'two in a bar' feel and so the piece is written in 2/2 rather than 4/4.

The original consists of 12 bars of C7♭9 followed by four bars of F minor. For this exercise we have divided the first 12 bars into three four-bar phrases, containing two bars of Gm7♭5 and two bars of an extended C7♭9. For an extended chord such as this you will sometimes see the abbreviation 'alt', as in C7alt. This means that the chord should be extended using 'altered' or non-diatonic extensions, such as the flat ninth, sharp eleventh, flat or sharp fifth, and flat thirteenth.

The bassline alternates between the root and fifth of the chord; above, the rhythm guitar plays inversions working progressively down the neck. All the chords are described in the chord symbols as being in root position because the root is being stated so clearly by the bass part. Watch out for the four flats in the key signature – we are in F minor.

Here is an analysis of the notes in each chord, figuring out their function. The first chord is Gm7♭5 in root position; from low to high the notes are G, D-flat, F, and B-flat. This is root, fifth, seventh, and third. In bars three and four the chord reads, again from low to high, E, B-flat, D-flat, and G-sharp. This is third, seventh, flat ninth, and sharp fifth over the C root note. Bars five and six have Gm7♭5 in third inversion: seventh, third, fifth, and root from low to high. Bars seven and eight retain the third of C7 at the bottom of the chord, while above we have the seventh, flat ninth, and flat fifth. This sort of analysis is great for getting beyond the point where chords are shapes to the point where chords are voicings. It takes time, but it comes with practice.

For bars 13 to 16 we have F minor with the common trick (used in Exercise 2.11) of a chromatic descending line from the root to the major sixth. The last two bars are a coda to bring the piece to a strong close.

THEORY: most of the Gm7♭5 chords in this exercise do not have the root note in the bass, and none of the C7 chords contain a root note at all. By analysing the chords and including the bass note we can see that these groups of notes are in fact Gm7♭5 and extended C7 chords.

TECHNIQUE: on the CD the track was played using fingerstyle, thumb, and fingers. Try it with the pick alone (think about upstrokes or downstrokes) and also with pick and fingers ('hybrid' picking, as it is sometimes called).

Exercise 3.28 CD TRACK 76 *Locrian ♮2 and altered scale, backing track*

PRO TIP

Use the backing track to practise both this and your own solo. You could also experiment by ignoring chord ii and treating the first 12 bars as if it were all C7alt. You should find that the altered scale fits both chords. Ignoring chord ii and treating a ii-V progression as being all chord V is often heard in jazz.

Exercise 3.29

Exercise 3.29 uses the sixth mode of the melodic minor scale, the Locrian ♮2, to play over Gm7♭5 and the seventh mode of the melodic minor scale, the Altered scale, to play over an extended dominant chord on C. The key is F minor, where Gm7♭5 is chord ii and C7♭9 is chord V. It's good to change keys; jazz is played in all keys and it is good practice to get used to thinking of the different modes in all keys too.

The Locrian ♮2 mode is the sixth mode of the melodic minor scale. To play this mode in G we would need the B-flat melodic minor scale, the sixth note of which is G.

The Altered scale is the seventh mode of the melodic minor scale, so to play in C we would use the D-flat melodic minor scale, of which C is the seventh note.

Using the shapes from Exercise 3.22, begin working out the shapes for B-flat and D-flat melodic minors. Treat G as the keynote for the B-flat minor scale and C as the keynote for the D-flat minor scale. It is a good idea to work progressively up the neck from the lowest possible scale. In this case, the lowest B-flat melodic minor scale would be shape five, starting at the first fret. For D-flat melodic minor, the lowest shape would be shape four, starting on G-flat on the second fret – assuming you exclude the idea of starting on the open string F-flat (E, in other words) with shape three.

Returning to Exercise 3.29, the first four-bar phrase is constructed by repeating a two-bar sequence of descending scale tones – these notes were chosen because they highlight the differences between the two scales we are using. The next four bars take the scales in an upward direction, so that we can hear the remaining notes of the scales against the background harmony. The third phrase, from bars nine to 12, begins with a one-bar sequence on the G Locrian mode, before arriving on the C Altered scale, emphasising the sharp nine and the major third. The dissonance and tension of the Altered scale is released by a flowing fourth phrase based on an F Dorian mode.

Exercise 3.29
CD TRACK 77
Locrian ♮2 and Altered scale, solo

THEORY: another way of looking at the Locrian ♮2 mode is that it is the same as the Aeolian mode or natural minor scale but with a flattened fifth.

Latin ♩=96

Gm⁷♭⁵   C⁷♯⁵♭⁹

Exercise 3.29 *continued*

Section 4
Symmetrical scales – and others

It is possible to create scales by repeating an intervallic pattern; these are known as symmetrical scales. Over the next few exercises we will look at the theory behind the whole-tone and diminished symmetrical scales, and then put them into practice in a musical context. As the next few exercises are theoretical and scale-based, we have saved space by not including them on the CD.

Exercise 3.30

The whole-tone scale is made up, as the name implies, entirely of whole-steps. Only two whole-tone scales are possible, one beginning on C and one beginning on C-sharp (or D-flat). The C whole-tone scale is identical to that which starts on D, E, F-sharp, G-sharp, and B-flat; similarly the C-sharp whole-tone scale is identical to the E-flat, F, G, A and B scale. Because every interval is identical, whole-tone scales cannot have modes.

The whole-tone scale has a major third and minor seventh, making it very suitable for playing over dominant chords. The other notes contribute a major ninth, sharp eleventh (or flat fifth) and flat thirteenth (or sharp fifth). In other words, like the Altered scale it contains some interesting notes.

Exercise 3.30
Whole-tone scale intervals

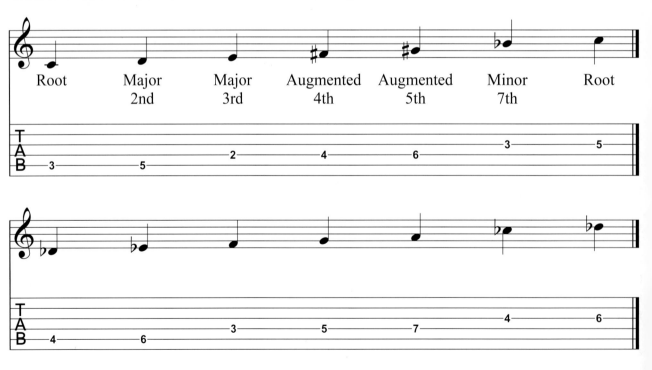

Exercise 3.30 outlines the notes of C and D-flat whole-tone scales together with the intervals that make up the scale. This sequence of intervals is the same for all whole tone scales.

THEORY: this scale also belongs to a group of scales known as hexatonics because it has only six notes.

Exercise 3.31

Exercise 3.31 is a whole-tone scale arranged on the guitar from the second fret on the sixth string to the sixth fret on the first string. It is only necessary to learn one whole-tone scale shape as the shape recurs every two frets. If you play the given shape starting with finger one at the fourth fret you will be playing exactly the same six notes but starting on G-sharp instead of F-sharp.

Whole-tone scale

TECHNIQUE: see if you can work out a shape for the whole-tone scale that has three notes per string – it fits under the fingers well.

Exercise 3.31
Whole-tone scale shape

Exercise 3.32

Another symmetrical scale is the diminished scale. This scale is constructed from alternate half-steps and whole-steps. Because there are two intervals involved in the construction of this scale, it is possible to have two modes. Exercise 3.32 demonstrates the mode that begins with a half-step followed by the mode that begins with a whole-step, and includes, as usual, the intervals created between the notes of the scale and the root. The first, half-step/whole-step scale is very suitable for playing over extended dominant seventh chords as it again has a major third and a minor seventh. The minor second and augmented second are equivalent to a flat ninth and a sharp ninth; other notes of the scale include the sharp eleventh and the natural thirteenth. Now that you have seen this scale you can see why some writers use the term 'diminished/whole-tone scale' to describe the Altered scale. The Altered scale begins with the same five notes.

The second scale in Exercise 3.32 is the whole-step/half-step. One way of looking at this scale is that it is an arpeggio of Cdim7 with each note being approached from a

SYMMETRICAL SCALES – AND OTHERS

Half-step/whole-step

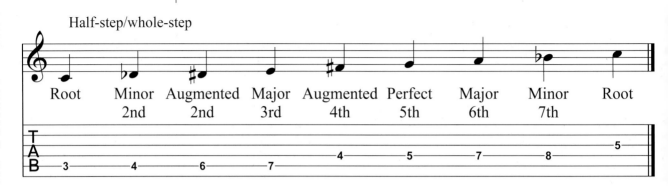

| Root | Minor 2nd | Augmented 2nd | Major 3rd | Augmented 4th | Perfect 5th | Major 6th | Minor 7th | Root |

Whole-step/half-step

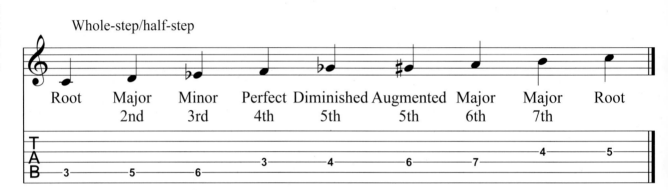

| Root | Major 2nd | Minor 3rd | Perfect 4th | Diminished 5th | Augmented 5th | Major 6th | Major 7th | Root |

Exercise 3.32

Diminished scale intervals

half-step below. This is the most appropriate scale to choose when soloing over a diminished chord.

THEORY: both these scales can be viewed as two interlocking arpeggios. C and D-flat diminished seventh arpeggios are found in the half-step/whole-step scale. C and D diminished seventh arpeggios are present in the whole-step/half-step.

Exercise 3.33

In the same way that there are only two whole-tone scales, there can only be three diminished scales, starting on C, C-sharp, and D. The scale starting on E-flat is the same as the C scale; the scale starting on E is the same as the C-sharp scale, and so on.

A possible shape for a diminished scale is shown in Exercise 3.33. This whole-step/half-step scale beginning on G is the same as a half-step/whole-step scale beginning on A. Any note of the Gdim7 chord (G, B-flat, D-flat, or E) could be the root of this scale and any note of the Adim7 chord (A, C, E-flat, or F-sharp) could be the root of the half-step/whole-step version of the scale. This means the shape recurs every three frets on the guitar; start at the sixth, ninth, or twelfth fret for the same scale in higher positions.

THEORY: these eight-note scales are sometimes known as octatonic scales. Each diminished scale contains four notes that could be roots of whole-step/half-step scales and four notes that could be roots of half-step/whole-step scales.

Exercise 3.34

As the scale recurs every three frets, there is no need to learn any other shapes; but because of their symmetrical structure, diminished scales can effectively be played four notes per string, as demonstrated in Exercise 3.34. Begin by sliding the first finger from the second to the third fret and then use fingers three and four; repeat the pattern on the next string and so on.

Exercise 3.33
Diminished scale shape (whole-step/half-step)

Exercise 3.34
Diminished scale shape (half-step/whole-step, four notes per string)

THE JAZZ GUITAR HANDBOOK

SYMMETRICAL SCALES – AND OTHERS

Exercise 3.35

Having studied the theory behind whole-tone and diminished scales, it's time to put them into practice. Exercise 3.35 demonstrates these two scales in use over the backing track that we used for the Altered scale in Exercises 3.28 and 3.29 (CD track 76). The first eight bars make use of the whole-tone scale and bars nine to 12 use the diminished scale (half-step/whole-step). The last four bars suggest F Dorian, although bar 16, with an E-natural, also hints at F melodic minor.

As well as learning the solo, use the scale shapes from Exercises 3.31, 3.33, and

Exercise 3.35
CD TRACK 78
Whole-tone and diminished scale solo

Exercise 3.35 *continued*

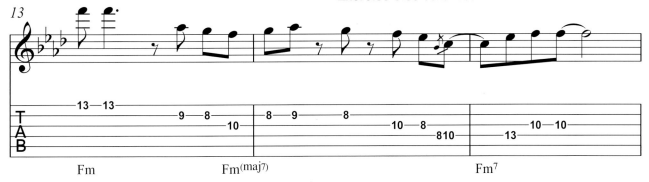

3.34 to improvise your own solo over CD track 76. You can switch between the two scales if you wish, but it might be better to take them one at a time, familiarising yourself with the sound of the whole-tone scale and then working on the diminished scale.

At this point we have covered all the scales in common use by jazz musicians. For the sake of completeness, Exercise 3.36 shows a few more that deserve a mention and which, in time, you may wish to experiment with.

Exercise 3.36a

Chromatic scale

Exercise 3.36a

The chromatic scale: the chromatic scale is in theory a symmetrical scale, being made up entirely of half-steps. Chromatic fragments can be used in improvising, particularly when using a 'target note' method to structure phrases, and can sound particularly good over dominant seventh chords.

Exercise 3.36b

Harmonic minor: we know that the harmonic minor scale produces useful minor key harmony, and it can certainly be played over a minor key ii-V-i. The augmented second between the sixth and seventh steps of the scale needs careful handling if we are not going to evoke the sounds of Arabia, and as a result most phrases in solos which appear to suggest the harmonic minor scale are made from arpeggios or decorated arpeggios of the underlying chords. The structure of a harmonic minor scale was looked at in Exercise 2.25. To create harmonic minor scale shapes on the guitar, either

Exercise 3.36b

Harmonic minor scale

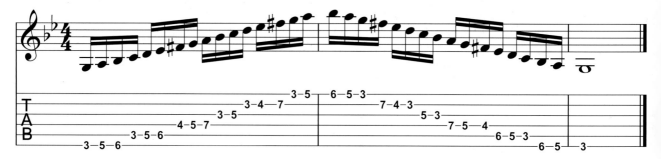

take an Aeolian mode shape and sharpen the seventh, or play a melodic minor scale shape and flatten the sixth. If you feel like experimenting you can also create modes from the harmonic minor scale.

Exercise 3.36c

Harmonic major: this scale exists in theory only. There is no harmonic major generating useful harmony in the way that the harmonic minor generates useful minor-key harmony. The scale gets its name from the idea that you can take a major scale and alter it to include the distinctive augmented second between the sixth and seventh steps of the harmonic minor. In other words, it is a major scale with a flattened sixth. Once again, the experimentally minded can create modes from this scale.

Exercise 3.36c

Harmonic major scale

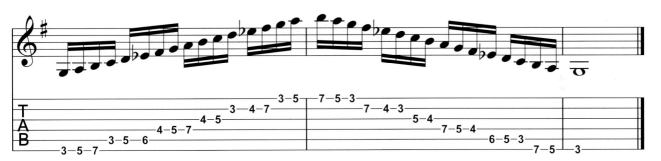

Exercise 3.37

Some guitarists like to play scale shapes that have three notes on every string, and therefore involve position changes. One example (shape one) is given in Exercise 3.37 to get you started; you should have no problem figuring out the rest of the shapes for yourself if this style appeals to you. Just beware of the temptation to play continuous triplet rhythms when you use this type of fingering.

Exercise 3.37

Major scale shape, three notes on every string

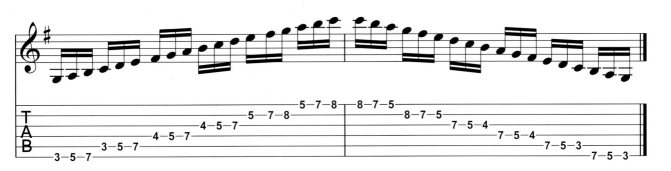

Exercise 3.38

Jazz musicians have for many years practised scales using melodic patterns. Not only do these make practising scales more interesting but also, ever since the days of bebop, these scale patterns have found their way into solos. Exercise 3.38 provides some scale-pattern ideas to get you started making up your own. These are written in eighth-note rhythms, but you should experiment with as many rhythmic ideas as you can come up with.

All of the examples use scale shape seven and begin on the root, G, at the third fret. They should be continued beyond the two-bar idea to the top of the scale shape and back. Then you should try them using other scale shapes. We begin with repeated notes; each note is played twice in bars one and two and played three times in bars

---

REAL BOOK AND FAKE BOOKS

Fake books originated in the 1940s and included the lyrics, melodies, and chords to popular songs of the day, including many from Broadway shows. Taken from the publishers' piano arrangements in the original sheet music, the chords were of little use as they mostly reflected an impression of the pianist's right hand, adapted for ukulele or guitar, rather than the underlying harmony. The *Real Book* was compiled by students at Berklee College in the 1970s, and included a mixture of standards, bebop, and contemporary tunes. A band, especially the rhythm section, needs only the correct chords, while the frontline instruments need only the melody line. The original *Real Book* is handwritten, with the lead line and *real* chord changes – a style of arranging known as 'lead sheet'.

Subsequently expanded to three volumes, these became the original underground *Real Books*, all photocopied and passed from musician to musician. Since then legitimate *Real Books*, modelled on the originals but paying royalties to the copyright owners, have been created by Hal Leonard and Sher Music Co among others, and there are now many other varieties, including a Latin version for Cuban and Brazilian music.

Most jazz musicians have a repertoire of jazz standards and *Real Book Volume One* is a great place to start building a repertoire of your own, particularly as the Hal Leonard edition is widely available and completely legitimate. Pick a tune, play through the melody (great for practising your sight reading), play through the chords, and then practise soloing over the harmony. Do this every day and you will soon build a collection of tunes that you can play confidently. Take your real book with you if you go to a jam session and you will have a lead sheet for many of the tunes that are called. Smartphone and tablet computer users can also find Real Book apps that include the chord sequences to a large number of jazz standards.

Exercise 3.38 *Scale patterns for practice*

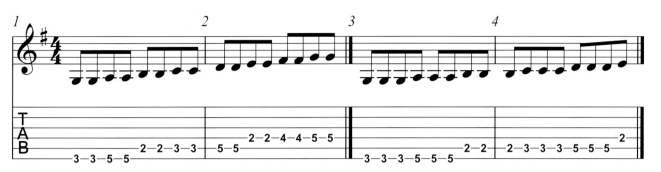

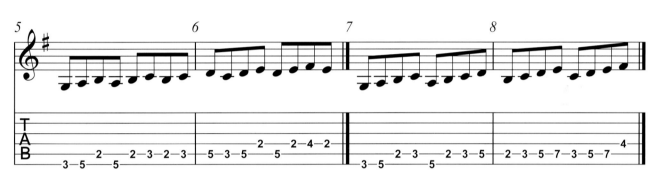

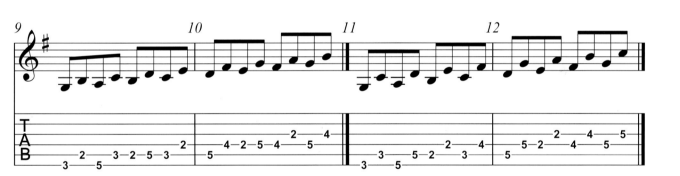

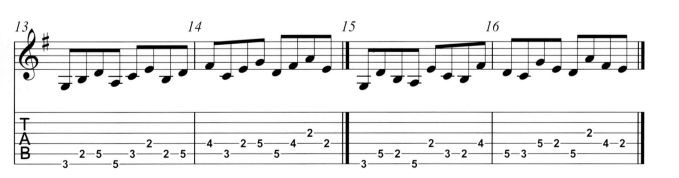

THE JAZZ GUITAR HANDBOOK

three and four. Played in a swing feel, bars three and four introduce an interesting across-the-barline rhythm.

Bars five to eight introduce short scalic runs of notes; three notes and four notes are shown ascending, but longer runs of five and six notes are possible and a descending pattern also works well.

Bars nine to 12 are based on the idea of playing scales in intervals. We begin with a rising third, followed by a falling second in bars nine and ten. This is followed by a rising fourth, followed by a falling third in bars 11 and 12. Both these ideas can be inverted and many other interval combinations are possible.

Bars 13 and 14 are based on a rising arpeggio of each triad. Bars 15 and 16 take the same notes but each chord is played root, fifth, and then third. Notice the 'across the bar' three-note pattern in these two exercises.

The speed and agility needed to be a jazz musician will take time to develop and scale practice using a metronome is one part of the process. When playing scales and arpeggios keep a note of the tempos you can play at and use the metronome to make very slight increases in speed – even one beat per minute is worthwhile as over time these small increments will add up to fast, fluent playing.

THEORY: an important point to remember when playing lead-sheet melodies is that they are not written for guitar and are written at sounding pitch. Guitar music (including the examples in this book) is written an octave higher than it sounds, so you must get used to reading and playing lead sheets an octave up.

Summing up

In this chapter we have covered all of the scales that are in common use in jazz soloing, and you should now be able to solo over the chords of any jazz standard or bebop tune. You can go far with the major scale modes, the Altered scale, and a good knowledge of arpeggios and decorated arpeggio licks. Add in diminished and whole-tone scales and a few characteristic blues phrases and you're well on your way. If you are looking for some more edgy or modern sounds then other modes of the melodic minor covered in this section are also available. In Part Four we take a look at a range of jazz styles and techniques, while also considering note choices when soloing and some more advanced harmony.

PART 4
Jazz guitar
styles

- Rhythm styles, chord/melody techniques, and time signatures

- Note choices and melody styles

Section 1
Rhythm styles, chord/melody techniques, and time signatures

I n Part Four we are going to develop technique by focusing on a selection of styles of jazz guitar, starting with a look at playing chord/melody style, which means playing chords and melodies at the same time. We begin by bringing things full circle and returning to the first exercise in the book, 'Kenny's Blues', and combining it with the rhythm track we learned in Part Two, Exercise 2.14. You may well have realised back in Part One that both parts of this tune would fit on one guitar as the chords are played only in the gaps left by the tune.

Exercise 4.01

Exercise 4.01 goes further than just joining Exercise 1.01 and Exercise 2.14; we figure you can probably get that together for yourself, so in this one we've added what are known as 'double stops', a term that comes from classical stringed instruments where two strings are played at once. There's also a hammer-on from a half barre at the third fret to the fourth and fifth frets simultaneously, using fingers two and three.

We mess with the timing a little in bar two, playing the riff half a beat late – and then have added, at the end, a little jazz cadenza around the blues-scale notes. (A cadenza is the part of a classical concerto where the orchestra stops playing and the soloist shows off in free time.) Remember there's a backing track you can use at CD12.

TECHNIQUE: as much as possible use the normal minor pentatonic fingering – just flatten your fingertips a little to hold down two strings at a time.

THEORY: you don't have to think only in terms of chords for accompaniment and single notes for solos. Two-note soloing can be very effective, particularly for blues-flavoured licks.

Exercise 4.01 CD TRACK 79 & 12 (BACKING TRACK) *'Kenny's Blues', parts together*

Exercise 4.02

Exercise 4.02 is based on the opening section of the jazz standard 'Autumn Leaves', played here in the key of E minor. Notice that it begins on Am7, the iv chord. The first eight bars are similar in style to Exercise 4.01, in that chords punctuate the spaces in the melody line. The accented rhythm part is played by the whole band in a style which jazz musicians often refer to as 'stops' (as in "Let's do this with stops"), because the band stops playing to leave space for each melodic phrase. The chord shapes should be recognisable from Part Two.

In the second eight bars, which would be the second A tune, the band swings through the stops and the guitar part comps with two-note chords. These two-note chords, technically known as diads, are useful for suggesting the chord movement in the midst of a melody without holding down a great many notes. Let's take a closer look at how this works.

In bar nine, the notes G and C progress to F-sharp and C. G and C are the seventh and third of Am7; by simply making a half-step change to the lower note we then have the third and seventh of D7.

In bar 11 the seventh and third of Gmaj7 become the third and seventh of Cmaj7, as the F-sharp moves down a whole step to E. In bar 13 we have three-note chords, and as the note E becomes D-sharp, we make the transition from F♯m7♭5 to B7♭9. In all the above cases, the root movement is provided by the bassline, leaving the guitarist free to suggest the chord movement by playing only the essential notes.

The exercise ends with harmonics, played at the seventh and 12th frets and outlining B7 and Em chords. With the fretting hand first finger, touch the strings very lightly as if making a barre all the way across the neck. Don't press the strings down and aim to get directly over the fret. Use the pick on the sixth string and use your m and a fingers on the top two strings.

THEORY: since the bassline provides the tonal centre for each chord, it is only necessary to play the third and seventh to outline its character. When roots are rising a fourth, the third and seventh of one chord tend to be very close to the seventh and third of the next chord.

TECHNIQUE: use the pick to play the single note melody; use pick and fingers to play the chords and diads, with the pick on the lowest note and the m, a, and e fingers on the upper notes.

Exercise 4.02 CD TRACK 80 *Chords with melodies, and comping with two- and three-note chords*

Exercise 4.03

Guitar players often play walking basslines, particularly when working in duos with singers and other instrumentalists. In fact, they often play walking basslines and comp chords at the same time – but that's coming up in Exercise 4.04. A walking bassline is the kind that tends to have a note on every beat and to be played legato.

In this exercise we have a simple pattern that you can use for making up your own basslines, focusing mainly on the first and last note of each bar. The first note of every bar is the root note of the underlying chord. The last note of each bar has to be a note which leads effectively to the first note of the next bar. The two notes in the middle are scale tones, chord tones, or chromatic passing notes. Exactly what makes a good leading note is a matter of opinion, but approaching the next note from a whole- or half-step above or below tends to sound good. A rising fourth, as between bar two and bar three, also works well.

Between bars one and two and bars three and four we have a diatonic whole-step approach note; in bars five and six you can see the effect of chromatic approach notes. As there are two chords per bar at this point every note is either a root note or an approach note. In bars seven and eight we just use the root note of each chord played twice, which can be effective for short periods if there is strong root movement. Once you get the hang of basslines, it is surprising how much you can get away with – even the rule that the first note must be the root can be fairly flexible – the third or fifth can be used or its arrival can be delayed for a beat.

TECHNIQUE: this track was played using the thumb of the pick hand.

THEORY: the harmony from these two eight-bar A-sections is from the 32-bar jazz standard that we first saw in Exercise 2.20. Compare this arrangement and the one coming up in Exercise 4.04 with the arrangement we used back then.

Exercise 4.03 CD TRACK 81 *Walking bass*

Exercise 4.04

Exercise 4.04 takes the bassline from Exercise 4.03 and fleshes it out with comped chords at the rate of one or two per bar. To make the two parts seem independent, some chords are cut short, but others, in bar two for example, are held while the bassline continues. Finding the right fingering is an important part of keeping the bassline swinging under the chords; in bars five and six, try using a barre for the Am7 and A♭m7 chords, as this will leave finger two free to play the approach tone, and then slide down a fret for the root note of the D9 or D♭9 chord.

The second eight-bar section is more challenging rhythmically, but the chord voicings are similar. At the end we use a rising sequence of chromatic chords to arrive on two different voicings of C6/9 chords – which makes the strange rising bassline at the end of Exercise 4.03 make sense. Check out any of the *Virtuoso* albums by Joe Pass, or solo albums by Martin Taylor, to hear geniuses at work with walking basslines and comped chords.

THEORY: in the notation stave the music is written out in two parts. The stems of the bassline notes point downwards, while the stems of the comped chords point upwards. Each part is fully accounted for with the correct number of beats and rests per bar. This is normal practice when writing in two parts on one stave.

TECHNIQUE: try playing the chords on their own over CD track 81, which supplies the walking bassline.

Exercise 4.04 CD TRACK 82 *Walking bass with chords*

RHYTHM STYLES, CHORD/MELODY TECHNIQUES, AND TIME SIGNATURES

Slow swing ♩=84

Staccato chords throughout

E♭maj⁷ Edim⁷ Fm⁷ B♭⁷ Gm⁷ C⁷♯⁵

Fm⁹ B♭⁷♯⁵ E♭maj⁹ E♭⁷/B♭ A♭maj⁶ᐟ⁷ A♭m⁶

rall.

Gm⁷ G♭m⁷ Fm⁷ B♭¹³ B♭⁷ E♭⁶ A♭m⁷/G♭ E♭⁶ᐟ⁹

Exercise 4.05
CD TRACK 83
Chord-melody,
Lenny Breau style

THE JAZZ GUITAR HANDBOOK

Exercise 4.05

Exercise 4.05 is a piece that combines a melody, chords, and a bassline in the style of the great fingerstyle guitarist Lenny Breau. Breau was a versatile all-round guitarist but his speciality was maintaining a chord accompaniment while adding a melody line above. It is important to play the chords (notice that the note stems point downwards) using thumb, index, and middle fingers of the pick hand. The ring finger (a) plays the melody. All of the chords are played slightly staccato by releasing the fretting-hand fingers immediately after the chord is plucked. Meanwhile the melody note (with note stems pointing upwards) must be held down to create a legato effect over the staccato chords.

The first eight bars are based on the A section of 'I Got Rhythm', a chord sequence often used in jazz and usually referred to as 'Rhythm Changes'. In this exercise we are in the key of E-flat major, but 'Rhythm Changes' is usually played in B-flat major; we will take a look at the full 32-bar chord sequence in Exercise 4.13. This 10-bar exercise is completed by the addition of a two-bar coda or tag using the minor version of chord IVc.

THEORY: extended chords are used to add interest to the melodic line in places (such as bars three and four) and an interesting bassline is maintained by occasionally choosing inversions or substitutions. Edim7 in the first bar is a substitute for C7♭9; G♭m7 in bar seven is a tritone substitution, also for C7♭9.

Exercise 4.06

We've tended to stick to four beats in a bar in all of the exercises so far. However, the more progressive forms of jazz have experimented with other rhythms since the 1960s. Pianist Dave Brubeck's 1959 album *Time Out* included the 5/4 tune 'Take Five' and others in 9/8 and 6/4. Guitarist composers such as John McLaughlin continued this experimentation, and have written in complex asymmetrical time signatures such as 7/8, 11/8, or 13/8.

Exercise 4.06 (over the page) is a jazz waltz arranged for solo guitar and written in 3/4 time. It is played with a swing feel suggesting 9/8 time: three eighth-notes per beat. The rhythm in bar two is common in a jazz waltz, but instead of being played as two equally-spaced dotted quarter-notes, the second chord is played slightly later, on the third eighth-note of the second beat.

The harmony for this exercise is inspired by the classic jazz waltz 'My Favourite Things', which has an unusually long form for a jazz standard. In this exercise there are just two 16-bar sections, with the second section being altered to bring the music to a conclusion on the key-chord of Em7.

The highest note of any chord is the most prominent to the human ear and we hear the highest notes of any sequence of chords strung together as a melody. The way to get this together in your own playing is always to prioritise the melody as the part that has most of the attention of the listener. The next most important part is the bassline; as demonstrated here, bringing out fragments of bassline whilst holding on to long

Exercise 4.06 CD TRACK 84 *Chord/melody solo arrangement in 3/4 time*

RHYTHM STYLES, CHORD/MELODY TECHNIQUES, AND TIME SIGNATURES

Exercise 4.06 *continued*

melody notes can be very effective. Creating a full counterpoint from the bass is not usually necessary, however, and furthermore the bass part can be surprisingly high in pitch at times, as in bar 29.

TECHNIQUE: the inner notes of the chords act as a middle part sandwiched between the melody and the bass. Not every note is harmonised: one or two chord voicings per bar, with the melody moving above, are plenty.

THEORY: in bars two and four there is a chord substitution which is only easy to spot if you know the original chord sequence, which normally has an F#m7 chord at this point. Known as 'chord quality substitution', it keeps the root note of the chord the same but changes the type of chord, in this case to the darker-sounding harmony of the m7♭5 chord. In this type of substitution, dominant chords are often used in place of minor sevenths or major sevenths, but in fact any replacement chord that works with the melody can be effective.

THE JAZZ GUITAR HANDBOOK

Section 2
Note choices and melody styles

Doubling up a single-note line with its octave seems to add emphasis. Octave guitar parts are rarely played particularly quickly, but they make up for this with their incisive and resonant quality. Django Reinhardt frequently used octaves in his solos, but it is Wes Montgomery who is chiefly remembered for his fluent bebop-inspired octave lines. He never used a pick, preferring to play everything with his picking-hand thumb.

Exercise 4.07

In Exercise 4.07 we return to the music of Exercise 4.02, but this time playing the melody in octaves and extending each phrase over the punctuating chords. Notice that the shape for an octave on the guitar changes depending on the location of the top note; it is a three-fret gap for the E- and B-strings, but a two-fret gap for the G- and D-strings. It is essential to damp not only the string in the middle but also the strings either side of the notes being held down. On the CD, the track is played 'Wes style', using a brushed downstroke of the thumb; try it using the pick too.

Bar eight is the lead-in to the second eight-bar section, which takes the form of a solo over the same chord sequence. Chromatic passing notes and approach notes are used extensively in both sections of this exercise; the final lick in bar 15 comes from the blues scale.

TECHNIQUE: playing in octaves involves an unusual amount of lateral movement from the fretting hand, and for this reason it is easy to hit the wrong fret when reading. Memorise the music phrase by phrase and then play it, looking at your hand. Do you prefer to watch the highest note, played with finger three or four, or the lowest note, played with finger one?

THEORY: there is another way to play octaves. The fifth fret on the top string can be doubled an octave down on the seventh fret of the D-string; but the two dead strings in between make this method less effective when using the pick or brushing with the thumb.

Exercise 4.07 CD TRACK 85 & 87 (BACKING TRACK) *Octaves, Wes Montgomery style*

Exercise 4.08

A chord solo is made up of an improvised melody that is spontaneously harmonised with chords taken from the underlying harmony. In Exercise 4.08 we use the same chord sequence as in Exercises 4.02 and 4.07 to demonstrate this style. When you try to create your own chord solo over the backing track (CD87) concentrate on the top notes of the chords, aiming for a smooth, linear progression which will come out as a melody.

Three- or four-note chords can be very effective in this style, in which no attempt is made to provide a bassline. Where a bass note is played separately, it is often to provide rhythmic interest, such as between bars two and three or in bar six. The focus is entirely on the melody, with almost every note harmonised. Chromatic slides are useful to easily add chromatic notes to the melody, such as in bars three and four, and a chord shape can occasionally be held while altering the top note as in bars five and 13.

THEORY: in this exercise we have switched from our normal practice of adding chord symbols beneath the stave that show the underlying harmony to adding chord symbols that show the name of the actual chord being played, taking into account the root note supplied by the bassline. Compare this exercise to the underlying harmony in Exercise 4.07; chords often arrive early (bar one, bar five, etc), or sometimes arrive late (bars nine/ten).

TECHNIQUE: a good knowledge of the inversions of chords and the possible additions to the upper notes of a chord shape are very useful in this style. However, almost all the chord shapes used in this exercise were first seen in Part Two and with some close analysis will look very familiar.

Exercise 4.08 CD TRACK 86 & 87 (BACKING TRACK) *Chord solo*

Exercise 4.09

Back in Exercise 2.37 we looked at the possibility of developing the chords of a 12-bar blues so that the harmony was more complex and the music modulated away from the tonic key in several places. Just for reference, here is the chord sequence we used in that exercise:

Cmaj7	C7		F9	F7		C7			Gm7	C7	
F7			F♯dim7			C7			A7		
Dm7			G7			Cmaj7	A7		Dm7	G7	‖

The presence of several ii-V-I or ii-V progressions means that there are several points where a new key centre is established or hinted at; for example, between bars four and five, bars eight and nine, and, to return to the tonic, bars nine to 12.

In the bebop era, tempos became generally faster and chord changes became more frequent, leading to further refinement of the blues chord sequence. Exercise 4.09 demonstrates an extended set of blues changes sometimes called 'Bird Blues', named after the saxophonist Charlie Parker, respectfully known in jazz circles as 'Bird'. Parker used a sequence like this in his composition 'Blues For Alice'.

Cmaj7			Bm7♭5	E7♭9		Am7	D7		Gm7	C7	
Fmaj7			Fm7	B♭7		Em7	A7		E♭m7	A♭7	
Dm7			G7			Cmaj7	A7		Dm7	G7	‖

Exercises 4.09 and 2.37 are both in the key of C major, making it easy to compare the two sequences. In 'Bird Blues', bars two to four have a descending pattern of ii-V chords; ii-V in A minor, ii-V in G, and ii-V in F, with this last 'two-five' resolving strongly to chord I in bar five. Bars six to eight are also changed to a descending series of ii-Vs, leading to the Dm7 chord in bar nine and a ii-V-I back to C major; the last four bars of the two sequences are identical.

Exercise 4.09 transcribes the first chorus of comping from CD track 88. As usual, the chord symbols for the underlying harmony are notated beneath the tab stave. We have also added smaller chord symbols between the staves, which describe the actual chord being used. Many chords are inverted, and in bar two we use an E7♯9 chord instead of E7♭9. Not every chord is played when comping; the fast tempo and the need to comp in phrases means that some chords are held while the bassline outlines the root movement, as in bar three or in bar six.

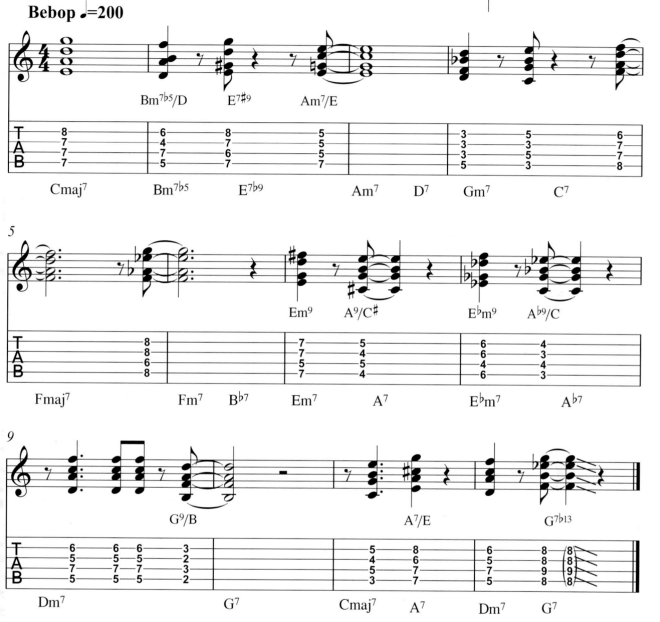

Exercise 4.09
CD TRACK 88
'Bird Blues', bebop blues changes in C

Exercise 4.10

The presence of so much modulation in a chord sequence is both an opportunity and a challenge to the improviser. On one hand, the rapidly shifting key centres invite the use of altered scales, chromatic extensions to the harmony, and suspension or anticipation of chord tones. On the other hand, they demand a high-level knowledge of chord/scale relationships, the ability to rapidly locate the notes on the instrument. and the ability to connect scale fragments and arpeggios to create interesting melodies. You can see why jazz musicians spend so much time 'woodshedding' those scales and arpeggios (the expression refers to being sent to the woodshed, where you could practice without annoying anyone).

In Exercise 4.10 we have a melody in the style of a bebop blues head, mostly made up of chord tones, with some chromatic extension tones and something which we have not yet discussed – encircling tones. For chord tones, let us take a look at the first three bars; the presence of several accidentals would suggest at first glance that there are many chromatic extensions; however, both the G-sharp and F-natural are found in the underlying E7♭9 chord and the E-flat in bar three completes a D7♭9 chord which we would expect to lead to G minor.

Chromatic extensions can be found in bar four, where there is a melodic sequence with the ninth, seventh, and fifth of G minor moving down a half step to become the sharp eleventh, third and flat ninth over C7. These two chromatic extensions are used at an important moment in the blues sequence, where it modulates to the subdominant.

In bar seven the F-sharp is the ninth over Em7, and the B-flat is the flattened ninth over A7. Overall, bars five to eight appear very chromatic, but many of the notes are in fact chord tones, as the chromatic slide of the harmony encourages the development of a chromatic melody.

Encircling tones are a common device in jazz. They add dissonance by anticipating or delaying the arrival of an expected note. In bar two, the A and F encircle the following G-sharp; at the end of the bar the D and F encircle the following E. In the first example we begin above, then go below the final note, and in the second example we begin below, then go above the final note. Encircling tones can be chromatic or diatonic. These examples introduce the idea; now experiment, and see if you can create some of your own licks using encircling tones.

TECHNIQUE: when you have mastered the head, try inventing your own solo over CD track 88. Solo over each chord using the appropriate scale or arpeggio, concentrating on the extended, upper notes of the chords and aiming to create long, fluent phrases. As an experiment, try ignoring all the ii chords. Treat each bar of ii-V as if it were just chord V, the dominant chord.

Exercise 4.10 CD TRACK 89 *Melody over 'Bird Blues' changes*

Exercise 4.11

'Hot Club' is an original style of jazz developed by guitarist Django Reinhardt and violinist Stefan Grappelli in France in the 1930s. Their Quintet of the Hot Club of France gave its name to Hot Club music that has now spread all around the world. Django Reinhardt was a Manouche gypsy and as a result this style is also called 'Gypsy Jazz' or sometimes 'Jazz Manouche'. These terms are widely applied to jazz involving acoustic guitars and a persistent, driving beat – most often with violin or clarinet as an additional lead instrument. The quintet consisted of two rhythm guitars and string bass in addition to Reinhardt and Grappelli.

In Exercise 4.11, we have an example of a typical Hot Club rhythm guitar part. Reinhardt was a phenomenal guitar player, not just for technique, but also for inventiveness. Injury to his left hand in a caravan fire at the age of 19 partially disabled fingers three and four; he made up for this by, when necessary, wrapping his thumb over the sixth string, occasionally stopping two strings with one finger, and by developing a repertoire of three-note chords played with fingers one, two, and four.

Exercise 4.11
CD TRACK 90
Hot Club and Gypsy Jazz

This exercise is inspired by the Django composition 'Djangology', and all of the chords from bars one to five can be comfortably played with three fingers. On the original track Django plays lead, not rhythm, but we can surmise that these voicings reflect how he would have demonstrated his composition to his two accompanists. It is

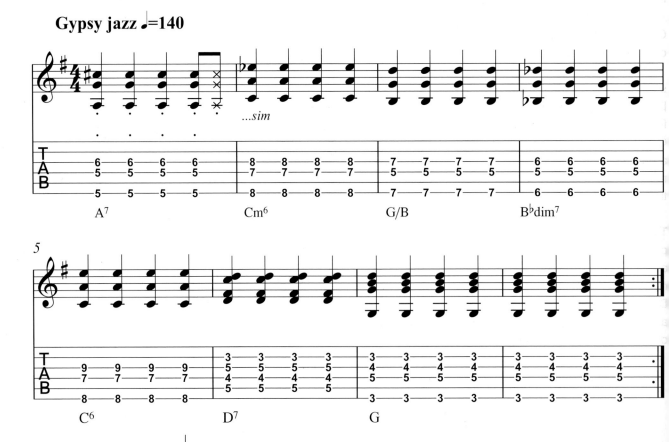

unlikely he would have used the voicing for D7 in bar six; to achieve a similar sound he most often omitted the top note and moved the bass note on to the E-string, giving D7/A, root omitted. The G major chord in bars seven and eight would have been played 'thumb over' the sixth string.

TECHNIQUE: a pile driver is the best comparison for Hot Club rhythm; strong, persistent, semi-staccato downstrokes played on an acoustic guitar with a heavy pick. In bar one there is an upstroke muted chord after the fourth beat; feel free to put this in occasionally in other bars.

THEORY: the three-note chords in bars one to five mostly just omit the fifth, the exception being the G/B chord, which is a triad and so should only contain three notes.

Exercise 4.12 (over the page)

Django could not finger many of the conventional jazz chords, but he made a virtue of his limitations and frequently came up with chord sequences whose logic on the guitar concealed the fact that they were harmonically eccentric. 'Djangology' is an example of this; the opening II7–iv6m–Ib–♭iii° makes little sense harmonically unless you view the Cm6 chord as a kind of D7♭9, with the missing D and F-sharp provided by the imagination. In that case the sequence begins to resemble an altered II7–V7♭9–Ib.

The last four bars of the sequence are, however, a simple ii-V-I in G major, with the C6 chord substituting for Am7. The B♭dim7 in bar four can then be viewed as a passing chord or approach chord between chord I in first inversion and chord II.

Improvising over a chord sequence like this is not straightforward; there is no one scale that will fit everything and each chord has to be treated as its own tonal centre. Django's original solo mainly uses arpeggios, and that is the approach we have gone for in Exercise 4.12. Notice the use of the ninth, B, over the A7 chord and A over the G/B chord in bars one and three. The notes in bar nine come entirely from a C♯dim7 arpeggio which, with an A bass, gives A7♭9. Frequent use of extended notes is very much part of Django's style. His original was recorded in 1935, some 10 years before the use of extended tones became commonplace with the emergence of bebop.

TECHNIQUE: entire books have been written about Gypsy Jazz picking; here is a paragraph to get you started. Use a heavy pick made of a hard material with no 'give' and pick nearer the bridge than usual. Use downstrokes whenever possible, reserving upstrokes for the second note when there are two notes per string. Descending arpeggios, which require the hand to move in an upward direction, are also played using downstrokes. For added power, follow through with each downstroke until the pick comes to rest on the string below.

Exercise 4.12 CD TRACK 91 *Django-style melody and improvisation*

NOTE CHOICES AND MELODY STYLES

Exercise 4.13

'Rhythm Changes' is a 32-bar AABA structure, derived from George Gershwin's jazz standard 'I Got Rhythm', that jazz musicians have used as a basis for composition and improvisation since before the bebop era. As with the blues, the chords can be substituted widely without losing the harmonic essence of the chord sequence, which can be adapted to many different styles.

In Exercise 4.13, the idea is that you use chord shapes of your own choice to play each of the chord sequences. The tab will give you some shapes to get you started, but you should experiment as much as possible using other shapes you know. You can play constant quarter-notes as notated, or play more freely, in a comping style.

Exercise 4.13.1

The simplest harmonisation for the A section, in the usual key of B-flat, is as follows:

Exercise 4.13.1
*'Rhythm Changes',
A-section in B-flat*

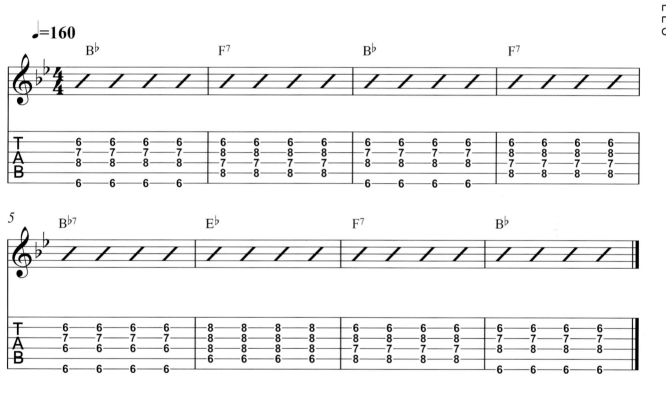

NOTE CHOICES AND MELODY STYLES

Exercise 4.13.2

However, jazz musicians developed these chords like this. This sequence adds a

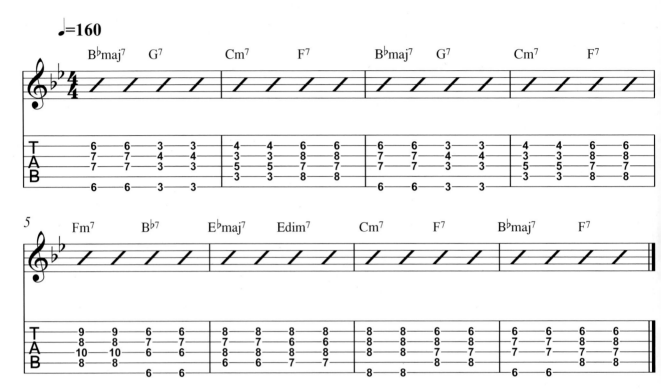

Exercise 4.13.2

'Rhythm Changes' with substitute chords

consistent two-chords-per-bar harmonic rhythm and ends on the dominant chord, pushing the music forward to resolve on chord I at the start of the second A section.

Exercise 4.13.3

This exercise demonstrates the possibilities for even more chord substitution, based on Exercise 4.13.2. Notice the use of diminished chords as substitutes for dominants (Bdim7 for G7) and tritone substitutions (B7 for F7). Chord character substitutions also work well: minor sevenths for diminished sevenths or dominants for minor sevenths and so on. The cadence in bar eight can be changed in the second A section to stay on the I chord.

Exercise 4.13.4

The middle eight of 'Rhythm Changes' is a sequence of dominant chords with roots rising in fourths, starting on chord III7, which is D7. This progression leads to chord V7, setting up the return to chord I in the final A section.

THE JAZZ GUITAR HANDBOOK

Exercise 4.13.3 *'Rhythm Changes' with more advanced chords*

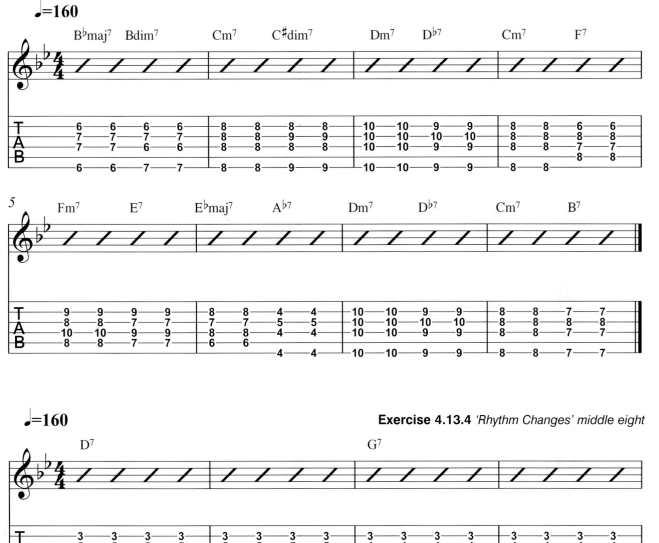

NOTE CHOICES AND MELODY STYLES

Exercise 4.13.5 *Use of ii chords in middle eight*

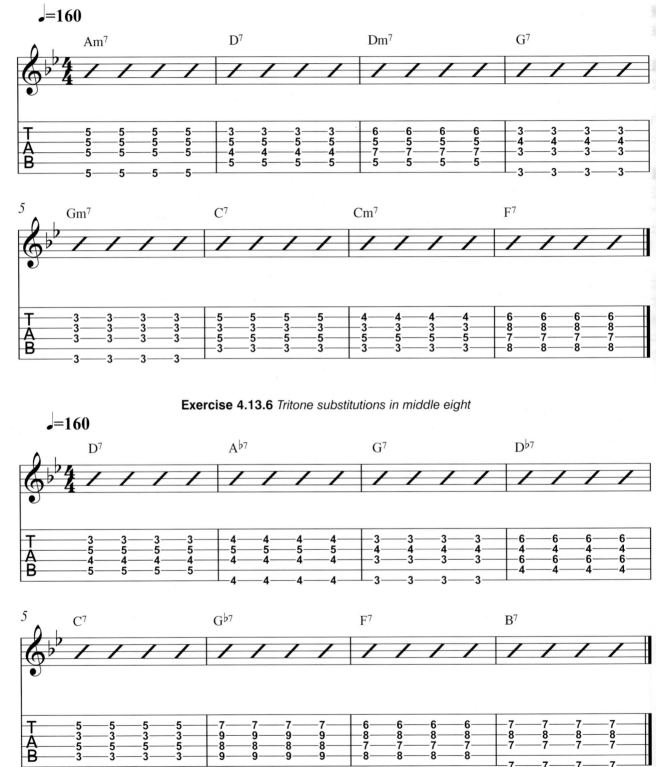

THE JAZZ GUITAR HANDBOOK

Exercise 4.13.5

Each of the dominant chords in the middle eight can be approached from chord ii.

Exercise 4.13.6

Or you can use tritone substitutions.

THEORY: Gershwin's 'I Got Rhythm' has a two-bar tag in the final A section. When playing 'Rhythm Changes', jazz musicians usually omit the tag.

Exercise 4.14

Exercise 4.14 is a melody in the style of a 'head' over 'Rhythm Changes' in a calypso rhythm. The time signature is 2/2, often known as 'cut time', as, in common with many other Latin rhythms, calypso has a 'two in a bar' feel. The use of a repeat sign and a 'Da Capo' or 'D.C' enables us to write 32 bars of music in a very compact way.

The CD track begins with four bars of triangle. You will need to count these four bars carefully when you play over the backing track, track 93, so that you enter at the right point. Technically, points to watch are the opening jump from the G-string to the A-string in bar one, and the large amount of string crossing caused by the arpeggio-based nature of the tune. This was played with a pick and alternate picking. There is a two-bar coda that is played on the CD track here but normally would be taken only after

Exercise 4.14
CD TRACKS 92/93/94
'Santa Margarita': calypso melody over 'Rhythm Changes'

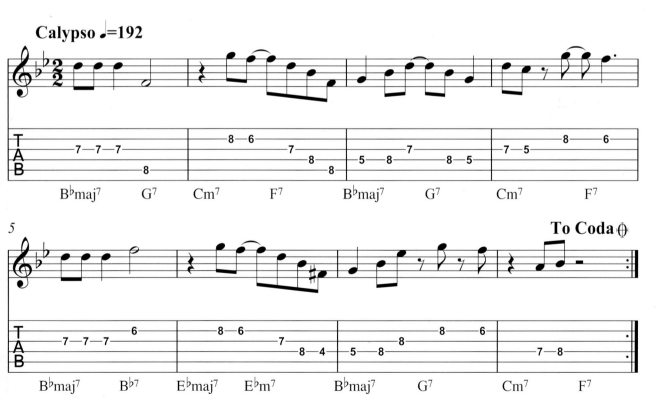

continued over page

NOTE CHOICES AND MELODY STYLES

Exercise 4.14 *continued*

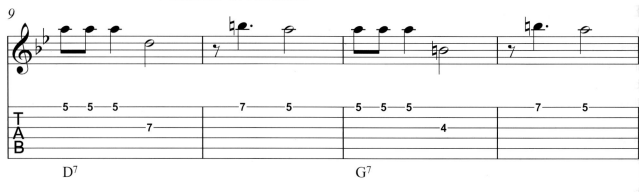

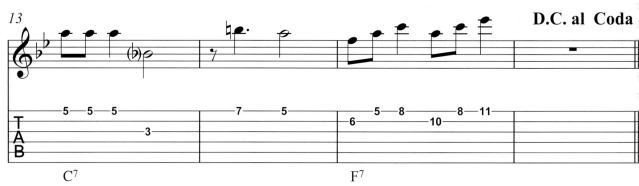

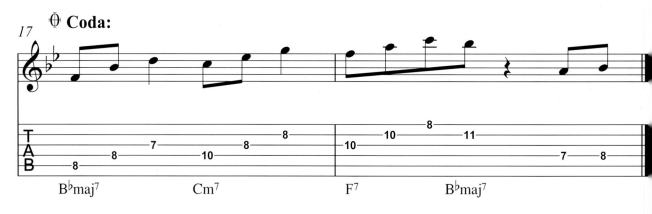

the last time through the tune; when played as a head, the coda would be omitted and the AABA form would be followed by solos on the entire form.

THEORY: get to know the 'Rhythm Changes' chord sequence and experiment with substitutions. Play them on the guitar so that you can recognise these common substitutions when you hear them.

TECHNIQUE: CD track 94 is 32 bars of 'Rhythm Changes' on bass and drums; you can use it to practise soloing, to practise Exercise 4.14, or to practise comping on the changes, making use of the substitutions outlined in Exercise 4.13.

Exercise 4.15

We have already met slash chords as chords that have a note other than the root in the bass. Up to now, most of the slash chords we have encountered have been chords in inversion: G/B, Gm/B♭ and so on. However, it is possible to create powerful harmony by using slash chords where the bass note is a 'foreign tone' – in other words, a note that does not belong in the chord.

Exercise 4.15 explores all the possible combinations of major triads over a C bass note. When a bass note is held stationary while chords change above it is often known as a 'pedal tone'.

Often the triad and bass note form an inversion of a recognisable chord and this has been notated in parenthesis beneath the slash-chord notation. For example, D♭/C is the same as D♭maj7 in third inversion; D/C is the same as D7 in third inversion; F/C is an F major triad in second inversion, and so on.

There are four combinations, however, that produce harmony of a kind that we have not yet encountered, containing various levels of dissonance. Progressing from the most consonant to the most dissonant they are G/C, A/C, B/C, and F♯/C.

Exercise 4.15

More slash chords: Triads with a 'foreign' bass tone

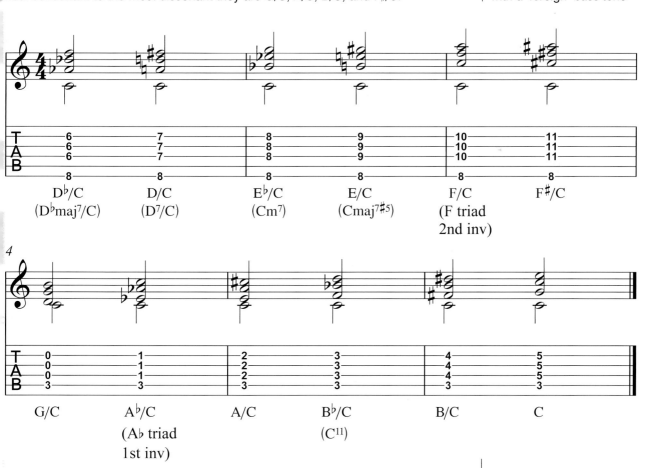

Exercise 4.16

Exercise 4.16 is the four-bar solo guitar introduction to CD track 95, an extended track with intro, 32-bar AABA head, guitar solo, and reprise of sections B and A with a coda to end. The piece as a whole makes extensive use of triads with a foreign bass tone, and the A section is based on the chords of the introduction.

A/C and B/D are the same chord a whole step apart; A/E♭ is the same as the F♯/C chord from Exercise 4.15, but this time in a close voicing. D♭/D is the same as the B/C chord from Exercise 4.15. This two-bar chord sequence works harmonically because both the triads and the bassline have their own logic; if you play the triad part of each chord, A, B, A, and D♭, you will hear that there is a strong progression. Similarly, the bassline C–D–E♭–D has a strong sense of direction. Combine the two and you have powerful harmony with a tense dissonance and strong harmonic rhythm.

Exercise 4.16

CD TRACK 95

'Slash Chord Thing', intro

Funky jazz swing 16s ♩=96

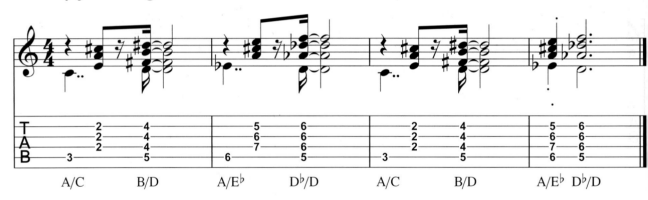

A/C   B/D   A/E♭   D♭/D   A/C   B/D   A/E♭ D♭/D

Exercise 4.17

After the four-bar intro in CD track 95 the two-bar chord sequence from Exercise 4.16 is developed into an eight-bar A section of a 32-bar AABA head. The bassline is the same as the intro, but the inversions of the triads are varied to create a melody. Chords, bassline, and melody are all played simultaneously on the guitar while the bass guitar enters to add weight to the bassline.

The middle eight or B section begins with a plain D major triad; it can be very effective to use a completely consonant triad in the midst of dissonant chords with foreign bass tones. With a succession of held chords over a chromatically descending bassline, the B section represents a moment of repose amidst the harmonic turmoil of the A section, which then returns to complete the head of the tune.

Funky jazz swing 16s ♩=96

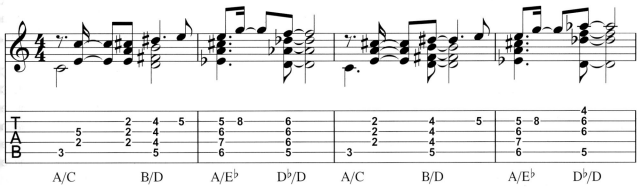

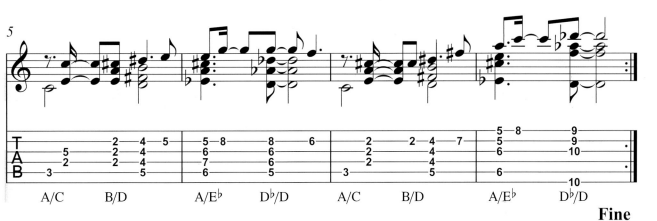

Fine

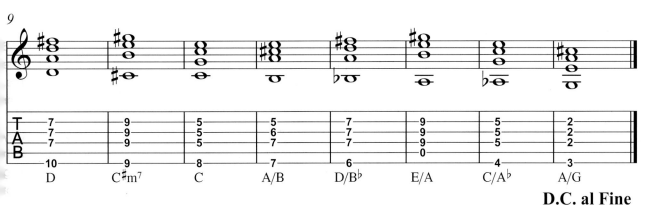

D.C. al Fine

Exercise 4.17
CD TRACK 95
'Slash Chord Thing'

THE JAZZ GUITAR HANDBOOK

Exercise 4.18

The guitar solo in CD track 95 is played over the same chords as the intro and the A section. In common with a great deal of groove-based jazz, it is open-ended, and the soloist can continue for as long as they wish – allowing for creativity and good taste. When playing this kind of solo the accompanying musicians have to be sensitive enough to respond to the soloist's dynamics and to realise when the solo is coming to an end, moving on to the next section of the song on cue. In this case the next section is the B section, which allows the soloist to wind down by playing a few choice sustained notes.

The conclusion of the piece sees the return of the eight-bar A section, played this time in single notes with the second and fourth phrases an octave higher. This takes the melody up to the 21st fret, which on many guitars will be the highest fret. There is then a three-bar coda, which is the last bar of the A section played three times, firstly at the usual pitch, then with an octave shift, and finally doubled in octaves.

Many of the note choices in the solo come from the arpeggios of the underlying chords, such as the A major arpeggios in bar 17; the fact that the chords are moving so quickly means that there are many possibilities for finding attention-grabbing melodies while staying within the chord tones. Often, interest is added by arriving early on a consonant note, such as the A-flat in bar six or the D-flat in bar 10.

There is no 'one scale' to fit this chord sequence, but as the A, B, and D-flat triads are a whole step apart, the whole-tone scale is useful, such as in bar 18; this is also hinted at in bar 23. Three-note chromatic runs can be found joining chord tones in bar 13 and bars 19/20. CD track 96 is a backing track from the solo to the end of the track. Make sure to try your own solo over this strange chord sequence.

THEORY: triads with foreign bass tones are not often found in such large numbers as in the A section of this exercise. The B section, which mixes other types of chord with slash chords, is the more common approach in contemporary jazz.

TECHNIQUE: there's some fast playing in this exercise for which you will need an efficient pick hand with minimal side to side movement when alternate picking. Sometimes it helps to imagine that you are trying to keep the pick in contact with the string; it is one way of getting used to making the smallest possible stroke.

If you have come this far you should be ready to play jazz to a high standard, with all the essential knowledge of chords, how they are constructed, and chord/scale relationships. Jazz is a lifelong challenge – you can always improve – but that is part of its fascination. You now have the tools you need to go out and play jazz with other musicians, whether for fun, at jam sessions, or perhaps, if it's your goal, professionally. In Appendix One you can find a complete list of the CD tracks, and there is an asterisk (*) beside each one that could be used as a backing track for practising your soloing. Keep learning, keep listening, and enjoy your music.

Exercise 4.18 CD TRACKS 95 & 96 *'Slash Chord Thing', solo*

continued over page

THE JAZZ GUITAR HANDBOOK

Exercise 4.18 *continued*

Exercise 4.18 *continued*

continued over page

THE JAZZ GUITAR HANDBOOK

NOTE CHOICES AND MELODY STYLES

Exercise 4.18 *continued*

Fingerboard chart: notes, letternames, and fret numbers

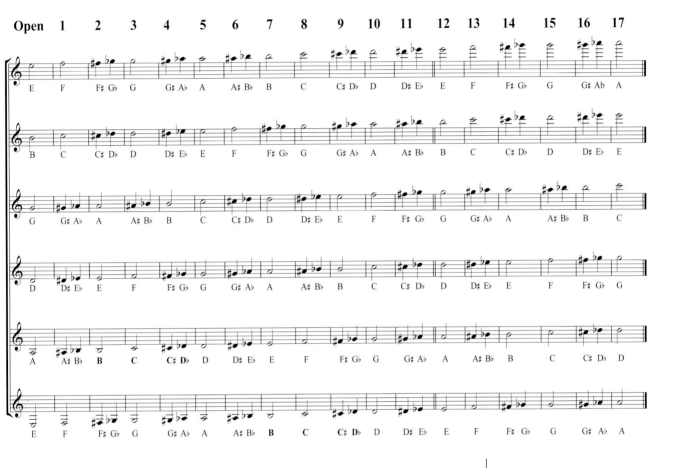

Spellings of jazz chords

Type of chord	Name of chord	Symbol	Spelling	Comments
Triads	C major	C	C E G	
	C minor	Cm	C E♭ G	
	C diminished	Cdim, C⁰	C E♭ G♭	
	C augmented	Caug, C+	C E G♯	
Sixths	C sixth	C6	C E G A	
	C minor sixth	Cm6, C-6	C E♭ G A	
Sevenths	C major seventh	Cmaj7, Cma7, C△7	C E G B	
	C seven	C7	C E G B♭	'Dominant seventh'
	C minor seventh	Cm7, Cmi7, C-7	C E♭ G B♭	
	C minor seven flat five or C 'half-diminished'	Cm7♭5, Cø	C E♭ G♭ B♭	
	C diminished seventh	C⁰7, Cdim7	C E♭ G♭ A (B♭♭)	
	C seven sharp five	C7♯5, C7+	C E G♯ B♭	C7+ symbol is less clear. Also C7♭5 = C E G♭ B♭
Ninths	C major ninth	Cmaj9, C△9	C E G B D	
	C nine	C9	C E G B♭ D	Dominant ninth, major key
	C minor ninth	Cm9, C-9	C Eb G B♭ D	
	C seven flat nine	C7♭9	C E G B♭ Db	Dominant ninth, minor key
	C seven sharp nine	C7♯9	C E G B♭ D♯	
	C add nine	Cadd9	C E G D	
	C minor add nine	Cm add9	C E♭ G D	
Elevenths	C eleventh	C11	C (E G) B♭ D F	
	C minor eleventh	Cm11, C-11	C E♭ (G) B♭ D F	
Thirteenths	C major thirteenth	Cmaj13, C△13	C E G B D A	(11th is omitted)
	C thirteenth	C13	C E G B♭ D A	(11th is omitted)
Suspended Chords	C suspended fourth	Csus4	C F G	
	C suspended second	Csus2	C D G	

CD track listing

Track	Exercise
1	1.01 'Kenny's Blues'
2	1.02 G minor pentatonic scale
3	1.03 G blues scale, shape 1
4	1.04 'Blue Note Blues'
5	1.05 'Kenny's Blues', octave up
6	1.06 G minor pentatonic scale, shapes 2 and 3
7	1.07 'Blue Note Blues', octave up
8	1.08 G blues scale, shapes 2 and 3
9	1.09 C major scale
10	1.10 G major scale
11	1.11 Blues solo, two choruses
12	* 1.11 'Kenny's Rhythm', backing track (also used for Exercises 1.21 and 2.14)
13	1.12 G minor pentatonic scale, shapes 4 and 5
14	1.13 G blues scale, shapes 4 and 5
15	1.14 C major intervals, two octaves
16	1.16 Intervals outside C major
17	1.17 F minor blues
18	*1.17 F minor blues backing track
19	1.19 B-flat blues with major pentatonics
20	* 1.19 B-flat blues backing track
21	1.21 G blues, major and minor pentatonics
22	1.22 Swing blues in B-flat
23	* 1.22 Swing blues in B-flat, backing track (also Exercise 2.22)
24	2.02 Five majors, three minors
25	* 2.03 Am7 D7 groove
26	2.07 and 2.08 Turnaround in G with melody
27	* 2.11 D minor descending minors
28	*2.15 'Kenny's Rhythm' higher shapes
29	2.16 C major in triads
30	2.17 C major in seventh chords
31	2.18 Cmaj7 chords, practical shapes
32	2.19 Gmaj7 chords, two ways
33	*2.20 32-bar jazz standard

Track	Exercise
34	*2.23 B-flat jazzy blues, chords
35	2.24 B-flat jazzy blues, arpeggio-based melody
36	2.25 Three minor scales
37	2.26 A harmonic minor, triads and sevenths
38	2.27 A minor chords, practical shapes
39	*2.28 'Bossa Blue', ii-V-I in C minor (also Exercise 3.13)
40	2.29 Ninth chords in C and A minor
41	*2.30 ii-V-I in A minor with ninth chords
42	*2.31 Tritone substitution, six ways
43	*2.32 Eight bars with tritone substitutions
44	2.33 Inversion and position
45	*2.35 Comping with triads
46	2.36 Seventh chord inversions
47	*2.37 Comping with seventh chords, 24-bar blues in C
48	2.38 Inversions of sixth-string roots
49	*2.39 Using sixth-string inversions
50	*2.42 32-bar jazz standard with sus4, 11ths, 13ths etc
51	*2.43 Eight bars of ii-V-I, chromatic extensions
52	3.01 G major scale, shape 1
53	3.02 Two-chord groove, Gmaj7 and Cmaj7
54	3.03 Seven major scale shapes
55	3.04 Modes in G
56	3.05 Dorian mode groove, solo
57	*3.06 Dorian mode groove, backing track
58	3.07 Lydian mode groove, lead
59	*3.08 Lydian mode groove, backing track
60	3.09 Modal chords in C
61	3.10 Mixolydian mode groove, lead
62	*3.11 and 3.12 Mixolydian mode groove, backing track
63	3.13 'Bossa Blue', lead (backing track CD39)
64	3.14 Seven arpeggios on shape 1

Track	Exercise
65	3.16 Gmaj7 and Cmaj7 groove using arpeggios
66	3.17 Chromatic decoration of arpeggios
67	3.18 Two notes per string arpeggios
68	3.19 Four other arpeggio shapes
69	3.20 C major and C melodic minor scales
70	3.21 Modes on G melodic minor
71	3.22 G melodic minor, seven scale shapes
72	*3.23 ii-V melodic minor modes, backing track
73	3.24 ii-V melodic minor modes, lead
74	3.25 Lydian augmented scale, solo
75	*3.26 and 3.27 Lydian augmented scale, backing track
76	*3.28 Locrian ♮2 and altered scale, backing track
77	3.29 Locrian ♮2 and altered scale, solo
78	3.35 Whole-tone and diminished scale, solo
79	4.01 'Kenny's Blues', both parts
80	4.02 Melody and chords, four- and two-note comping
81	4.03 Walking bass
82	*4.04 Walking bass with chords

Track	Exercise
83	4.05 Chord-melody, Lenny Breau-style
84	4.06 Chord-melody, jazz waltz
85	4.07 Wes-style octaves
86	4.08 Chord solo
87	*4.08 Chord solo, backing track
88	*4.09 'Bebop Blues', backing track
89	4.10 'Bebop Blues', lead
90	*4.11 Hot Club/Gypsy jazz rhythm and chord shapes
91	4.12 Hot Club/Gypsy jazz lead
92	4.14 'Santa Margarita' / 'Rhythm Changes', lead
93	*4.14 'Santa Margarita' / 'Rhythm Changes', backing track
94	*4.14 'Santa Margarita'/ 'Rhythm Changes', 32 bars for solo
95	4.16 and 4.17 'Slash Chord Thing', complete
96	*4.16 and 4.17 'Slash Chord Thing', backing track for solo

* = tracks that can be used as backing tracks for soloing

THE JAZZ GUITAR HANDBOOK

More Titles in the Popular Handbook Series

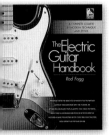

The Electric Guitar Handbook
by Rod Fogg

Combines a two-part book and an audio CD in a practical, lay-flat binding for ease of reference when playing. Newly written exercises in the book and on CD cover rock, country, blues, soul/funk, indie/alternative, and metal.

978-0-87930-989-3 • $29.99 • 9.25" x 11" • 256 pages • Hardcover w/CD • HL00332846

The Fiddle Handbook
by Chris Haigh

This treasure trove of information spanning the whole range of fiddle playing includes the most commonly played styles in America, the British Isles, Eastern Europe and beyond. A wealth of musical examples are faithfully reproduced on the accompanying CD to give you a taste of each style.

978-0-87930-978-7 • $29.99 • 9.25" x 11" • 288 pages • Hardcover w/CD • HL00332749

The Piano Handbook
by Carl Humphries

With clear and easy-to-understand exercises, this book provides fresh material and techniques in styles ranging from classical to jazz, rock, bebop and fusion, and gives new players everything they need to learn and enjoy the piano. This book's innovative tutorial approach covers classical and contemporary music styles in an integrated way, and the companion CD brings the playing techniques and concepts to life.

978-0-87930-727-1 • $29.99 • 10" x 12" • 290 pages • Hardcover w/CD • HL00330987

The Piano Improvisation Handbook
by Carl Humphries

A comprehensive overview of the practical skills and theoretical issues involved in mastering all forms of piano improvisation, including classical, jazz, rock, and blues. An accompanying CD contains musical examples for the series of graded tutorial sections, and an appendix of useful scales, chords, and voicings provides a quick reference guide.

978-0-87930-977-0 • $29.99 • 9.5" x 11" • 488 pages • Hardcover w/CD • HL00332750

The Home Recording Handbook
by Dave Hunter

Dave Hunter shows you how to make pro-sounding recordings without pro budgets. Packed with tips and techniques born out of years of recording experience, supported by specially recorded audio tracks on the accompanying CD, this is an essential volume for the working musician.

978-0-87930-958-9 • $29.99 • 9" x 11.25" • 256 pages • Hardcover w/CD • HL00332982

The Keyboard Handbook
by Steve Lodder and Janette Mason

This step-by-step course in keyboard playing for musicians of all levels begins with the basics of posture and technique. It offers a series of more than 80 specially written exercises and covers styles from blues to rock, soul to funk, gospel to synth-pop, and more. Includes a CD featuring audio tracks of the examples in the book, along with a range of different keyboards.

978-1-61713-104-2 • $29.99 • 8.75" x 10.75" • 160 pages • Hardcover w/CD • HL00333243

The Blues Guitar Handbook
by Adam St. James

Author Adam St. James traces the evolution of blues guitar from the humble beginnings into the hands of the electric blues kingpins, the blues-rockers of the '60s, '70s, and '80s, and finally to the flame-keepers and not-quite-traditionalists of today. A comprehensive tutor for mastering electric and acoustic blues follows this historic overview.

978-1-61713-011-3 • $29.99 • 9.25" x 11" • 256 pages • Hardcover w/CD • HL00332863

The Bass Handbook
by Adrian Ashton

This indispensable handbook helps players of all levels produce better, more creative, and more varied bass lines. Divided into two sections – Playing Your Bass and Knowing Your Bass – this book provides an unrivaled digest of bass information that might otherwise take an entire career to amass.

978-0-87930-872-8 • $27.99 • 9" x 11" • 256 pages• Hardcover w/CD • HL00331295

Backbeat Books

0513